AF007567

Winter Climbs in the Cairngorms

Selected snow, ice and mixed climbs in the Cairngorms and Creag Meagaidh

by Blair Fyffe and John Lyall

Juniper House, Murley Moss,
Oxenholme Road, Kendal, Cumbria LA9 7RL
www.cicerone.co.uk

© Blair Fyffe and John Lyall 2023
Seventh edition 2023
ISBN: 978 1 78631 125 2
Sixth edition 2011 (Allen Fyffe and Blair Fyffe); Fifth edition 2000, Fourth edition 1987, Third edition 1981 (all Allen Fyffe); Second edition (with John Cunningham) 1976; First edition (John Cunningham) 1973

Printed in Turkey by Pelikan Basim using responsibly sourced paper.
A catalogue record for this book is available from the British Library.
All photographs are by the authors unless otherwise stated.

© Crown copyright and database rights 2023 OS AC0000810376

Updates to this guide

While every effort is made by our authors to ensure the accuracy of guidebooks as they go to print, changes can occur during the lifetime of an edition. Any updates that we know of for this guide will be on the Cicerone website (www.cicerone.co.uk/1125/updates), so please check before planning your trip. We also advise that you check information about such things as transport, accommodation and shops locally. Even rights of way can be altered over time. We are always grateful for information about any discrepancies between a guidebook and the facts on the ground, sent by email to updates@cicerone.co.uk or by post to Cicerone, Juniper House, Murley Moss, Oxenholme Road, Kendal, LA9 7RL.

Register your book: To sign up to receive free updates, special offers and GPX files where available, create a Cicerone account and register your purchase via the 'My Account' tab at www.cicerone.co.uk.

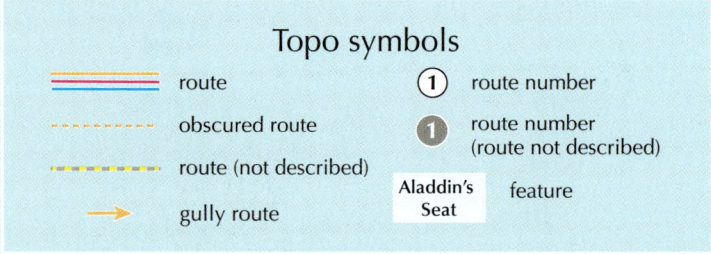

Front cover: Scott Grosdanoff enjoying sunny ice on Central Gully, Lurcher's Crag (photo: Alex Riley)

Heading up The Seam on Fiacaill Buttress, Coire an t-Sneachda

Contents

Topos key... 4

INTRODUCTION 11
Weather and conditions... 11
Types of winter climbs: snow, ice and mixed............................ 15
Ethics.. 24
Logistics... 26
Equipment 26
Navigation.. 28
Mountain rescue 30
Avalanches 30
Using this guide.. 35

NORTHERN CAIRNGORMS... 43
Northern Cairngorms overview map....................................... 44

The Northern Crags 46
    Creagan Cha-no 47
    Coire an t-Sneachda 57
    Coire an Lochain 79
    Lurcher's Crag 96
    Sron na Lairige 103

The Loch Avon basin 108
    Stac an Fharaidh 109
    Stag Rocks... 116
    Hell's Lum Crag 124
    Garbh Uisge Crag... 131
    Shelter Stone Crag... 134
    Carn Etchachan 141

The Ben MacDui crags... 150
    Creagan a'Choire Etchachan 151
    Coire Sputan Dearg 159

The Cairn Toul/Braeriach amphitheatre.............................. 166
    Angel's Peak 170
    Corrie of the Chokestone Gully 172
    Garbh Choire Mor 175
    Garbh Choire Dhaidh 182
    Coire Bhrochain 186

Beinn a'Bhuird 193
        Coire na Ciche. 196
        Garbh Choire 200

SOUTHERN CAIRNGORMS 207

The Loch Muick crags 208
        Lochnagar 212
        Creag an Dubh Loch 239
        Eagles Rock 248
        Broad Cairn Bluffs 252

Glen Clova 253
        The Winter Corrie. 254
        Corrie Fee 257

CREAG MEAGAIDH 262
        Coire Ardair 265

Appendix A   Useful contacts. 285
Appendix B   Route summary table by area 286

Warning
Mountaineering is a dangerous activity carrying a risk of personal injury or death. It should be undertaken only by those with a full understanding of the risks and with the training and experience to evaluate them. Mountaineers should be appropriately equipped for the routes undertaken. While every care and effort has been taken in the preparation of this guide, the user should be aware that conditions, especially in winter, can be highly variable and can change quickly. Holds may become loose or fall off, rock fall can affect the character of a route, snow and avalanche conditions must be carefully considered. These can materially affect the seriousness of a climb, tour or expedition.

Therefore, except for any liability which cannot be excluded by law, neither Cicerone nor the author accepts liability for damage of any nature (including damage to property, personal injury or death) arising directly or indirectly from the information in this guide.

Map scales
Crag approach maps have been scaled at 93 per cent (resulting in a scale of 1:53,500).

Dave Sharpe on Fingers Ridge, Coire an t-Sneachda

Well rimed conditions on Lochnagar (photo: Paul Noble)

Lightly rimed conditions on the crux pitch of Ventriloquist, Coire an Lochain (photo: Iain Ballantyne)

Introduction

Coire an Lochain on a fine spring day

The major climbing venues of the Cairngorms provide some of the finest winter routes in Britain. From the readily accessible Northern Corries – the collective name for the north-facing corries of Cairngorm, including Coire an t-Sneachda and Coire an Lochain – to the magnificent cliffs of Lochnagar, Creag an Dubh Loch and Shelter Stone, to the wild and remote corries of Braeriach and Beinn a'Bhuird, and the icy Creag Meagaidh, every aspect of winter climbing is to be found.

Building on previous editions of this guide, we have tried to select the best routes in each area. Where possible we have included a selection of routes of all grades up to Grade VII, with the odd harder route too. Where there is a choice, several climbs of a similar standard are detailed to allow for some choice should conditions or availability dictate a change in plan. Many of the routes selected follow natural lines which, once embarked upon, should be relatively easy to follow. The exception to this is some of the more recent hard mixed routes, which require a more detailed description.

Weather and conditions

Scottish winter climbing can be a hazardous pastime. The weather is often unfavourable and can change with startling suddenness, transforming a pleasant excursion into a battle for survival. Too many people have underestimated these mountains and found themselves in trouble. However, when the weather, the conditions and the climb are right, then winter climbing in the Cairngorms can offer an unforgettable experience.

Good climbing conditions can occur in this area any time between

Heavy going on the approach. In conditions like these approach times will be significantly longer than those quoted in this guide

November and April, with February and March tending to be the most reliable months. In some years winter climbs can be in condition as early as October and as late as May. Winter ascents have even been made in June!

The Cairngorms are generally further from the sea than other Scottish winter climbing areas, and many of the crags are quite high with bases above 1000m. Conditions tend to fluctuate less rapidly in the Cairngorms than elsewhere. Summit temperatures can remain below freezing for long periods with fewer thaw-freeze cycles than further west. This has various advantages and disadvantages.

Being high, rocky and exposed to northerly winds, the Northern Corries of Cairngorm and the other higher crags are among the first in the country to come into condition. A north or north-easterly wind in late October or during November with snow showers can build up rime rapidly, bringing snowed-up rock routes into condition very quickly.

However, for routes that rely on vegetation it is very important to wait for the turf to be properly frozen before they are climbed to minimise damage to the ground. Some routes in the Northern Corries, such as Invernookie, are getting progressively harder as the turf disappears due to them being climbed in unfrozen conditions. It can be a frustratingly long wait for the ground to freeze properly in the autumn, especially if snow falls and insulates unfrozen turf. Once frozen, however, the turf takes a long time to thaw out again.

As the season progresses, conditions tend to evolve. The gullies will

Weather and conditions

begin to fill in and ice will start to form. With fewer thaw-freeze cycles, the build-up of good snow-ice can take longer to develop than on Ben Nevis, for example. During periods of sustained cold weather, deep soft snow can remain unconsolidated, making the approach to the crags arduous. However, tracks to the more popular crags will soon appear. During these periods ice tends to form well in the drainage lines. These are the times to visit some of the lower crags.

After a period of mild weather or a big thaw, the best option is to go high. The higher crags will hold onto snow and ice for the longest. Enclosed corries and gullies that face north and northeast often retain the cold air, so there is less thaw than in locations of comparable altitudes that are exposed to the mild south or south-westerly winds. The high crags of the Cairngorms can retain winter conditions while many other areas are stripped bare. In general, the steep buttress routes tend to be the first routes to come into condition, but are also the first routes to be stripped in a thaw.

Some routes, particularly the gullies, require a number of thaw-freeze cycles to bring them into good condition. These are often in their best condition mid to late season after a number of these cycles have built up the ice. This is particularly true of many of the routes on Creag Meagaidh. Best conditions here are likely to be from mid January through to March. Some routes, The Fly Direct for example, are frustratingly slow to form and only come into good condition every few years. However, this does make an ascent of a route like this very special when it's found in nick.

Through March and April, the days get warmer and the Sun's rays get

A lone figure in clearing conditions (photo: Paul Noble)

progressively stronger. Sunshine has more of an effect on south-facing crags. It is for this reason that the likes of Hell's Lum and Stag Rocks have a shorter season than other shadier crags of similar altitude.

Part of the challenge of winter climbing is predicting weather and conditions, and then choosing suitable objectives accordingly. Knowing when, for example, it is better to go for a buttress route rather than a gully, or when to try something well within your capabilities rather than push your grade, can make the difference between a great day's climbing and an unpleasant and potentially dangerous expedition. However, predicting conditions can be tricky, particularly for those based far from the mountains.

In the old days the decision of where to climb might be based on how many snowflakes the TV weather forecaster placed on the weather map at the end of the evening news. The knowledge of how conditions were developing was often hard won, with many climbing trips ending in disappointment due to poor conditions. These days, however, with a plethora of mountain weather forecasts, up-to-date conditions blogs, webcams and winter climbing forums, it is much easier to keep up with current weather and climbing conditions.

At the time of writing both the Mountain Weather Information Service (www.mwis.org.uk) and the Met Office (www.metoffice.gov.uk/weather/specialist-forecasts/mountain) provide free mountain weather forecasts for the areas of interest. The Met Office run automatic mountain weather stations on the summits of Cairngorm, Cairnwell and Aonach Mor that can be useful for monitoring actual conditions. Although the latter is outside of the area covered by this guide, it is less than 20 miles as the crow flies from Creag Meagaidh, and thus can be useful to judge conditions there. For the more advanced user the likes of www.wetterzentrale.de, www.ecmwf.int and www.netweather.tv give a plethora of charts, graphs and predictions to keep weather watchers entertained for hours.

In terms of conditions many climbers and instructors maintain a blog or conditions page. These tend to be regularly updated, often with photos, and can be a great source of information about current conditions. However, these can sometimes portray a somewhat optimistic view of conditions. Be warned that once the word is out that a particular climb is in good condition, it can lead to a honeypot effect with lots of teams heading to the same area and route.

Less specific to climbing, but useful for an overall picture of weather and snow conditions, are the web pages of the ski areas. Cairngorm, the Lecht and Glen Shee ski areas all provide webcam images and snow and weather reports on their web pages.

The SAIS avalanche reports and blogs, discussed in more detail in the avalanche section, are another useful source of information about weather and conditions.

Types of winter climbs: snow, ice and mixed

Every route in this guide has been assigned a category to indicate its overall style/character. There are, of course, overlaps and crossovers, but the aim is to give an idea of the usual type of route, and what it takes to bring it into condition.

Snow

The great snow gullies of the Cairngorms and Creag Meagaidh are obvious and alluring objectives which drew the attention of the early mountaineers. They can offer journeys through impressive rock formations on reasonable ground. However, they tend to collect a lot of fresh snow, can steepen to around 45 degrees and often form cornices at their tops. This combination makes them prone to avalanche, and so great care should be taken when venturing into these gullies.

The snow on these routes is transformed over time by thaw-freeze cycles, which consolidate and harden the snowpack. Soft snow that can make upward progress nearly impossible soon after it has accumulated is turned into firm snow that supports your weight and can hold a boot print. Kicking and cutting steps in the snow like this is a time-honoured mountaineering skill that should be practised by everyone and is very rewarding.

Further transformation of the snow can make it hard and icy, demanding good crampon technique. Climbing, and especially descending, these gullies on hard icy snow is a serious business. There can be a lack of good rock or ice belays so an understanding of how to build snow anchors and how to belay to reduce shock loads onto them

The top section of Fiacaill Couloir, Coire an t-Sneachda

is useful. Snow gullies can occasionally have icy steps in them early in the winter season when there is little snow cover.

The approaches to many of the climbs, such as those in Coire an Lochain, involve Grade I snow slopes, so it is important that climbers become comfortable moving around on these big, serious snow slopes.

The crux of a snowy gully can often be the cornice. Cornices are often biggest in the centre of snow gullies and smallest (or non-existent) above the buttresses to each side of the gully. So, if faced with a big cornice, try to move onto the buttress at the side to reach the top. Or descend the climb! Tunnelling through cornices was once popular but is dangerous and lost its appeal a long time ago.

Ice

Ice climbs can be sub-categorised into two styles.

Snow-ice climbs

Scotland's most common and most famous style of winter climbing is snow-ice climbing in gullies. Smith's Gully on

Pete Trudgill climbing the middle section of Smith's Gully, Coire Ardair (photo: John Trudgill)

Types of winter climbs: snow, ice and mixed

Creag Meagaidh, Polyphemus Gully and Raeburn's Gully on Lochnagar, and Hell's Lum on Hell's Lum Crag are all classic examples of snow-ice climbs.

Snow-ice does not form with cold weather alone. Instead, snowfall combined with the correct wind direction is required to fill the gully up with snow. A thaw, with perhaps a bit of rain thrown into the mix, is then required to make the snow wet (but not too much otherwise all the snow will melt) followed by a good freeze to make it solid. Too little thaw before the freeze will result in firm snow rather than solid snow-ice, or a surface layer of snow-ice on top of softer snow.

However, good snow-ice rarely forms as a result of a single thaw-freeze cycle. It normally requires many such cycles to change the structure of the snow and to build the snow-ice sufficiently. The winter brings a continuous succession of thaw-freeze cycles of differing lengths and depths, resulting in ever-changing snow and ice conditions. The Cairngorms tend to be slightly drier and colder than the mountains further west, so the formation of good snow-ice can be slower than on Ben Nevis, for example.

At its best, snow-ice can offer the perfect combination of 'plastic', dependable ice that does not shatter when you place a pick but is sufficiently solid to place good ice screws. The honeycomb structure provided by millions of tiny air-pockets in the snow creates a texture that absorbs the strike of a pick instead of shattering like cascade ice. At its worst, a snow-ice climb can be vertical snow that is too soft to hold an ice axe, let alone an ice screw.

Cascade ice climbs

Elsewhere in the world, ice climbing is usually cascade ice climbing. In persistent cold temperatures, waterfalls

Contemplating the various options on the crux of Window Gully, Lurcher's Crag North (photo: Findlay Cranston)

freeze to form cascades of pure, hard water-ice. A steady source of water and reliably cold weather without too much precipitation create ideal conditions for forming this kind of ice. In Scotland we do occasionally experience such conditions, but they rarely stay with us for more than a few weeks.

Cascade ice is dense and can be brittle. It can also form beautiful shapes and features. Its density demands sharp picks and ice screws, and an accurate swing with an ice axe. The shapes and features often help by providing useful places for hooking and placing front points. The density of this ice also makes it quite durable in a thaw. However, cascade ice can become detached from the rock behind it and large chunks can fall off in thaw conditions. It is best to avoid cascade ice in mild conditions and to be careful after it has refrozen, making sure it's securely held in place. Sunshine in the spring can also create unpleasant conditions on cascade ice due to the partial warming of the ice by solar radiation.

Devil's Delight and The Chancer on Hell's Lum Crag, Funeral Fall on Broad Cairn Bluffs, and The Last Post on Creag Meagaidh are cascade ice climbs. These climbs need significant periods of below-freezing temperatures at their altitude to come into condition. Take sharp picks and crampons, and lots of ice screws.

Variations and combinations

While many climbs fall neatly into one of the above categories, there are also plenty that are, or can be, a mixture of snow, snow-ice and cascade ice. The Pumpkin and South Post Direct on Creag Meagaidh can have pitches of cascade ice followed by a snow-ice gully and final snow slopes to finish.

Mixed

Mixed climbs can be sub-categorised into the four styles below.

General mixed climbs

Mixed climbs feature a combination of rock, ice and turf in varying degrees. Mixed climbs that include all of these, and do not have a strong characteristic towards any one of those components, will be referred to simply as general mixed climbs.

Mixed climbing has always been pursued in the Cairngorms, but has become more widespread in the last few decades. It was developed to a much higher level in the Cairngorms than in other areas, due in part to the more vegetated nature of the cliffs and the granite which lent itself to this style of climbing. Eagle Ridge and Parallel Buttress on Lochnagar and Sticil Face on Shelter Stone Crag are hard and highly sought-after lines which were first climbed in the '50s. The colder conditions in the east also mean that soft snow lies for longer on the cliffs, so mixed climbing can be done while the gullies are full of soft unconsolidated snow.

Modern mixed climbing has diversified and specialised in the same way that all aspects of climbing have evolved. Whereas in ice climbing there

Types of winter climbs: snow, ice and mixed

Mixed climbing on The Lamp, Coire an t-Sneachda

is a limit to the level of difficulty due to the nature of how ice forms, in mixed climbing there is virtually no limit.

Mixed climbs need to be white and frozen to be in acceptable condition. By consensus that has been reached over many decades, and due to the damage caused, dry tooling is not considered acceptable on Scottish cliffs away from some low-level training crags. In the mountains, the crag needs to be wintry in appearance, white with snow or rime, and frozen. This is the ethical approach that has developed over many years and is specific to Scotland. Many foreign climbers are baffled by these restrictions, but we abide by them to maintain the quality of experience and challenge. Waiting until the crag is properly frozen protects turf from excessive damage, and any loose blocks are more likely to be frozen in place.

Rocky mixed climbs

Rocky mixed climbs often make a good choice for the first climbs of the winter season because they're early to freeze, don't require any thaw-freeze cycles and can offer reasonable protection. Even so, a thaw and refreeze can provide the snow-ice required to hold blocks and chockstones in place. They can be a bit rattly before this happens.

'Snowed-up rock climb' is an unhelpful name for this style of climb. It is rime that is more effective at making the climb white and that will provide better climbing conditions. Rime is a type of ice crystal that grows on any surface exposed to humid air being blown onto it in a sub-zero temperature. It is often seen on fence posts and, perhaps confusingly, grows into the wind. You need a wind blowing cloud onto the crag and the temperature to be below zero. After a wind from the north-east, off the North Sea, choose a crag that faces that direction and has been in the cloud, like Coire an Lochain or Lochnagar.

Sufficient rime to make crags and climbs white enough to climb can form overnight. Twelve hours of strong winds blowing freezing clouds onto the crag is enough to form a couple of centimetres of rime over every surface, even under overhangs.

Over time, rime can grow to be a metre thick, and it turns very icy after thaw-freeze cycles. This type of rime makes life difficult if you want to climb the rock underneath it and very bold if you climb over it. In thick, icy rime it can be a monumental struggle to clear the rime off the rock for a whole pitch.

Thaw-freeze cycles create dribbles of water that run into cracks and refreeze. Such iced-up cracks can make it difficult to uncover protection. Snowed-up rock climbs can be good early in the season when the cracks are still clear of ice and the rime is not too thick.

Snowfall can also make a crag white in appearance. Cold, dry snow will not stick to the rocks; it will pile up on ledges, making the crag look white from above but not from below. However, if the snow is a bit wet (this happens when

Types of winter climbs: snow, ice and mixed

Rocky mixed conditions on Short Ridge, Creagan Cha-no

the temperature is at or just above freezing) it can stick to the rocks and make the whole crag go white. This wet snow can also freeze into an unhelpful icy crust that is hard to clear from the rocks when you're climbing.

Snow on ledges is helpful on all mixed climbs, especially if it has transformed to snow-ice after thaw-freeze cycles, and provides ice axe placements to pull on and a more secure surface to stand on with crampons.

Pygmy Ridge and The Message in Coire an t-Sneachda, and Savage Slit and Ventriloquist in Coire an Lochain are all excellent rocky mixed climbs.

Turfy mixed climbs

Turf freezes slowly. Small tufts of turf freeze first and freeze most quickly when they're exposed to a cold wind. Big patches of turf can take many weeks to freeze properly, especially when covered in deep snow, and can be damaged or even completely removed from the crag if climbed on when not frozen. Turf in chimneys, corners and gullies takes longer to

Andy Nisbet making the most of frozen turf on the first ascent of Polar Bear, Sron na Lairige

Types of winter climbs: snow, ice and mixed

freeze as these features retain warmer air and running water.

Turf normally takes a couple of weeks of sub-zero, windy conditions to freeze properly. Even then, it benefits from a couple of thaw-freeze cycles to consolidate properly. If the turf is very dry it will not be good to climb on, even if it's frozen. It becomes very crumbly and easy to break up if it's too dry. Wet turf freezes into a much more solid medium. Turf can be wet from rain that fell before the freeze, or it can be made wet by thaw-freeze cycles with rain or drainage in the cliff running onto the turf.

In any case, turf must be frozen to climb. Since it is difficult to assess the quality of the turf at the start of the winter without climbing on it, it's worth waiting a while to make sure. Don't head out at the first sign of snow or rime.

However, once properly frozen, turf will stay frozen through some quite substantial periods of thaw. In a thaw, water will dribble down below the turf and will freeze into ice of one sort or another in the refreeze, so turfy mixed climbs can become quite icy over the course of the winter. There's nothing more satisfying than placing a pick in a solid, icy lump of turf!

Turf commonly holds snow on top of it, and this is transformed into snow-ice with thaw-freeze cycles. So, turfy mixed climbs quite often turn into true mixed climbs over the course of a good winter, with a mixture of turf, rock, ice and snow-ice.

Turfy mixed climbs, like any mixed climbs, should look wintry and white. Rime and snow should cover the rocks. There's an argument that only the turf needs to be frozen and icy, that the rocks don't need to be white as they are not used for climbing. This is mostly the case on sandstone crags found in the far north-west and is also a matter of opinion. It might be easier to say that all mixed climbs should be white and wintry in appearance with the rocks covered in rime or snow.

Arch Rival at Creagan Cha-no and Tough-Brown Traverse on Lochnagar are good examples of turfy mixed climbs.

Icy mixed climbs

Mixed climbs are found on buttresses and ridges and therefore don't

Nice ice on the crux of Sticil Face, Shelter Stone Crag

normally form very much ice. However, some mixed climbs benefit from or rely on a certain amount of ice. The ice is normally snow-ice, which requires snow to collect on the route followed by a thaw-freeze cycle to saturate the snow and turn it into ice. Some routes require a short section of cascade ice to form and are much harder without this. Good ice can form on routes that follow ramps, grooves (mini gullies) and corners, easing progress.

Doctor's Choice in Coire an t-Sneachda, Sticil Face on Shelter Stone Crag and Vertigo Wall on Creag an Dubh Loch are superb icy mixed climbs.

Combinations and variations

Mixed climbs have a combination of rock, ice and turf with varying amounts of each of these ingredients. Some climbs like Sticil Face require frozen turf, ice and rocky mixed conditions to be in condition, but the crucial crux section is icy mixed, so the route is described as such. Other climbs will be given two styles of climbing, like Trail of Tears on Lochnagar, which is given icy mixed and rocky mixed, as both conditions are required to climb the crux sections of the climb.

Ethics

Winter climbing ethics are strongly held in Scotland, especially when it comes to mixed climbs on buttresses, faces and ridges. To be in acceptable winter condition, buttresses should be generally white, there should be snow on the rocks, and turf should be well frozen. **Climbing routes when the turf is not well frozen destroys the route and should be avoided**. Snow on the ledges and dry rocks is generally not held to be sufficient, and neither is a coating of hoar frost when snow is not present. Dry tooling is the preserve of a very few crags in the glens that have been agreed as suitable.

The short daylight hours, the variability of conditions and the seriousness of the environment means that the ethics around using aid tend to be less rigid than in summer. However, speed and aid are not always compatible. The more aid used, the longer time taken and the increased risk from approaching darkness. The use of aid is becoming generally less accepted than it once was.

Although pegs are still required in some situations, climbers should attempt to apply modern rock-climbing ethics to winter climbs as far as possible. It is often in the gullies, where the rock tends to be of a poorer quality, that pegs are required. Many of the buttress routes can be adequately protected with nuts and the like. Attempts should be made to limit the use of pegs on all climbs, especially those that are also popular summer climbs.

For both safety and enjoyment, when choosing which route to climb it is worth considering both conditions and other teams. If climbing behind other parties on an ice route, there is often a danger of being hit by ice dislodged by the team above. In thawing conditions there can also be a very real danger from natural ice and rock fall. This is particularly the case in gullies

Ethics

where the rock may be of poorer quality and falling debris tends to be funnelled. The top of Red Gully in Coire an t-Sneachda is bad for this. Hooking and torquing axes behind blocks can lever them off, especially if the ground is not well frozen. There have been serious accidents resulting from both rock and ice fall.

Access rights

The Land Reform (Scotland) Act 2003 established statutory rights of responsible access to land and inland water for outdoor recreation and crossing land. These are known as Scottish Access Rights. The Scottish Outdoor Access Code gives detailed guidance on the responsibilities of those exercising access rights and of those managing land and water. The Act sets out where and when access rights apply, and how land should be managed with regard to access. The Code defines how access rights should be exercised.

The three principles for responsible access apply to both the public and land managers.

- Respect the interests of other people – be considerate, respect privacy and livelihoods and the needs of those enjoying the outdoors.
- Care for the environment – look after the places you visit and enjoy, and care for wildlife and historic sites.
- Take responsibility for your own actions – the outdoors cannot be made risk-free for people

The walk into Coire Ardair, Creag Meagaidh

exercising access rights; land managers should act with care for people's safety.

Logistics
Starting times
Due to the short daylight hours, early starts are a must in Scottish winter climbing. For big routes, or if climbing in some of the more remote locations, consider walking in in the dark. When pushing your grade routes tend to take a long time. When darkness falls things slow down even more. Starting an hour earlier can save two or three hours in the evening. Don't forget to bring a head torch.

Later in the season the amount of daylight increases significantly. At the winter solstice around 21 December there are less than seven hours between sunrise and sunset. By the time of the spring equinox around 21 March there are over 12 hours between sunrise and sunset. Thus, late in the season you can climb without the sense of urgency required in the early season.

Accommodation and transport
Due to the early start required, many climbers find it preferential to stay in the area the night before a day's climbing. There is a wide variety of accommodation available from 5-star hotels to soggy campsites. Details can be found online. For one or two days of climbing, people often find it convenient to stay in their vehicle, particularly with the increase in popularity of campervans. This has the advantage of flexibility. However, large numbers of vans parking up in laybys and car parks in popular areas have caused problems with local residents, and care should be taken to be as unobtrusive as possible.

Scottish winter climbing is hard work, and the opportunity to recover and fully dry kit will likely improve performance and enjoyment on subsequent days. Therefore, for anything longer than a night or two, staying somewhere large and warm enough to allow the drying of kit and the opportunity to relax and recover after a long day on the hill will be appreciated.

Most climbers access the area via car. Cars and vans should be parked with consideration to other visitors and locals alike. Do not block driveways and roads or create a hazard for other road users. Do not drive down private roads without permission.

Bicycles can be very useful for approaches that include significant sections on tracks. This is particularly the case for some of the crags accessed from Deeside. However, they can cause erosion on footpaths and on open hillside, so should only be used on forest roads and estate tracks. The use of bikes is covered by the Scottish Outdoor Access Code mentioned previously.

Equipment
Ice axe and crampons are essential for any winter outing, whether walking or climbing. For climbing it is assumed that two tools are used, with either curved or inclined picks. Climbing with leashless tools is now popular. The

greatest benefits of leashless climbing tend to be in the higher grades. Unless very confident, lanyards connecting your tools to your harness are recommended.

Crampons should have front points and be adjusted accurately to fit the boots. They should be securely attached to the boots by either straps or a clip-on arrangement. The boots themselves should be rigid with a good sole for step-kicking and be able to take crampons. Ill-fitting crampons are a real danger in winter.

A helmet should be considered mandatory on steep ground in winter as a slip on snow or ice can quickly develop into something more serious. When climbing there is always the risk of being hit by falling ice, even from the most skilled and considerate leader. Besides, a helmet provides good insulation from the cold!

A normal rack of gear covering a reasonable range of crack sizes is usually sufficient. Camming devices can still work well on granite in winter if the interior of the crack is ice-free, but should always be treated with more caution than in summer. Although a few pegs may be beneficial on some routes, most routes, particularly buttress routes, can be done safely without them. Ice screws are obviously needed on ice routes. One or two drive-in/screw-out pegs – such as warthogs or bulldog-style ice hooks – that can be hammered into frozen turf or icy cracks, can be quite useful. Hooks should be avoided in corner cracks as they torque and are impossible to then remove. Try to match the gear to the climb and avoid being burdened by unnecessary weight.

A complete water- and wind-proof shell outer layer is necessary, as is spare clothing and food. A synthetic belay jacket which can be pulled on over a waterproof shell is also useful. As the name suggests this can be worn by the belayer, who then seconds the pitch wearing it, and then passes it over to his/her partner before starting to lead the next pitch. Also essential is a head torch and adequate battery power. A bivi bag of some type and a small first aid kit are also worthwhile additions. An extra pair of dry gloves is extremely useful, especially if the temperature is around or above freezing and gloves are likely to get wet. Wet gloves will lead to cold hands! Even the best climbers will not be able to enjoy (or even complete) their route if they do not learn what to wear, and how to wear it, to remain warm and comfortable.

Smartphones

These days most people carry smartphones on the hill. These can be useful for a variety of purposes: uploading your latest heroic photos to Instagram, letting your family/friends know you are back at the car, and calling out the emergency services. However, users should be aware of their limitations. The batteries have a habit of dying in the cold, so the phone should be kept in a warm inner pocket. Signal can be poor when tucked away in a deep corrie; often an exposed summit or ridge will provide better signal.

Winter Climbs in the Cairngorms

Assuming signal can be found, the procedure for requesting a rescue involves dialling 999 and asking for the police and then asking for mountain rescue. Further details on this process and information to give are covered in the mountain rescue section.

Sometimes there will only be enough signal to send a text message. You can still contact the emergency services using a text from your mobile, but only if you have already registered with the emergency SMS text service. To register text the word 'register' to 999. You will get a reply and should then follow the instructions you are sent. This will take about two minutes of your time and could save your life. Texting is also a useful way of preserving battery life.

Alternatively, the smartphone app EchoSOS (echosos.com/en) is simple to use and delivers accurate info about location even with a weak signal. It also automatically sources the emergency services in any other country you visit.

Navigation

The size and scale of the crags and the approaches make the ability to navigate essential, even for a visit to the most accessible of crags. Bad weather and winds of over 100mph are common on the summit plateaus of both the Cairngorms and Creag Meagaidh, which are notoriously featureless. In a whiteout, accurate navigation is sometimes needed to find the cliff and more often required to find the way back after the climb.

The climbing areas described in this guide are covered by a range of maps in the Ordnance Survey 1:50,000 Landranger® series. The Lochnagar/Creag an Dubh Loch area is covered by Sheet 44, entitled *Ballater & Glen Clova*. The Cairngorm area is covered by Sheet

Atmospheric conditions around the top of Coire an t-Sneachda

36, entitled *Grantown & Aviemore*. Part of the area is also on Sheet 43, *Braemar & Blair Atholl*. Creag Meagaidh is covered by Landranger Sheet 34 *Fort Augustus*, and is also on Sheet 42, *Glen Garry & Loch Rannoch*.

The OS Explorer® maps, at 1:25,000 scale, also cover the area. Sheet OL57 *Cairn Gorm & Aviemore* covers the Central and Northern Cairngorms. Sheet OL58 *Braemar, Tomintoul, Glen Avon* covers Beinn a Bhuird and Sheet OL53 *Lochnagar, Glen Muick & Glen Clova* covers the areas in its title.

Creag Meagaidh is on OS Explorer Sheet OL55, entitled *Loch Laggan & Creag Meagaidh*.

Harvey Maps produce the 1;25,000 Superwalker series maps. Three of these, *The Cairngorms & Ben Avon*, *Lochnagar & Glen Shee* and *Ben Alder*, cover most of the crags in this guidebook. They also produce a series of 1:40,000 Mountain Maps of which *The Cairngorms & Lochnagar* sheet covers most of the area.

The ability to use a map and compass correctly is essential for all winter mountaineers and climbers!

A GPS device, which are now built into many smartphones, can provide a useful backup to more traditional map and compass skills, but should not be relied on as the sole navigational aid. Walking on the bearing obtained from a traditional compass will nearly always be steadier than following that from its satellite-driven GPS cousin. Inbuilt compasses on GPS are not reliable but getting the bearing (or location) off a GPS and putting it into your compass can be useful in a whiteout – so always have a compass. Also, there is no battery in your compass to die at an inconvenient moment.

Mountain rescue

Mountain rescue teams are made up of experienced and skilled local mountaineers who undergo regular training in mountaineering and remote-care first aid skills. Rescues are coordinated by the police.

Mobile phones will usually be the fastest way to contact the emergency services. If doing this, dial 999 and ask for **police**, then ask for **mountain rescue**. It is worth noting that if your own mobile phone carrier/provider doesn't have a signal in your location, you may well manage to call 999 using another 'roaming' provider. If this is the case, the **police/mountain rescue cannot call you back** to follow up, so be very sure you have conveyed detailed info about the incident.

When contact is made with the rescue services, by whatever process, they will require as much concise information about the incident as possible. The following is a list of useful information to provide:

- Who is calling: name, phone number, location. Even if the caller doesn't know where the party are, giving information on where they are parked and the make/model/registration of their vehicle can be a huge help in a search.
- What happened?
- When and where did the accident happen?
- How many are in the party?
- How is the party equipped?
- The nature of the injuries and whether there is anybody with the casualty.
- Is a group shelter being used and if so what colour is it? Group shelters stand out well in poor visibility thus aiding the rescue team finding you.

In the event of an avalanche accident, additional information will be useful:

- The time of the incident, and how long the victims have been buried.
- How many completely buried victims there are.
- Whether avalanche transceivers are worn by the victims.

If it is not possible to make a call or attract anyone else by shouting, by whistle or by torchlight, and your party is made up of only two people, it is a difficult decision whether to go or stay. This will depend on the nature of injuries, the location, weather, equipment and perhaps other considerations. If the casualty is unconscious, then this decision is even more difficult. If you go for help, however, make sure the casualty is as well-equipped and comfortable as possible and in as sheltered and well-marked a location as you can find or create.

There is a mountain rescue box on Lochnagar on a small flattening midway between the loch and Central Buttress (NO 250 857). Likewise, there is one in Coire an t-Sneachda just south of the lochans (NH 993 032). Both contain avalanche probes and shovels plus other rescue kit. Both these locations are favourite gearing-up spots.

Avalanches

Avalanches occur every year in the Scottish mountains. In the vast majority

Avalanches

of avalanche accidents, the avalanche is triggered by either the victim or another member of the victim's party. A basic understanding of avalanches and how to avoid them is necessary knowledge for Scottish winter climbers. The ability to judge the likelihood and consequences of an avalanche, and knowing what to do if one occurs, can save lives.

Snow and avalanches

Scotland's highly variable winter weather tends to build up a layered mountain snowpack. Avalanches usually occur when the bond between adjacent layers fails. This failure can be brought on by a change in the properties of the snowpack or by additional loading.

Avalanches release on slopes between about 20 and 60 degrees, with slopes between about 30 and 45 degrees the most common. The greatest danger of both avalanches and cornice collapse usually exists during, and for approximately 24 hours after, a period of heavy snowfall or during periods of thaw, especially when accompanied by rainfall.

Avalanche types

Various types of avalanches occur under different conditions and present different degrees of hazard.

Powder or loose snow avalanches tend to occur during, or right after, snowfall. Usually the failure spreads out down the slope in an inverted V-shape. These avalanches are generally small, but in the confines of a gully they can be unpleasant and sometimes large enough to knock a climber off.

Dry snow slab avalanches can be a substantial size and are the most

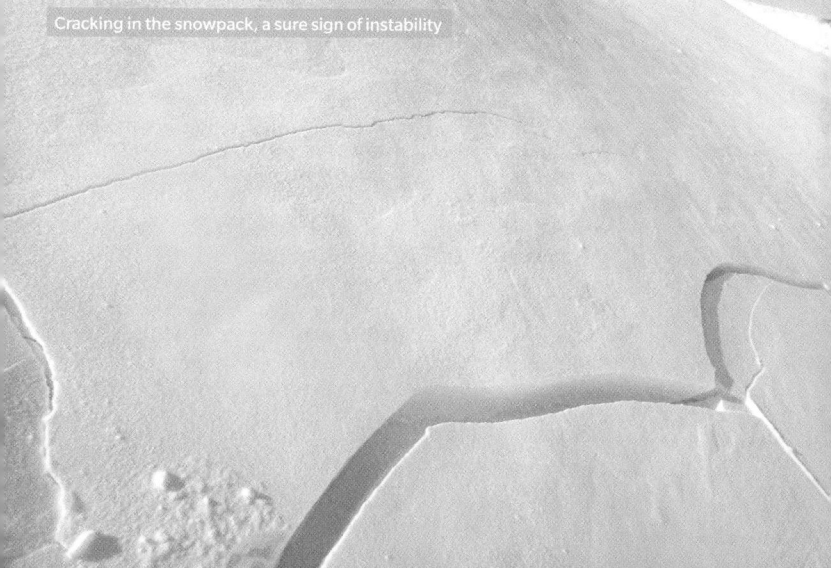
Cracking in the snowpack, a sure sign of instability

Avalanche debris in the Southern Cairngorms

common and most hazardous type of avalanche. They occur when a cohesive slab of snow slides due to the failure of a weak layer. These slabs are formed when wind-transported dry snow is packed onto lee aspects to form a cohesive layer of snow known as windslab. Although most common on lee slopes, particularly below cornices, pockets of windslab can build up in unexpected places, even on windward slopes. It can vary from soft to hard, and can be firm enough to walk on without sinking in so may feel stable to the unwary. It tends to have a dull, chalky appearance, and may squeak or creak when walked on or probed with an axe.

A weakness in the snowpack might well be strong enough to support an overlying layer of windslab in its undisturbed state. However, adding a small stress concentration to undisturbed windslab, such as a person walking on the slope, can initiate a shear crack which can grow rapidly, causing the failure of the whole slope. The slope is just waiting for a trigger, which could easily be a person. Many avalanche victims trigger the avalanche they are involved in.

Wet snow avalanches occur during periods of thaw, particularly if there's rainfall too. Wet snow tends to be denser and more viscous, making these avalanches particularly destructive. However, they tend to occur in their own time and are less prone to being triggered by people.

Cornices, overhanging lips of snow that form at the tops of slopes and gullies, can be prone to collapse, particularly during periods of formation or of thaw. They can become very large, and a cornice collapse can be very hazardous to those below. Additionally, the load produced by a cornice collapse may be enough to trigger an avalanche on the slope below.

Avalanche avoidance
Planning
Avalanche avoidance should start long before the mountains are reached. By gathering information on mountain weather and snowpack conditions before your excursion, you will be better equipped to make sensible decisions when on the hill. Heavy snowfall accompanied by wind is a sign of potential hazard. Long periods of cold temperatures will tend to maintain the hazard, while a freezing level that rises and falls rapidly will tend to create a period of instability followed by a significant consolidation of the snowpack. The greatest danger is likely to be on lee slopes, so be aware of recent and forecasted wind directions. Consult the SAIS avalanche forecast and consider possible alternatives should conditions turn out to be worse than expected.

Your mountain journey
You should already have a good understanding of the avalanche hazard before you set out. Throughout the day, continually observe weather and snow conditions both underfoot and around you – and consider its effect on avalanche hazards along your planned route.

Signs of recent avalanche activity are the most significant indicators of an avalanche hazard and should not be ignored. On the approach, observe the nature of the snow on the ground and in the air. Snow blocks cracking and breaking away beneath your feet indicates windslab and instability.

Other signs of danger are fresh snowfall and spindrift, which shows snow is being transported and is likely to be deposited as windslab in sheltered locations such as gullies and on lee slopes.

Another danger sign is a rapid rise in temperature, particularly when accompanied by rain or sleet. Areas of windslab will go through a period of instability for the first 24 hours or so of thaw. A heavy thaw will also increase the hazard of rock and ice fall on the crags.

Route choice and safety precautions
Route choice is not just about the climb, but about all your movement in the mountains. Ridges, buttresses and flat ground tend to be safer than open slopes and gullies. Windward slopes will generally be safer than lee slopes. However, local variations in topography can create a localised avalanche hazard even on windward aspects. Gullies will tend to concentrate avalanche depth and power. Even a very small area of windslab can represent a hazard if the run-out is into rocks, over a drop or into a terrain trap such as a stream bed or hollow, where the debris can build up to a considerable depth. Some very serious avalanche accidents have occurred when the size of the slab which released was only a few metres across.

Avalanche-prone slopes should be avoided by thorough planning and a willingness to change objective or retreat. If, for whatever reason, you find yourself in avalanche terrain, then reduce the risk as much as possible. If a slope must be crossed, traverse it high up to reduce the amount of snow above you. It is better to be carried further but be buried less deeply. Travel one at a time between safe areas and keep an eye on the person crossing the slope. Where possible follow other people's tracks but never assume that a slope is stable because one person has crossed successfully. Tighten clothing and remove wrist loops. If near rocky terrain and a good belay, consider putting the rope on and pitching across the slope.

If caught in an avalanche

If you feel the snow slope around you move, shout to alert others. Try to stay in place for as long as possible as the more snow that slides past you, the less there is above to potentially bury you. Once moving attempt, if possible, to roll out to the side, and try to get your head uphill. As the avalanche slows make a desperate effort to get to the surface or thrust a limb out of the snow. If some part of your body protrudes from the surface it will be quicker for rescuers to find you and dig you out. Make every effort to create a breathing space in front of your face.

As the snow comes to a halt it tends to harden up very rapidly, making self-escape almost impossible. If buried, try to remain calm to conserve oxygen and energy and do not shout; the sounds you make will not be heard on the surface.

If you see others being avalanched then try to keep them in sight. Note their starting position and where they were last seen, and attract the attention of other people in the area. Beware of further danger when approaching the area. Mark the position where the victim was last seen, as this can indicate the most likely burial area. Make a thorough search of the debris for surface clues. Probe the most likely burial spots then conduct a systematic search, probing with ice axes or walking poles with the baskets removed. If you have phone signal call mountain rescue but remember **the initial search is vital**. If a buried victim is not suffering any serious trauma injuries, they have about a 90 per cent chance of survival if dug out in the first 15 minutes. After 35 minutes, this drops to only about 30 per cent. The importance of the first search cannot be stressed too strongly.

SAIS avalanche forecasts

The Scottish Avalanche Information Service (SAIS) has an invaluable source of up-to-date avalanche information at www.sais.gov.uk. From mid December until mid April daily hazard reports and forecasts are produced for areas including Creag Meagaidh, Northern Cairngorms and Southern Cairngorms.

The avalanche forecast consists of a report about conditions observed on the day and a forecast for the following day. However, it should be remembered that the avalanche forecast is **dependent on the weather forecast**. Mountain weather is very complex and difficult to forecast. If the weather

Using this guide

Climb style categories

- ◇ snow
- ⊗ snow ice
- ⊛ cascade ice
- ⊠ mixed
- 🪨 rocky mixed
- 🟩 turfy mixed
- 🧊 icy mixed

forecast is inaccurate, then the avalanche forecast may also be inaccurate. The forecasts are meant as a guide and do not absolve climbers of the responsibility of making their own decisions and assessing the avalanche hazard.

Be Avalanche Aware (BAA) guidelines have been developed by the SAIS to encourage sensible avalanche behaviour, including a free app with various tools to help encourage safe travel and links to the SAIS forecasts. More information can be found at http://beaware.sais.gov.uk.

Using this guide

Each venue has an overview description, as well as an info box which provides the following: grid reference of the crag, starting point and approach time, crag altitude and aspect, typical route lengths and a summary of the style(s) present at the venue. There are also approach and descent directions, and details of typical conditions. Grid reference, base altitude and aspect are listed separately for specific buttresses within that venue.

The climbs are then described individually under headings which include name, route length, overall and technical grade, star rating and style categories. First ascent details are provided where available. The route is shown on a photo topo unless otherwise indicated.

Style categories

Every route in this guide is assigned a category to indicate the overall style of that route. There are three basic categories:

- Snow
- Ice
- Mixed

Almost all winter routes will have snow on them. However, only when snow is significant to the overall character of the route (mainly the easier gully lines) is the snow ◇ category used.

The following subcategories are given for ice climbs:

- snow-ice ⊗
- cascade ice ⊛

In addition, some mixed climbs ⊠ have a particularly strong characteristic and are given a subcategory:

- rocky mixed 🪨
- turfy mixed 🟩
- icy mixed 🧊

There are no subcategories for snow routes in this guide.

Ridges, like this remote location in the northern Cairngorms, can provide the safest and more enjoyable routes in poor snow conditions

Pete Trudgill climbing in lean conditions on Raeburn's Gully, Lochnagar (photo: John Trudgill)

There are various routes in this guide where the whole character of the route can change depending on conditions. Some routes that are usually climbed as mixed or ice routes early in the season can bank out to become snow routes later in the season. There are also some rocky and turfy mixed routes which sometimes become much icier in character. In these cases two symbols – separated by **or** – are given to indicate that these routes can be of different character according to the conditions. Other routes can contain crux sections of for example both ice and rocky mixed; such routes are shown with two symbols side-by-side.

The dynamic and ever-changing nature of the environment is one of the appealing aspects of Scottish winter climbing. The same route can feel very different under different conditions. For this reason, it would be impossible to accurately describe all the possible conditions that could be found on a particular route. Therefore, this classification, a bit like winter grades, is meant only as a rough guide to indicate what's likely to be found most of the time.

Grades

The usual winter climbing two-tier grading system has been used throughout this guide. The first number given (a Roman numeral such as III, IV or V) indicates the overall difficulty of leading the route considering, among other things, the seriousness, technical difficulty, protection, route finding and sustained nature.

Full Conditions in Raeburn's Gully (photo: John Trudgill)

OVERALL GRADES

- **Grade I**: Uncomplicated snow climbs which have no pitches under average conditions. However, cornice difficulties can be encountered, there can be dangerous run-outs and the avalanche hazard is often high in the snowy confines of a Grade I gully.
- **Grade II**: Gullies which have individual or minor pitches or high-angled snow (cornices can be difficult), or the easiest buttresses under winter conditions.
- **Grade III**: Gullies which contain ice in quantity. There is normally one big pitch and often several smaller ones. The buttresses will be fairly sustained.
- **Grade IV**: Routes of sustained technical difficulty. Short vertical steps, or longer sections of 60- to 70-degree ice expected in gullies. Buttresses require a good range of climbing techniques or are long and sustained.
- **Grade V**: Climbs which are difficult, sustained and generally serious. On ice climbs long steep and sustained pitches are to be expected. Buttresses will require winter techniques such as axe hooking and torquing combined with competent rock-climbing ability.

- **Grade VI**: Ice climbs will have long vertical sections or be thin and tenuous. Buttress climbs will include everything in Grade V, but there will be more of it.
- **Grade VII**: Usually buttress or face routes that are very sustained or technically extreme. If ice is involved, it will be extremely steep and/or thin and serious.
- **Grade VIII and above**: Very hard and sustained mixed routes. By the time you are considering this sort of grade, you should have a fair idea what will be involved.

The technical grades, which are given by the Arabic numeral, are based on the technical difficulty of an ice route of that level of overall difficulty. A technical grade lower than the overall grade suggests the route will be serious and committing, while the opposite would suggest a shorter and better-protected mixed route. For example, a V,4 would be a technically easy but serious Grade V route, probably on ice; V,5 would be a classic ice route with adequate protection; V,6 would be likely to be a classic buttress route – harder but better protected than a V ice route; V,7 would have a technically very difficult but short crux and good protection. It is unlikely that the technical grade will

Garbh Choire Mhor, probably the snowiest place in the UK

vary by more than two from the overall grade.

Grades are given for average conditions, which may or may not exist. A big build-up of snow and ice may make gully climbs easier but buttresses harder as more clearing is required to find holds and protection. The grades of some routes can vary dramatically, and on some of the harder climbs conditions are occasionally such that routes may be one or even two grades easier than that given. The absence or presence of even one good placement can make a big difference to the difficulty of some climbs. Occasionally a split grade is used to indicate a climb whose difficulty varies according to the build-up. An example of this is The Vent II/III in Coire an Lochain. Early season has a steep section past a chokestone, but later in the season this tends to bank out and it becomes a much easier proposition.

Route lengths

Route lengths are given for all routes. For some routes, especially easier gullies, this value is approximate as often there is not a clearly defined boundary between the approach slopes and the start of the route. Pitch lengths are given on some routes to help with route finding.

For most routes, 50m ropes are sufficient. However, 60m ropes can be useful, particularly on many of the ice routes on Creag Meagaidh.

Recommended routes

Since this is a selective guide, some routes have had to be excluded. While all the climbs included are worthwhile and have some positive features, a star rating (*, ** or ***) has been used to indicate quality. This has been done by considering all the features which make up a climb: its length, line, escapability, how sustained it is, and the quality of

AMENITIES

Aviemore and Braemar are well supplied with all the necessary facilities required by climbers.

Transport

There are several coaches each day to Aviemore from Edinburgh, Glasgow and Inverness. Daily trains serve Aviemore; it's common for climbers from London to catch the sleeper on a Friday evening, climb on Saturday and Sunday, then head back to work on the Sunday night train! Glasgow and Edinburgh airports are both approximately two and a half hours' drive from Aviemore, with Inverness airport about 40 minutes away.

From Aviemore there are several buses to the Cairngorm car park.

For venues approached from the Dee, there are buses from Aberdeen to Ballater and Braemar, but this still leaves the issue of getting to Loch Muick.

There is no bus service to Aberarder for Creag Meagaidh.

Most climbers find that a car is required to access the start points for each crag.

Shops and food

Specialist climbing gear can be bought in Tiso's, Nevisport and Cairngorm Mountain Sports (all on the Aviemore high street), and Braemar Mountain Sports on Invercauld Road, Braemar.

There are a number of supermarkets in Aviemore that remain open late into the evening. Smaller convenience stores can be found in Braemar and Ballater. For Creag Meagaidh, the nearest shop is in Newtonmore. There are also a variety of chip shops, bars and restaurants in various villages.

Accommodation

There is a wide variety of accommodation available, from 5-star hotels to soggy campsites. Details can be found online.

The one specific mountaineering hut in the area that can be useful is the Raeburn Hut near Laggan, which is owned and run by the SMC. Bookings can be made directly through them: www.smc.org.uk/huts/raeburn.

---

the climbing. However, route quality is a subjective measurement at the best of times. Scottish winter conditions are very variable, meaning that the same route can give very different climbing experiences on different days. It should be remembered that quality of a route will vary with conditions and is at best subjective, so the number of stars per route should be viewed as a rough guide.

Maps, diagrams and route numbers

Each of the main climbing areas features an approach map showing the best routes to the crags. These maps have been scaled at 93 per cent (resulting in a scale of 1:53,500). All the main crags have photo topos. However, some routes are not shown, either because they are outside of the photographed area or to avoid overcrowding. For these climbs, the text is sufficient to locate and follow the route. A broken line on a topo indicates that a section of the climb is hidden. The numbered routes offer good reference points for adjacent non-numbered climbs. An index of climbs is at the back of the guide.

Most crags have the routes described from left to right. However, a few, such as Hell's Lum and Stac an Fharaidh, are described from right to left. This is because the normal approach to these crags is from the right (when looking up at the crag). This is clearly indicated in the text. All directions refer to a climber facing the cliff, unless otherwise stated (such as for the descent).

Northern Cairngorms

The Hoarmaster, Coire an Lochain (photo: Murdoch Jamieson)

The Northern Crags

This area lies between the deep valleys of Strath Nethy in the east and the Lairig Ghru in the west, with the large expanse of the Cairn Gorm/Ben MacDui plateau to the south. These crags give the most popular and easily accessible climbing in the guidebook and, with ease of access from the Cairn Gorm ski road, can lull people into a false sense of safety and security. This can still be a very harsh environment. The crags face from east through north to west.

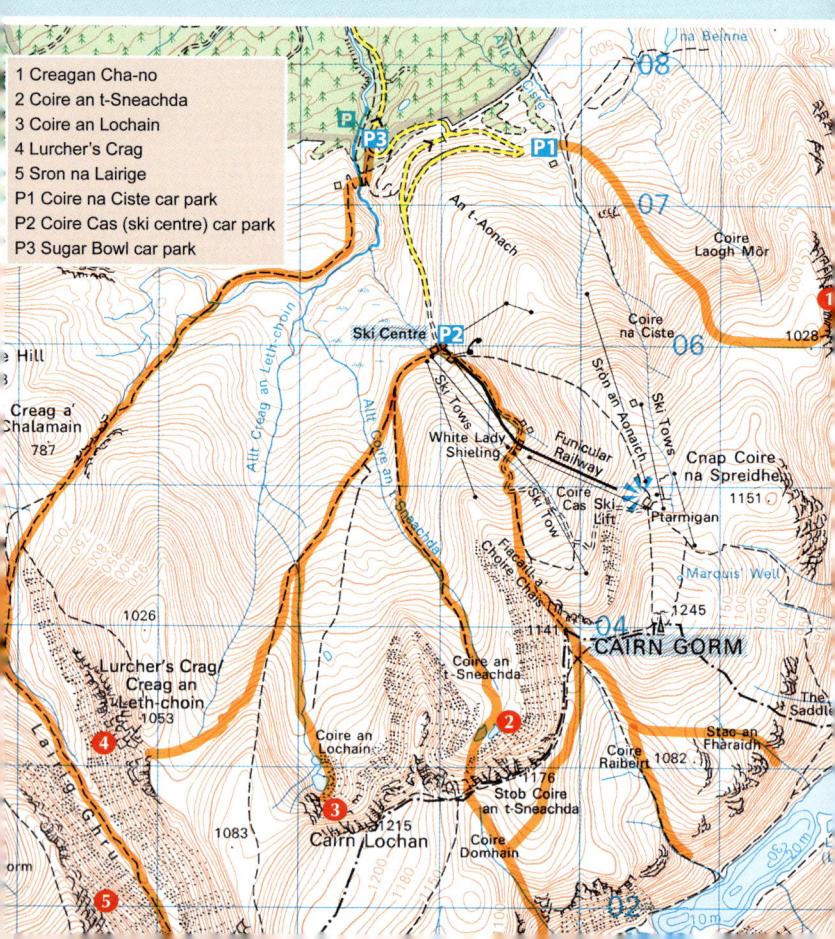

1 Creagan Cha-no
2 Coire an t-Sneachda
3 Coire an Lochain
4 Lurcher's Crag
5 Sron na Lairige
P1 Coire na Ciste car park
P2 Coire Cas (ski centre) car park
P3 Sugar Bowl car park

Creagan Cha-no (NJ 017 063)

Start	Coire na Ciste car park NH 997 074
Time	1hr 15min
Crag base altitude	950m
Aspect	East
Route lengths	30–55m
Style	A relatively new venue. Short mixed routes.

This line of small cliffs lies high up on the east flank of the north ridge of Cairn Gorm (Sron a' Cha-no), overlooking the deep upper glen of Strath Nethy. It is made up of a series of individual buttresses facing from north-east to south, with some good well-protected features and abundant turf. Cutty Sark Area and Chimney Rib are south of Recovery Gully, while Anvil Buttress, Arch Wall and Tower Buttress are to the north.

This has become a popular venue, with the attraction of being able to do several routes in one day.

Approach
The approach starts from Coire na Ciste ski car park (NH 997 074) and heads halfway to the ski building then goes left down a wooden staircase to cross the Allt na Ciste. Follow a path up the spur (Creagan Dubh) on the east side and cross a flat section. From here, go up in a south-east direction until the 1000m contour, then head east to Pt.1028m. Go north, parallel with the cliff edge, to reach the top of Recovery Gully, which lies just south of the protruding Anvil Buttress (NJ 01722 06310). A GPS device is useful, and care should be taken near the cliff edge as large cornices can form. Recovery Gully can be descended from the top of Anvil Buttress, while a 50m abseil down Anvil Gully, from a thread belay, takes you down the gap right (south) of the prominent Anvil Block.

Descent
Reverse the approach route.

Conditions
It can be windy on top of the crag so finding a sheltered gearing-up spot can be hard, with the outcrops of Pt.1028m being one option. The wind leaves big cornices and windslab in the gullies and slopes below the cliffs, so great care is required when

Coiling ropes at the top of Creagan Cha-no

Creagan Cha-no – Cutty Sark Area

1. Short Ridge IV,4
2. Mainmast IV,5*
3. Cutty Sark IV,4**
4A. Direct Start V,6
4. Auld Reekie IV,4

there are large quantities of new snow. Conditions can change very quickly on a sunny day, with the east- and south-facing walls softening but the north-east facing Arch Wall and Tower Buttress remaining in the shade and giving better climbing.

Cutty Sark Area   NJ 017 062 Crag base altitude 950m East facing

These small, squat buttresses have prominent lines and are the furthest left, lying 100m south of Recovery Gully.

Short Ridge 45m IV,4
J. Preston, J. Lyall and A. Nisbet, 12 December 2011
The squat buttress and short ridge, left of a prominent pinnacle and right of a wide snow gully. Climb a short chimney on the left side of the squat buttress and then up right to the ridge which is easy to the top.

Mainmast 35m IV,5*
J. Lyall, A. Nisbet and J. Preston, 12 December 2011
Right of the prominent pinnacle is a chimney-crack which is climbed to its top, then pull out left and follow the gully behind the pinnacle to exit right of the cornice (or continue up Cutty Sark from the top of the chimney).

Short Ridge

Cutty Sark 35m IV,4**

J. Lyall and A. Nisbet, 18 January 2011

The prominent corner right of Mainmast and the fault above, finishing by the left side.

Auld Reekie 30m IV,4

J. Lyall and E. Pirie, 13 January 2012

Climb an icy groove on the steep right flank of the buttress, then move left and pull into a short deep chimney, exiting left of the capping roof.

Direct Start 10m V,6

N. Adams and G. Lynn, 22 January 2012

A wide crack left of Auld Reekie's normal start leads directly into the chimney.

Chimney Rib 40m III,4*

R. Webb and S. Richardson, 21 November 2010

Climb the chimney up the rib on the left of Recovery Gully, then descend from the pinnacle and climb easily to the top.

Recovery Gully 50m I

The broad gully gives the easiest ascent, with the cornice passable on the right at the top of Anvil Buttress.

Anvil Buttress   NJ 017 063 Crag base altitude 950m East facing

This buttress is steep on the left side, with a longer south-facing wall to the right, containing Anvil Corner, before becoming less distinct further right.

Frozen Planet 40m IV,6

A. Nisbet, J. Preston and J. Lyall, 12 December 2011

An escapable line. Start up two short, steep corners leading left to a wide, open chimney and climb this to a ledge. Go up the bulging flaky edge above and move left behind a block to the top.

Anvil Gully 45m IV,4*

J. Lyall and A. Nisbet, 18 January 2011

Climbs up left under the impressive south-facing wall to a notch left of the Anvil Block. Climb up a V-groove and finish on the left at the top. An easier start can be made on the left and a harder finish on the right.

Anvil Gully (photo: Allen Fyffe)

Anvil Corner 50m VI,6**
S. Simpson and S. Richardson, 14 November 2010
The shallow corner line up the middle of the south-facing wall. Go up three steep steps to gain and climb the corner to a notch in the crest, then up this to the top.

Wile-E-Coyote 50m IV,4*
(no photo topo)
S. Crawford and A. Parmentier, 19 January 2012
The deep groove right of the crest of Anvil Buttress, gained from the right.

Duke's Rib 55m II/III*
(no photo topo)
R. Webb and S. Richardson, 21 November 2010
This easy-angled rib lies 15m before a col that leads to Arch Wall. Easy ground to a rock window which then leads to a steep left-facing corner and the top.

Arch Wall and Tower Buttress NJ 017 064 Crag base altitude 950m North-East facing

This rightmost section retains snow better than the other faces and has a lot of vegetation. The longest, most sustained routes are here, but the lines are less well defined.

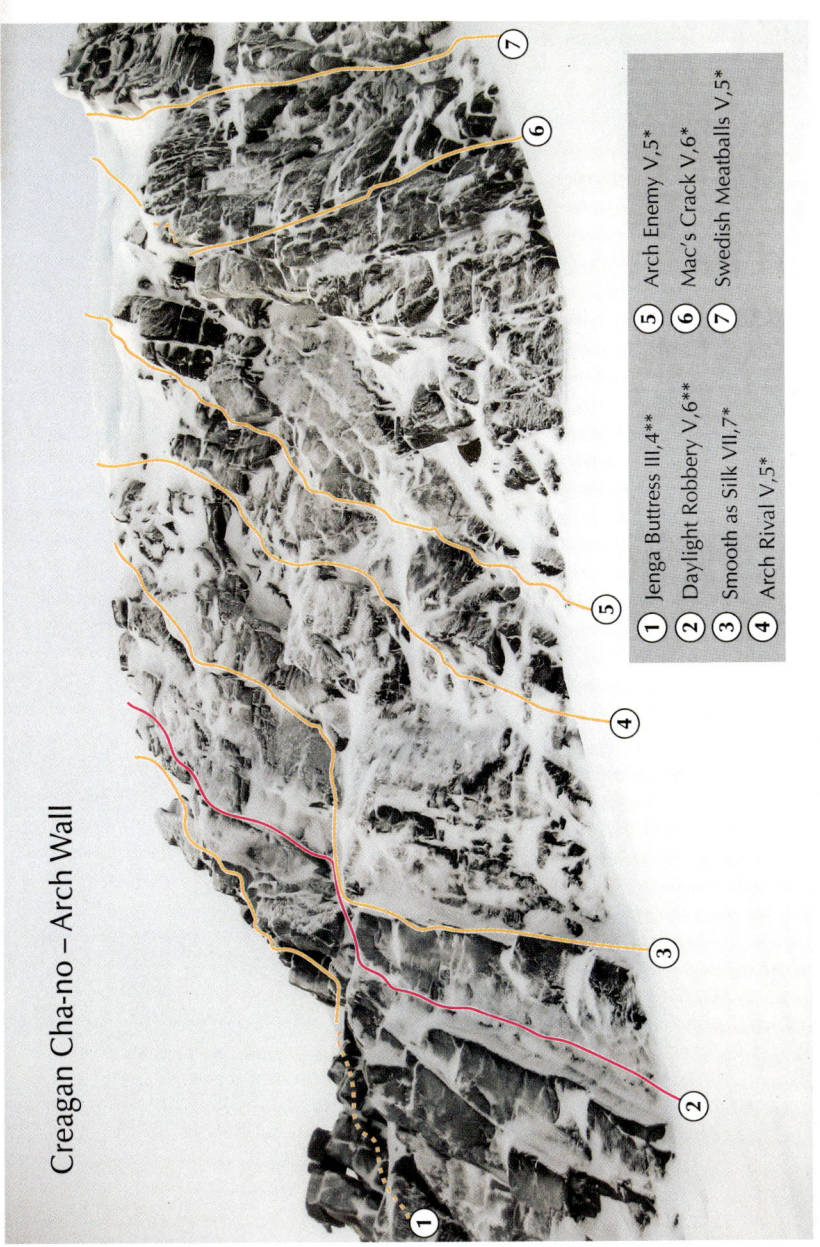

Winter Climbs in the Cairngorms

Jenga Buttress 55m III,4**
S. Simpson and S. Richardson, 14 November 2010
Start just to the left of the col and go up a gully to gain the rib, then over a step and continue up two stepped corners on the right of the crest. Climb a groove in the crest then a short gully and final wall to the top.

Daylight Robbery 55m V,6**
J. Edwards, S. Richardson and R. Webb, 8 January 2011
Start on the left side of Arch Wall up the left hand of two right-facing corners to a ledge. Continue up the right-facing corner at the left side of the ledge and finish close to Jenga Buttress.

Smooth as Silk 55m VII,7*
S. Richardson and I. Small, 12 December 2010
Climb the right-hand corner to the ledge and move right to belay under an off-width crack. Go up a left-facing groove, a steep crack, then an off-width to a roof where moves left lead to turf and a groove which is followed to the top.

Arch Rival 50m V,5*
S. Baboud and S. Richardson, 26 January 2012
Take a right-trending series of ledges to a short steep corner. Go up this to a belay ledge. Go up right to climb a turfy corner to a bay, then left to a short corner and the top.

Arch Enemy 50m V,5*
J. Lyall and A. Nisbet, 18 January 2011
A right-slanting line, going up a narrow chimney past a chokestone, then continue right up two steep steps and a short gully to finish on the right.

Mac's Crack 50m V,6*
A. Huntington, R. Clothier and G. McEwan, 30 December 2011
This awkward off-width crack is hidden on approach from the left and leads up the wall to finish up easier ground.

Swedish Meatballs 45m V,5*
R. Mathers and E. Mellergard, 27 January 2012
A left-facing corner leads up to a ledge under the bulging tower, which is passed by a steep corner on the left, then follow easier ground to the top.

Coire an t-Sneachda (NH 993 032)

Start	Coire Cas (ski centre) car park NH 989 060
Time	1hr
Crag base altitude	1000–1060m
Aspect	North-west to north-east
Route lengths	35–180m
Style	Popular and accessible venue. A good range of mixed buttress routes and snow/ice gullies which tend to be in the lower grades.

This is the most accessible of the climbing corries in this area. A somewhat broken and sprawling set of buttresses are ringed round the corrie edge. Of the Northern Corries of Cairngorm, this corrie contains the widest selection of good low grade winter routes and as such is the most popular of all the cliffs, especially at peak holiday times when it can be worth avoiding. However, there is a good selection of routes of all grades and of most styles of climbing. There should be something climbable most of the winter season and some of the rockier routes come into condition very quickly.

On the far left of the corrie is the Mess of Pottage with the straight gash of Jacob's Ladder on its right flank. Next is an area of broken ground and in the centre of the corrie is Aladdin's Buttress which is defined on its left by the big dog-leg gully of Aladdin's Couloir. This buttress consists of a lower dome-shaped mass of rock with more broken ground above. Here are several ridges, the rightmost one, Pygmy Ridge, being the most obvious. Next is Fluted Buttress, which gives the longest routes in the corrie. Fluted Buttress merges into Aladdin's Buttress and is cut by a number of gullies and faults. On its right side it runs into the snow slopes of the Goat Track, the wide slope leading to the col at the head of Coire Domhain. Last is the Fiacaill Buttress, which lies in a subsidiary part of the corrie high on the right and forms the side of the Fiacaill a'Choire an t-Sneachda, usually just referred to as the Fiacaill Ridge, which separates this corrie from Coire an Lochain.

Approach

From the car park in Coire Cas follow the good path, heading first west then south round the Fiacaill a'Choire Chais, for several hundred metres to a junction. Take the left fork into the corrie; this path is not marked on some older maps. The right fork continues to Coire an Lochain. Follow the path south into the corrie where it peters

The top of Coire an t-Sneachda (photo: Allen Fyffe)

out at the start of the boulder field, then go on to the small lochans below the centre of the cliff. It is unusual for there to be no track in the snow even if the path is buried. A less obvious alternative is to go from the car park to the White Lady Shieling then follow the track which zig-zags up Coire Cas until the Fiacaill a'Choire Chais can be crossed and a slightly diagonal line taken down into the corrie.

In thick and misty conditions it may be difficult to identify some of the climbs but from the mountain rescue box (NH 993 032) just south of the lochans, the magnetic bearings to some of the main gullies are:

- Aladdin's Couloir – 100 degrees
- Aladdin's Mirror – 112 degrees
- Trident Gullies – 154 degrees
- Goat Track Gully – 193 degrees
- Fiacaill Couloir – 246 degrees

Descent

From the top of the climbs the usual descent is to follow the plateau rim round to descend the Fiacaill a'Choire Chais into Coire Cas and so to the car park. The Goat Track, the slope west of Fluted Buttress, gives a steep but convenient return to the

Coire an t-Sneachda

corrie floor, but can be an avalanche risk. For climbs on the left of the corrie it is possible to descend from the col east of the Mess of Pottage and go down diagonally below that buttress. For climbs on the Fiacaill Buttress, the Fiacaill Ridge or the Goat Track give convenient descents.

Conditions

A high and accessible north-facing corrie whose buttress routes come into condition quickly. The easier gullies do not take much longer to form either. However, the ice development mostly depends on freeze/thaw and snow melt so routes can take longer to come into condition. Because of the popularity of this corrie many routes are becoming harder as vegetation is destroyed, especially by ascents in lean or thawing conditions. However, this can mean the route is well marked with crampon and tool placements. There can be some serious rock-fall danger in thaw conditions, particularly in the area of Fingers Ridge and Red Gully.

In windy conditions, especially with westerlies, the top of the cliffs, especially the Mess of Pottage, can be very exposed. The Fiacaill Buttress is much more sheltered, but the approach slopes can have dangerous slab build up in these conditions. With a northerly airstream these cliffs are often shrouded in cloud.

Mess of Pottage NH 998 032 Crag base altitude 1060m North-west facing

The leftmost buttress; the main section is seamed with cracks and corners while the right side is slabby low down and easy angled above. In the centre of the main section a big, stepped fault slants up slightly left and is used by several routes.

The Opening Break 100m IV,5
A. Cunningham and A. Fyffe, November 1990
The obvious left-facing corner on the left of the buttress: low in the grade. Start below the corner and climb cracks up the initial slabby steps with a detour right then back left at the first bulge. Climb the corner, which can be icy. Above, go right to easy ground and follow a fault up left below a steeper wall till twin cracks lead to more easy ground and the top. It is possible to avoid the first pitch and the crux by slanting in rightwards to the corner from higher up, making it a Grade III.

Honeypot 90m IV,6**
J. Lyall and M. Sclater, 25 March 1989
Lies near the left edge of the buttress and takes the obvious square-cut chimney near the left side of the top wall. Start in a recess where awkward moves give access to a right-slanting line. This leads to easier climbing up a gully which is followed to the

Coire an t-Sneachda – Mess of Pottage

1. The Opening Break IV,5
2. Hoheypot IV,6**
3. Wachacha VI,7*†
4. No Blue Skies VI,7**
5. The Melting Pot V,7**
6. The Message IV,6***
7. Pot of Gold V,6***
8. Mariella VI,7*
9. Droidless VI,6**
10. The Messenger V,6*
11. Sharks Fin Soup V,6
12. Yukon Jack IV,5*
13. The Haston Line III,4
14. Hidden Chimney III**
14A. Direct Start IV,5**
15. Jacob's Edge II
16. Jacob's Ladder I*

On the top pitch of Wachacha (photo: Keith Ball)

upper wall. Climb the square-cut chimney, passing the roof steeply on the right wall. The left side of the roof can also be climbed (V,6).

Wachacha 90m VI,7*

J. Lyall and A. Nisbet, 6 January 1990

Takes a line to the right of Honeypot and has two possible starts. Either begin about 6m right of Honeypot and climb a right-slanting crack to gain easy ground leading to the steep top wall, or climb an obvious right-facing corner further right again. Where it steepens, swing onto the left rib then continue up the crack line to the top wall (this is the summer line). Follow a crack and left-facing corner system then trend left to below the upper roof and come back right to the crack going through the roof. Follow this to the top.

No Blue Skies 100m VI,7**

A. Fyffe and L. Healey, 20 December 1990

A good but somewhat devious climb. Start at the first obvious left-slanting line, which has a steep right wall. Climb the diagonal corner until a traverse left to gain a right-facing corner can be made. Climb this then exit left onto a ledge by a horizontal slot. Continue up the crack line above to easier ground below the upper wall. Climb up to a fine right-facing flake crack which is climbed to a ledge. Go to its left end (at this point it joins Wachacha) then through the walls above by the crack, which is followed to the plateau.

The Melting Pot 90m V,7**

A. Cunningham and A. Nisbet, February 1987

The main feature of this route is the steep groove in the middle of the upper wall which is gained by a fairly direct line. Start midway between No Blue Skies and the main diagonal fault taken by The Hybrid. Climb leftwards into a short obvious groove with a tall, steep left wall. Leave the groove over a bulge and go left round an arête to more broken ground leading to the diagonal fault, which is followed to a large bay. Climb the overhanging groove then continue up the crack line to finish.

The Hybrid 100m IV,5*

(no photo topo)

Makes use of the diagonal fault. Start as for The Message and climb the obvious diagonal stepped fault for a pitch. Continue up and left as for The Melting Pot to the ledge system below the top wall. Move awkwardly up right to a higher ledge or traverse out right at a lower level to gain the front face and go left and up to a big ledge. This is the crux. Finish up the top pitch of The Message.

The Message 90m IV,6***

A. Cunningham and W. Todd, 23 January 1986

A good, popular and well-scarred route which takes the deepest groove in the centre of the face right of the diagonal fault. Start at the top of a large bay right of the lowest rocks and climb the stepped diagonal fault till the deep corner can be gained. Climb a short wall into the corner (this can be difficult) and follow the corner to the top and then go left then up to the upper ledge. Climb the right-facing corner to a bulge, swing left onto the edge and climb cracked slabs to the top. Alternatively climb the crack in the slab to its right.

Pot of Gold 90m V,6***

J. Lyall and S. Spalding, 26 November 1988

An interesting if escapable route up the edge of the buttress right of The Message. Climb the first pitch of The Message until a traverse right gains cracks and a narrow chimney on the buttress edge. Climb up till near The Message then climb up right to a large ledge. Climb the wall above by shallow corners and flakes to finish up a shallow chimney.

Mariella 90m VI,7*
C. Forrest, G. Ettle and A. Nisbet, 6 January 1991
Takes the deep red groove capped by an overhang and is high in the grade. Start as for The Message then climb into the groove. Follow this to a swing left below the roof and continue up a crack line to a ledge shared with Droidless (30m). Continue up the left-hand crack line (15m). Move left and climb walls and slabs to the plateau.

Droidless 90m VI,6**
C. Forrest and G. Ettle, 21 December 1990
The parallel crack line 3m right of the deep red groove of Mariella. It has a sustained first pitch. Start just on the right of Mariella and gain the main fault by a slanting corner just on its left, then follow the fault over the bulge to a ledge below parallel cracks (30m). Continue up the right crack, a difficult start, to an easing in angle in a bay below an obvious right-facing corner (20m). Climb the corner then easier ground (40m).

The Messenger 90m V,6*
G. Ettle and C. Campell, 15 November 1991
Takes the obvious left-facing corner some 10m right of the previous routes. Climb the corner, pulling left past the obvious roof with difficulty (35m). Trend right into an open fault and climb this and then a steep right-facing corner (35m). Easier climbing leads to the top (20m).

Sharks Fin Soup 90m V,6
J. Preston, G. Ettle and I. Taylor, 10 December 1999
Between the lines of The Messenger and Yukon Jack are three crack lines. The middle one has an obvious huge flake at its foot (the right crack is Despot V,7). Climb up onto this huge fin and up the crack line above. Continue in the same line to join The Haston Line and finish up that.

Yukon Jack 90m IV,5*
M. Sinclair and C. Schiller, 30 December 1993
Takes the main right-facing corner in the lower slabs leading to the diagonal fault of The Haston Line. Under powder snow conditions it will feel hard for the grade, but in icy conditions it can give an amenable Grade III. Gain the obvious right-facing corner via a crack. Climb the corner and cross The Haston Line to the steep upper rocks and finish up a wide chimney in the same line.

The Haston Line 120m III,4
D. Haston and party, 1965
The obvious lower left-slanting fault starting from the right corner of the buttress. There is an awkward corner moving up to easier ground and a choice of finishes on the upper snow slopes.

The Slant 120m II ◇ or
(no photo topo)
A diagonal snow line running left across the buttress. Start a pitch up Jacob's Ladder at a big recess. Climb up and left by the obvious line to open slopes on the front face and continue going left to finish up the big upper snowfield.

Hidden Chimney 110m III**
Climb The Slant for about two pitches to gain the right side of the most continuous upper buttress. Climb the chimney on its right side to the top passing over a prominent chokestone.

Direct Start 40m IV,5**
A good pitch that can be climbed for its own sake. Climb the prominent right-facing corner starting from the toe of the buttress. Ice makes it easier.

Jacob's Edge 90m II
Start up The Slant for about a pitch then slant back rightwards to finish up snow slopes overlooking Jacob's Ladder. Alternatively, go almost to the foot of Hidden Chimney and slant back right towards the edge.

Jacob's Ladder 100m I* ◇
A. Henderson and F. Mitchell, Easter 1939
The straight gully defining the right edge of the Mess of Pottage is steepest at the top and the cornice can be large. In lean conditions there may be a short chokestone pitch.

Aladdin's Buttress   NH 994 031 Crag base altitude 1000m North facing

This is the obvious buttress in the centre of the corrie and consists of a lower dome-shaped mass of rock, which is cut by a series of left-facing corner lines. The chimney fault of Patey's Route on the right side of the buttress is obvious. Above and to the right is an easier section of ground topped by several roughly triangular ribs, Pygmy Ridge being the rightmost rib. Aladdin's Seat is the 10m pinnacle above the lower

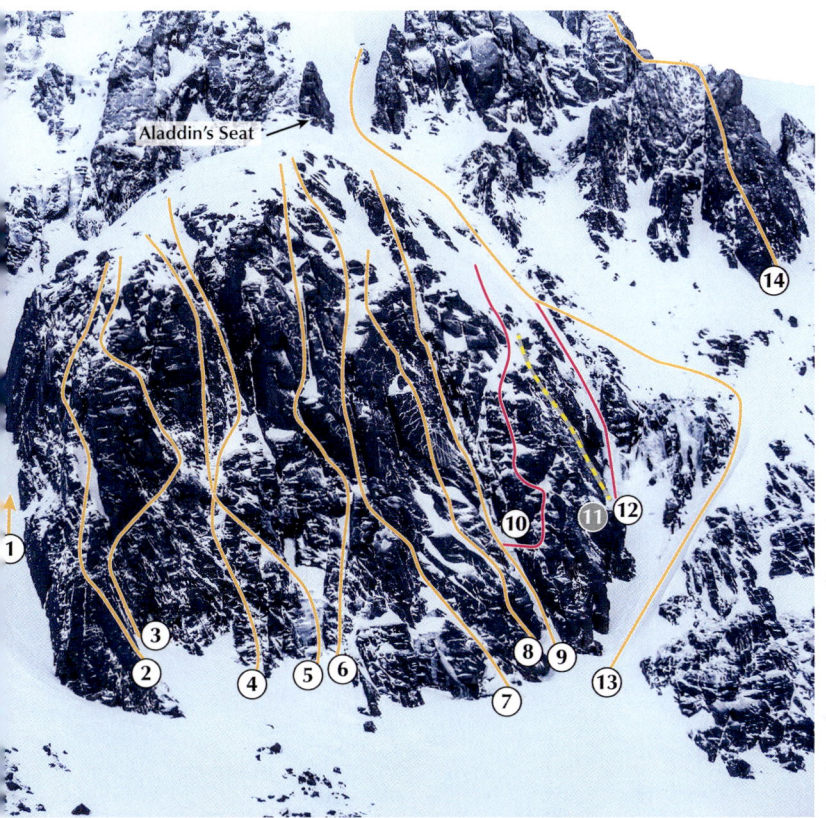

Coire an t-Sneachda – Aladdin's Buttress

1. Aladdin's Couloir I
2. Original Route IV,5**
3. The Lamp V,6*
4. The Prodigal Principal V,5
5. Doctor's Choice IV,5**
6. Doctor Janis V,7**
7. The Genie V,7***
8. Salvation VI,7**
9. Patey's Route IV,5**
10. Terms of Endearment III
11. Honour Among Thieves IV,4
12. Aladdin's Mirror Direct IV,4**
13. Aladdin's Mirror I
14. Pygmy Ridge IV,5**

buttress. For routes on the lower buttress either continue up, or descend, Aladdin's Mirror or Aladdin's Couloir. Alternatively, independent finishes can be found through the upper rocks at a choice of grades. There may be an equipped abseil point in some huge boulders at the top of Original Route; a single 50m abseil runs down into Aladdin's Couloir below the smooth wall by the bend.

Aladdin's Couloir 180m I ◇ or ⊗
A. Henderson and E.M. Davidson, 24 March 1935

The large dog-leg gully which flanks the left side of Aladdin's Buttress. There may be a small ice pitch at the bend. Sometimes a good ice pitch develops on the left wall just by the bend. Above this the gully widens and at a col above Aladdin's Seat, is joined by Aladdin's Mirror.

Original Route 100m IV,5**
W. March and B. Manson, 13 February 1972

Lies on the left side of the buttress and overlooks Aladdin's Couloir. Start 5m above and right of the toe of the long narrow rib that forms the lowest rocks on the left of the buttress. Climb a shallow corner with a couple of moves on its right to a prominent flake, well seen in profile from the right, and continue to a large snow ramp running up the flank of the buttress. From the top of the ramp climb up to some big blocks, then take the obvious ledge going left and up a series of steps on the wall overlooking Aladdin's Couloir. An alternative start begins at the foot of the lowest rock and climbs a groove onto the crest (V,6).

The Lamp 100m V,6*
A. Liddell and party, January 1988

A zig-zag line up the left side of Aladdin's Buttress. Start at an open corner just right of the long rib of rock. Climb the open corner, sometime moving onto the right wall, to its top. Go diagonally right on the obvious ramp to gain the large central bay. Take the diagonal fault leading left to easier ground and the top of the buttress and a choice of finishes.

The Prodigal Principal 100m V,5
G. Reid and J. Lyall, 19 November 1985

An ice route dependent on freeze/thaw for its formation. Start left of Doctor's Choice at ice runnels going up slabs and ramps before moving leftwards to a snow bay where Doctor's Choice is joined. Ice lines can also develop at either side of the usual first pitch, giving alternative starts. From the main bay climb the narrow chimney left of the big corner of Doctor's Choice – a good pitch.

Doctor's Choice 110m IV,5**
W. March and N. Dilley, 12 February 1972
A good climb which takes a huge detour to reach the largest left-facing corner in the upper part of the buttress. Start below this upper corner and climb up the fault to the big cave. Belay in the top left corner of the cave. Move down and go left onto the rib and follow the diagonal break left for a pitch into a snow bay. Leave this first bay on the right and gain easy ground. Go right and finish up the big corner (better with ice). If there is little ice, the narrow chimney of The Prodigal Principal provides a fine alternative finish.

Doctor Janis 120m V,7**
J. Grosset, J. Lyall and A. Nolan, 4 April 1987
Takes a series of corners on the right of the big fault of Doctor's Choice. Start on the right side of the bay below Doctor's Choice. Climb the main groove slanting right, cross an overlap and traverse up left to a bay. Take the hanging ramp (crux) on the right, slanting left up the steep wall, then a short corner to step right to a ledge.(The hanging ramp can be avoided on the left in icy conditions.) Follow the long final corner to the top.

In icy conditions a combination of the lower groove of Doctor Janis and the upper groove of The Genie gives a very fine icy climb at V,5.

The Genie 110m V,7*** or
G. Smith and G. Ball, 1979
The central of the three main corners right of Doctor's Choice gives a good climb. Start at the foot of Patey's Route and follow the lower of the slabby ramps going left and then follow open corners to where the cliff steepens up. A short crack running up to below a roof leads into a left-facing corner. This is climbed to a stance below the main corner which is followed to the top of the buttress.

Looking for gear on The Genie (photo: Ali Rose)

The Magic Crack 100m VII,7**
(no photo topo)
A. Cunningham and A. Nisbet, 7 December 1985 (White Magic); A. Huber and A. Mullen, 10 March 1999

Takes the eye-catching thin crack right of The Genie. Climb The Genie for two pitches to the belay below its main corner (60m). Traverse right to gain the finger crack and follow it to the overlap and a belay on the left (20m). Strenuous but well protected. Gain a right-slanting crack over the overlap then another crack leading back left to thin moves onto the final slab (20m). Finish easily or descend in two abseils from in situ gear. The original winter line (White Magic VI,7) climbs the first three pitches as described. The fourth pitch traverses right under an overlap to a ledge, and then finishes up a narrow chimney as for Damnation.

Salvation 100m VI,7**
J. Lyall and A. Nisbet, 27 December 1989

This route is on the cracked slabs right of The Magic Crack and main corner of Damnation (VI,6* and taking the rightmost left-facing corner). Start at the foot of Patey's Route and climb about 5m up the higher slabby ramp going left. Leave the ramp via a short chimney/groove then pass left of a short wall to a broad ramp. Break through the big overlap above at some flakes and climb thin cracks up the slab. The overlap can also be climbed about 3m right of the flakes. Move up right to a block, then follow the continuation right-facing corner to the top.

Patey's Route 120m IV,5**
T.W. Patey, February 1959

The wide chimney on the right side of the buttress is a very popular and reliable route. Generally, the more ice, the easier it is. There is bulge at about mid-height which is difficult. The top chokestone is usually turned by going out left then returning right by a long move back into the chimney line.

Terms of Endearment 100m III
A. Liddell and party, 1981

The buttress edge overlooking Patey's Route. Climb the start of Patey's Route a short way to just above the initial narrowing, then traverse a ledge right to its end and make a slabby move onto the front of the buttress. Once on the crest, follow the easiest line to join Aladdin's Mirror which can be followed up or down.

Aladdin's Mirror Direct 45m IV,4**
A direct start which climbs the ice pitch on the right of the buttress (25m). An easy chimney then leads to the parent route. The difficulty and length varies with build-up and it is extremely popular. There may be other short ice pitches to its right.

Coire an t-Sneachda

Aladdin's Mirror 180m I ◇ or 🟢

E.U.M.C. party, Easter 1946

An exposed snow route which skirts the right edge of the steeper rocks. Climb the open gully, slanting right to turn the steep rocks, then trend back left above them to join Aladdin's Couloir above Aladdin's Seat. Finish up the couloir.

Pygmy Ridge 90m IV,5** 🟢

Above the easy snow of Aladdin's Mirror are several roughly triangular buttresses. This is the most defined right-hand buttress, gained from Aladdin's Mirror or Central Left Hand. Start at a wide crack at the toe of the buttress and follow the crest on clean rock. Go across a horizontal section and finish up the final tower, although it is easy to escape right.

Fluted Buttress   NH 993 030 Crag base altitude 1020m North facing

This buttress is separated from Aladdin's Buttress by Central Gully, the left-hand of the three Trident Gullies which spring from a large snow bay extending high into the cliff. Right of this the cliff is steeper and slabbier and the pinnacles of Fingers Ridge are very distinctive. Right of Fingers Ridge are more gullies before the buttress diminishes in height and ends by the Goat Track. Because of the slabby nature of the foot of this buttress, the length of the routes can vary as a lot of ground can be buried in some conditions.

Central Left Hand 150m I* ◇ or ⓧ

This ascends the broad open rib on the left of Central Gully to finish up the defined gully right of Pygmy Ridge. A choice of lines is available, and the left side of the upper gully may contain a steep but avoidable ice pitch.

Central Gully 150m I ◇

T.E. Goodeve and A.W. Russell, 1 April 1904

The leftmost of the Trident Gullies starting from the snow bay. It slants left and the cornice is easily avoided. Can be interesting in lean conditions when short pitches may be encountered.

The Runnel 150m II** ◇

E.U.M.C. party, Easter 1946

The central straight, well-defined gully. High up there is a steep narrow chimney which constitutes the crux. The grooves on either side are climbable at about the same grade.

Coire an t-Sneachda – Fluted Buttress

1. Pygmy Ridge IV,5**
2. Central Left Hand I*
3. Central Gully I
4. The Runnel II**
5. The Grooved Rib III,4*
6. Crotched Gully II
7. Spiral Gully II**
7A. Direct Finish III*
8. Fluted Buttress Direct IV,5***
9. Broken Gully III*
10. Red Gully II/III**
11. Western Rib III,4
12. Goat Track Gully II*

The Grooved Rib 150m III,4*

This is the buttress between The Runnel and Crotched Gully. Start at the base of the rib and climb the prominent groove to easier snowfields. There is an easy finish parallel to The Runnel from here. The route takes either of the two steep grooves in the crest of the buttress. The left groove has a smooth start and is entered from the left and followed past a small chokestone. The right-hand groove is climbed direct and steepens to an awkward bulge which leads to a platform overlooking Crotched Gully. Step left into a narrow chimney leading to an easy finish.

Crotched Gully 150m II ◇
E.U.M.C party, Easter 1946
From the snow bay, go up the right branch which has a steep section near its top. This leads into a broad but well-defined upper gully which can have a large unavoidable cornice.

Vortex 60m IV,5*
(no photo topo)
G. Ettle and J. Lyall, 10 January 1992
The rib between the top part of Crotched Gully and the Direct Finish to Spiral Gully, reached by climbing Spiral Gully to the slanting gully and the foot of the rib. Climb the shallow groove up the rib and turn the roof on the right or left. Finish up a well-defined arête.

Spiral Gully 150m II** ◇ or ☀
T.W. Patey, February 1959
The main feature of this route is the right-slanting narrow gully cutting the upper rocks. Start up broken ground on the left of the buttress, heading for twin deep grooves which lead to easier ground and the foot of the slanting gully. Climb this to a small col then finish up a short pitch to the top.

Direct Finish 40m III* The wide groove above the start of the right-slanting upper gully gives a mixed pitch, although sometimes it can be icy and very good. Other harder finishes are possible up grooves further right.

Wavelength 150m III,4**
(no photo topo)
A. Fyffe and D. Bowen, 13 February 1985
Takes the left branch of the Y-shaped fault taken by Fluted Buttress Direct on the left side of the steepest slabby rocks and becomes more defined with height. Climb up to the foot of the twin grooves of Spiral Gully and climb diagonally up and right, taking in a short steep corner to gain a diagonal fault which goes right into the main fault where it splits. Climb the left fault to an open corner at the top which can be climbed or turned on the left (easier). Continue up the ridge to finish or cross Spiral Gully and climb the groove opposite.

Fluted Buttress Direct 150m IV,5***
A. Fyffe and S. Crymble, 18 March 1978
A good route up the narrow but prominent Y-shaped chimney system on the left of the steeper slabby rock. Climb a pitch of easy broken ground to the chimney and follow this to the fork where the fault gets bigger – can be harder under powder conditions. Take the right fork which leads onto the crest and follow this to the plateau.

Broken Gully 130m III*
T.W. Patey, J. McArtney and J. Cleare, February 1967
The gully between the main part of the buttress and Fingers Ridge is good to start, then the upper section is wide and straightforward. Start from the top of the first bay right of the lowest rock. Climb steeply up and right until it's possible to go left by a short wide crack onto the top of a slabby pillar near the top of the initial gully. Move left into the main funnel-shaped upper gully which is easy and offers a choice of lines.

The **Left-Hand Start** climbs directly into the upper gully by a narrower fault and is generally harder but needs ice.

Fingers Ridge 130m IV,4**
(no photo topo)
J.R. Dempster and J. Wallace, 19 January 1969
The slabby ridge between Broken and Red Gullies has two prominent pinnacles high up where the buttress narrows. A popular route, although the upper part of the ridge has many loose blocks and is best avoided in thaw conditions. Start just at the foot of Red Gully and go diagonally left for a pitch to a good ledge by a short deep corner on the left side of the buttress. From the left side of the ledge climb the blunt rib close to Broken Gully. Trend right and climb a flake to gain the obvious open groove. Climb the right-facing groove (escape into Broken Gully is possible here) then the pinnacled ridge to a narrow col then to the top. The short wall at the end of the col may be the crux if climbed direct but can be avoided on the left side.

Red Gully 120m II/III**
The gully on the right of Fingers Ridge is narrow and well defined at the bottom, and often very busy. Climb the initial chimney, usually on ice, then follow the funnel-shaped upper gully to finish. Again, in thaw conditions, the blocky nature of the upper gully can provide serious rock-fall danger.

Western Rib 120m III,4
The rib on the right of Red Gully is usually gained from above the mushroom-shaped pinnacle a pitch up Goat Track Gully. Climb the blocky and escapable broad rib to the top. Sometimes possible to climb the rib all the way from the start of Red Gully if icy.

Goat Track Gully 120m II*
Starts close to Red Gully and slants right below a big vertical left wall. At the steep section climb the right corner, which can be awkward but well protected if bare of ice. Above the gully is less defined and open to variation.

Coire an t-Sneachda

Fiacaill Buttress   NH 989 030 Crag base altitude 1060m North-east facing

This lies high on the right of the corrie flanking the Fiacaill Ridge which itself gives a pleasant route of Grade I to II depending on the line taken. The Fiacaill Couloir, which is hidden from many angles, slants up leftwards dividing the buttress into two contrasting parts. The left section is split by the midway ledge, above which are some prominent, slabby ramps. The right section has several large vertical features and obvious snow ramps. As the highest cliff in the corrie, it may be in condition when other buttresses are not and can also be sheltered from westerlies. However, the open approach slopes can be avalanche prone.

Escapologist 55m IV,6
G. Ettle and J. Lyall, 10 March 1992
Start 8m left of the main left-slanting groove of Houdini. Slant up left before moving right over a slab to an obvious ledge. Climb up left to a large block (30m). Stretch (or jump) from the top of the block to reach turf and continue up a corner and easier ground to the terrace (25m).

Straight to Jail 50m V,5*
D. Jarvis and B. Ottewell, April 1996
The steep groove above the start of Escapologist. Follow Escapologist to above the obvious ledge. Move right to gain a steep groove and climb this to the midway ledge. Needs ice to be at this grade.

Houdini 160m VI,7***
A. Cunningham and A. Fyffe, February 1990
An intricate but excellent line up the left face. Start in the middle of the lower tier and climb the main left-slanting groove then trend left to the midway ledge. Climb a short wide corner to a big ledge with flakes and traverse delicately right to gain ramps which are followed a short way to reach the left side of a big block. Go right

Houdini (photo: Guy Steven)

Coire an t-Sneachda – Fiacaill Buttress

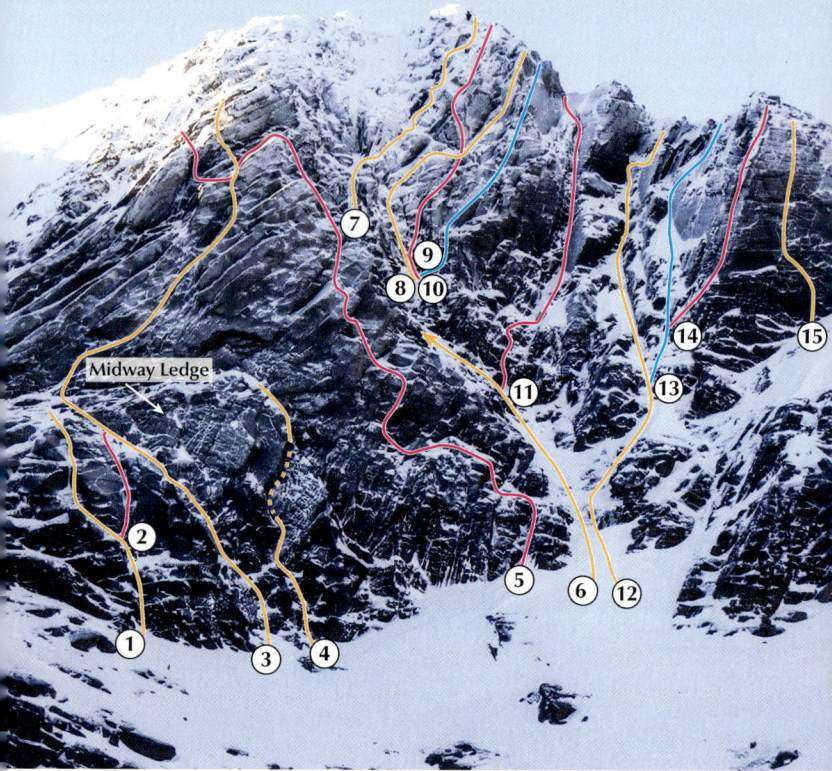

Midway Ledge

1. Escapologist IV,6
2. Straight to Jail V,5*
3. Houdini VI,7***
4. Stirling Bomber V,7**
5. Smokestack Lightnin' VI,7*
6. Fiacaill Couloir II/III***
7. Trampled Underfoot IV,4
8. Rampant IV,5**
9. Physical Graffiti IV,6**
10. Burning and Looting V,6*
11. Belhaven V,6**
12. Invernookie III,4**
13. Short Circuit IV,5**
14. The Seam IV,5***
15. The Hurtling XI,11

and climb the groove/ramp going right, and above a chokestone head up by thin climbing to below the final wall. Climb this wall by going left into a niche then up to gain the step.

Stirling Bomber 55m V,7**

A. Cunningham and A. Fyffe, 4 January 1990

The obvious right-facing crack and chimney line on the lower buttress gives a good but unusual climb, finishing on the midway terrace. Start right of the chimney and climb up and left to gain and follow the flake crack into the chimney. Climb the chimney which gradually widens (difficulty can be height dependent) and curves over to form a roof above which a ramp is gained and followed to the midway ledge.

Jailbreak 110m VII,7* or

(no photo topo)

A. Fyffe and A. Liddell, 31 January 1986

Takes the obvious ramp leading to the midway ledge and then has a serious and intricate pitch leading to the more featured upper part of the buttress. Start about 15m left of Fiacaill Couloir and climb the stepped ramp to the ledge. Go left about 10m and climb up and right until moves left lead to a short groove-cum-ramp running right (fairly direct and shares some of the upper part with Houdini). At the top of the groove, move left to the right side of a large block (Houdini also belays here then goes rightwards.) Climb the obvious ramps and corners above to below the vertical top wall. Move right of the obvious chimney (or climb it, as an easier finish) to climb the wall diagonally left via a niche to finish by the step in the top wall (as for Houdini).

Smokestack Lightnin' 140m VI,7*

A. Cunningham and A. Fyffe, 16 February 1990

A fine but escapable route which zig-zags up the buttress to the left of Fiacaill Couloir. Start in a bay just left of the base of Fiacaill Couloir and climb this to a ledge. Traverse left to some large blocks. Climb a corner on the left, and then trend back rightwards to another ledge. Traverse left to below a deep overhung corner. Either climb this corner (strenuous but well protected), or gain a hanging flake on the left and use it to pull left round on to the front face. Either way, a slanting corner above gives access to the crest of the ridge. Climb this to a barrier wall and make a descending leftward traverse for about 10m (crossing Houdini) to a chimney which is climbed to easier ground.

Fiacaill Couloir 150m II/III*** or

T.W. Patey, 17 January 1958

The big diagonal gully offers a choice of lines to the top, where the final chokestone can be hard if the build-up is poor. It can be interesting and icy or steep snow. Above the col go diagonally left to gain the plateau.

Winter Climbs in the Cairngorms

> The next six routes all climb the wall above Fiacaill Couloir and are accessed by climbing this, almost to the top in some cases.

Trampled Underfoot 60m IV,4
G. Ettle and J. Lyall, 13 January 1992
Starts about 8m up Fiacaill Couloir from the big ledge at the foot of Rampant. Climb steeply up on vegetated ledges then move left to climb a short corner. Follow a ledge right and climb a large right-slanting ramp to the ridge (or, more easily, up a gully). Directly above the short corner is a chimney which gives a good finish (IV,5).

The top pitch on Rampant (photo: Guy Steven)

Rampant 75m IV,5**
A. Fyffe and T. Walker, 1 March 1979
Takes narrow left-leaning ramps then a big right-facing corner. It starts about two pitches up Fiacaill Couloir where the left end of a large ledge system is gained by a short wall. Climb the right of two ramps, initially going up left then up right to a corner to gain a ledge below a steep wall. Go right round the edge and follow the main corner, passing under a huge chokestone at the top.

Physical Graffiti 70m IV,6**
A. Fyffe, and J. Lyall, 7 February 2007
A direct line up the vague buttress below the big top corner of Rampant. Start as for Rampant on the big ledge and after a couple of moves up Rampant go straight up right to a V-shaped niche. From the top right-hand corner make awkward moves to exit left then follow the fault, passing the left side of a block roof to a ledge (35m). Climb up to the foot of the main groove of Rampant and take a short chimney on the left to gain a pinnacle. From

its top, move up to a niche below an overhang and climb the slanting groove on the right leading to blocky ground and the top (35m).

Swan Song 70m V,6*
(no photo topo)
G. Ettle and J. Lyall, 17 February 2007
Takes a line parallel to Physical Graffiti to finish up cracks in the side of the pillar between Rampant and Burning and Looting. Start on the big ledge and climb the fault left of the big block and continue up into a curving corner. Go up a thin crack in a slab to gain an awkward short slot leading to a ledge (35m). Climb the ramp on the right (below Rampant) and pull out left and climb the crack left of the sharp rib to finish on the rib (35m).

Burning and Looting 70m V,6*
Pitch 1: G. Reid and J. Hepburn, January 1988; as described: A. Cunningham and A. Fyffe, 13 February 1991
The rib between the corners of Rampant and Belhaven. Start at the big ledge as for the previous routes, and from near a big block on the ledge go up to a ledge leading right then go into a hanging groove capped by a block. Enter the slot (strenuous but interesting) or turn it on the right. Climb the rib above by cracks and blocks, mostly on the right.

Belhaven 75m V,6**
A. Fyffe and K. Geddes, 19 February 1979
The main corner system in the wall directly above the bend in the Fiacaill Couloir gives interesting climbing. Climb the couloir until big ledges lead right into the corner which is then followed throughout. If there is a good build-up, the corner can be gained direct.

Invernookie 120m III,4**
K. Spence and J. Porteous, 4 January 1969
A good, popular and well-marked route that takes the main left-slanting ramp line on the wall overlooking Fiacaill Couloir. Start just right of the couloir and go up and right to gain the ramps. Climb these with some short, steep steps to where they end below an impending wall. Go up the corner into the chimney-cave. Traverse the ledge right and finish up a short groove.

Short Circuit 110m IV,5*
S. Monks, G. Reid and A. Fyffe, 9 February 1987
This route takes the snow ramp above and parallel to Invernookie. Start up Invernookie but go further right to gain the higher ramp. Climb this to its top then climb thin ice in the corner, or go left and climb the cracked edge to a snow patch.

Climb a short wide crack into the right of two grooves. Climb the crack in the slab to its right to finish.

Seam-stress 100m IV,6**
(no photo topo)
J. Grosset, J. Lyall and M. Sclater, 13 December 1987
The parallel fault just left of The Seam, which leads to a spectacular finish through the roof.

The Seam 100m IV,5***
J. Grosset and J. Lyall, 2 January 1986
An excellent route up the obvious chimney fault immediately left of the steep triangular wall on the right of the buttress and right of a long white streak. Climb Invernookie for a pitch then trend up right into the chimney, which is followed to the top.

The Hurting 35m XI,11
D. McLeod, 19 February 2005
One of the hardest routes of its type anywhere, this takes a line up the centre of the triangular wall right of The Seam. Exceptionally hard, strenuous and serious, with ground-fall potential and tenuous and blind climbing. Not one for the faint-hearted. Start at the obvious detached flake and climb the faint groove line for 10m to a ledge and runners. Continue straight up some hollow flakes then go right to the roof. Climb the left-hand side of the roof and traverse right to a hidden flake crack. Go to the top of this then move left then diagonally right into a niche and the finish.

Coire an Lochain (NH 983 029)

Start	Coire Cas (ski centre) car park NH 989 060
Time	1hr 30min
Crag base altitude	1100–1150m
Aspect	North-west to north-east
Route lengths	50–150m
Style	Another popular and relatively easily accessible venue. One of the first crags to come into condition. Mainly mixed buttress routes with a few gullies in the easier grades.

This is the most westerly of the Northern Corries of Cairngorm and consists of a compact headwall of cliffs lying below the summit of Cairn Lochain and overlooking a huge pink slab – the Great Slab. This is a slope prone to avalanches and should be treated with caution.

The buttresses themselves are numbered one to four from left to right and are separated by obvious gullies. On the left is The Vent, initially narrow but opening out into a wide funnel above. In the centre of the cliff is the wide diagonal of The Couloir and tucked into the right-hand corner of the corrie are the two branches of Y Gully, separated by a narrow rock pillar. The rock in this corrie is very blocky and split by a succession of prominent crack and corner lines, which give some very fine mixed buttress routes.

Approach
From the ski area car park in Coire Cas, contour round the Fiacaill a'Choire Chais, initially as for Coire an t-Sneachda but take the lower track at the fork after a few hundred metres. Cross the stream and continue on one of several paths (not all shown on the map) which lead roughly south into the corrie. It is surprisingly easy to miss the corrie in poor visibility and careful navigation is recommended in bad conditions. To gain the foot of the routes it is best to ascend the slope to one side or other of the Great Slab, depending on where your chosen route lies.

Descent
Follow the corrie edge going roughly south-west to avoid the cliff edge, then north-west to a plateau. From here a steep descent back into the corrie is possible just north

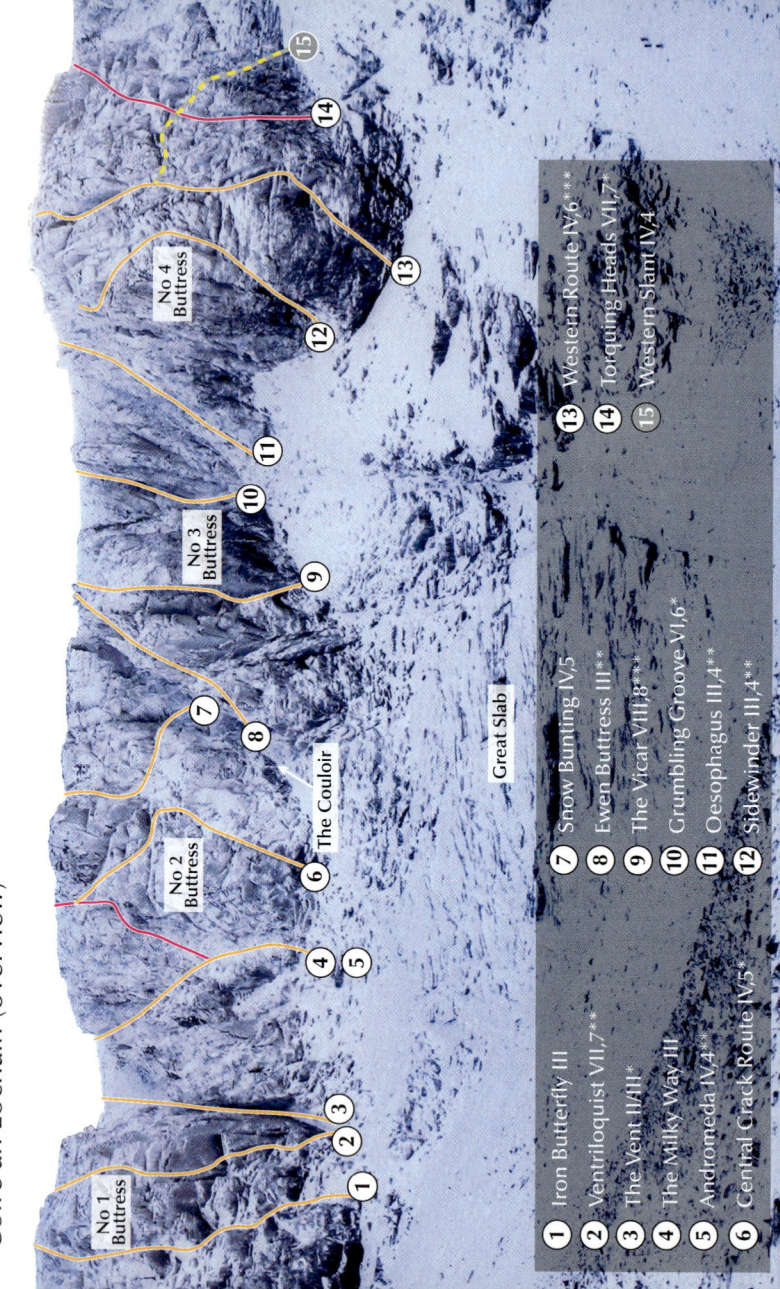

Coire an Lochain (overview)

1. Iron Butterfly III
2. Ventriloquist VII,7**
3. The Vent II/III*
4. The Milky Way III
5. Andromeda IV,4*
6. Central Crack Route IV,5*
7. Snow Bunting IV,5
8. Ewen Buttress III**
9. The Vicar VII,8**
10. Grumbling Groove VI,6*
11. Oesophagus III,4**
12. Sidewinder III,4**
13. Western Route IV,6***
14. Torquing Heads VII,7
15. Western Slant IV,4

of twin burns, or go northwards down the ridge. The latter is safer when there is any avalanche risk. Alternatively the Fiacaill Ridge can be descended, or the plateau rim can be followed to eventually descend into Coire an t-Sneachda by the Goat Track or continue round and down the Fiacaill a'Choire Chais.

Conditions

This is a high cliff with its base at around 1100m. It comes into condition very quickly with snow and cold weather. However, good conditions can also extend well into the spring. Mixed routes are the first to be climbable, with the snow and ice routes taking a little longer to form. With a huge snow-collecting plateau above the cliff, there can be a substantial build-up of snow. This, combined with the cliff's northerly aspect and height, may mean that occasional routes, such as the branches of Y Gully, are climbable into June some years, while some of the buttresses may be good in October.

Avalanches can be a real hazard, both below the cliff and from cornices that build up at the top. The Great Slab is a notorious avalanche slope, and a huge full-depth avalanche occurs here each spring. At other times it becomes sheathed in ice, and it is worth avoiding this slope most of the time.

Number 1 Buttress   NH 985 027 Crag base altitude 1100m North-west facing

This buttress, the left-hand one, is cut by some deep and prominent corners; the right side is a steep wall overlooking The Vent. The front face is also steep but merges into broken ground on the left.

Iron Butterfly 150m III

(see overview topo)
S. Docherty and B. Gorman, 31 December 1969
Climbs the more broken ground bounding the left side of the most continuous rock. Start in a huge open corner about 40m below and left of The Vent. Climb a groove to a ledge below an obvious crack in a steep wall. Step up right then up to below another steep wall. Move left then up to below another steep wall. Go rightwards and gain a wide gully and follow this to the plateau.

Coronary By-pass 110m V,7*

A. Fyffe and J. Hepburn, 20 April 1994
Takes a line right of the upper gully of Iron Butterfly and left of Auricle. Start on the right, about 5m above the lower corner of the buttress. Climb the chimney line and slant diagonally left to below the big corner of Auricle (35m, as for Auricle). Go left below a steep wall into an open corner (10m). Climb this, crux (10m). Ascend

a narrow flake chimney. Move right then go up a deep corner crack. Continue up the same line, passing a rock crevasse (30m). Climb the crack in the corner and continue up the slot and corner, or slant right in the rock crevasse to easy ground (25m).

Auricle 90m VI,7*
C. MacLean and A. Nisbet, 29 November 1984
Lies on the front face of the buttress and takes the big right-facing corner. Start about 5m up from the corner of the buttress and climb a corner/chimney to reach easier ground slanting up left to below the main corner (35m). Climb this strenuously, passing several chokestones (15m). Continue up the corner above to a large flake. From the top of the flake climb an overhanging recess to the top of the buttress. Cross the rock crevasse to finish (40m).

Ventriloquist 90m VII,7**
J. Lyall and A. Nisbet, 21 December 1990
A fine sustained route climbing cracks in the wall just right of Auricle. It is strenuous and well-protected with big cams if not verglassed. Start as for Auricle and climb the chimney-crack, then move right to climb a bulging crack into a recess. Pull steeply out of this and up to the wide crack (35m). Climb the crack line (crux) right of Auricle's groove (10m). Climb two short corners to a ledge (10m). Climb the thin crack on the right, making a short detour on the right at the steepest section. Cross the crevasse and finish up a deep crack (35m).

Ventricle 90m VII,8**
C. MacLean and A. Nisbet, 27 December 1984
Very hard but well-protected pitches separated by big ledges and taking prominent grooves and cracks on the left wall of The Vent. Start about 5m right of the corner/chimney of Auricle and climb a short overhanging crack. Move right along a ledge and go up a wall near the right edge to a small mossy recess (15m). Climb a thin crack on the right and swing left into the top of an overhanging groove. Go up to a larger overhanging groove and climb this to a big corner (20m). Climb this to a big ledge (15m). In the corner is a wide crack: climb just to the right of this then step left into it and climb it (15m). Go left to finish up The Ventriloquist (25m).

Daddy Longlegs 70m VIII,9**
B. Davison and A. Nisbet, 25 February 1991 (Big Daddy); P. Benson and G. Roberston, 7 December 2002
Hard and strenuous climbing starting up the obvious steep groove just inside The Vent. Climb the groove, then step right into a second groove and climb it to ledges (35m). Scramble up left to the base of a big corner containing a wide crack (10m).

Coire an Lochain – Number 1 Buttress

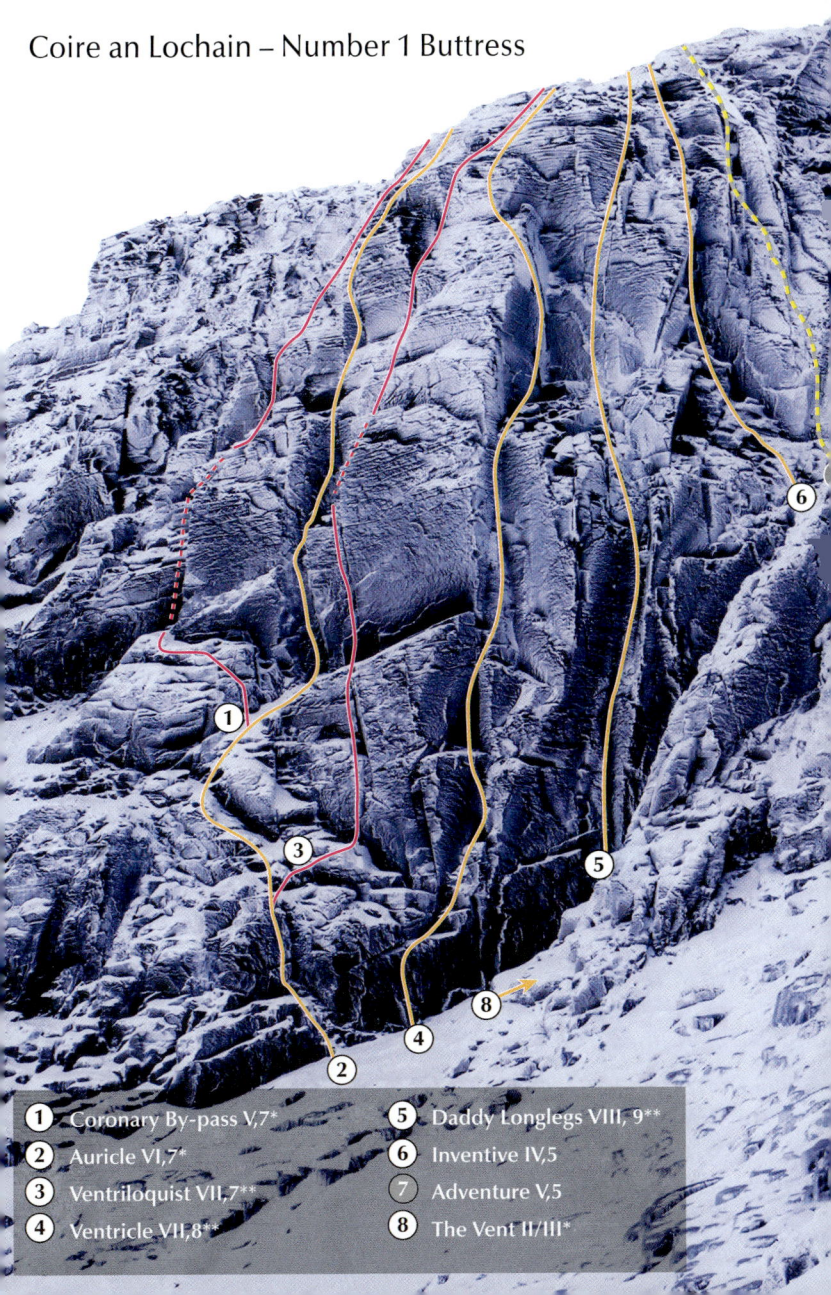

1. Coronary By-pass V,7*
2. Auricle VI,7*
3. Ventriloquist VII,7**
4. Ventricle VII,8**
5. Daddy Longlegs VIII, 9**
6. Inventive IV,5
7. Adventure V,5
8. The Vent II/III*

Seconding the first pitch of Daddy Longlegs (photo: Pete MacPherson)

Climb two consecutive, vertical cracks in the wall right of the corner (crux) to easier ground (25m).

A fine variation (**Big Daddy 80m VII,8**) avoids the top pitch by finishing up the wide corner crack as for Ventricle.

Inventive 70m IV,5
A. Fyffe and J. Hepburn, 20 April 1994
The deepest corner in the left wall above the chokestone in The Vent. From below the chokestones climb a groove into the corner. Climb the corner to easier ground and so to the plateau. With less of a build-up, climb The Vent to above the chokestone and traverse left into the corner.

The Vent 100m II/III*
E.M. Davidson, R.F. Stobbart, M. McBain, J. Geddes and H. Harrison, 13 April 1935
A popular route with short although very variable difficulties. Can be even harder if very lean. The lower narrow gully has a chokestone pitch near its top; this varies with build-up and ice. Above, the gully opens out into an easy funnel.

Number 2 Buttress   NH 985 026 Crag base altitude 1150m North facing

This wide buttress stretches between The Vent and The Couloir. The left side has more features while the central portion is composed of steep walls separated by ledges. The wide diagonal shelf of The Milky Way is conspicuous on the left. To the right of the upper section of The Milky Way is a prominent, steep tower which is a useful landmark. There is a steep wall split by The Crack just below the plateau which is also a useful marker.

Ventilator 100m II/III*
D.S.B Wright and party, 1969
The right side of The Vent is a defined rib. This route takes the corner on the right of the rib. Start in a snow bay about 30m right of the rib and from its top traverse into the corner and climb it to the top of the rib. Finish up The Vent. Can be easier if there is consolidated snow on the slabbier sections.

Chute Route 90m V,5*
M. Harris, D. Scott and R. Shaw, 24 December 1968
The corner at the head of the snow bay can give a fine ice pitch. The left wall of the corner is distinctively smooth. Above the corner join The Milky Way to finish.

Coire an Lochain – Number 2 and Number 3 Buttresses

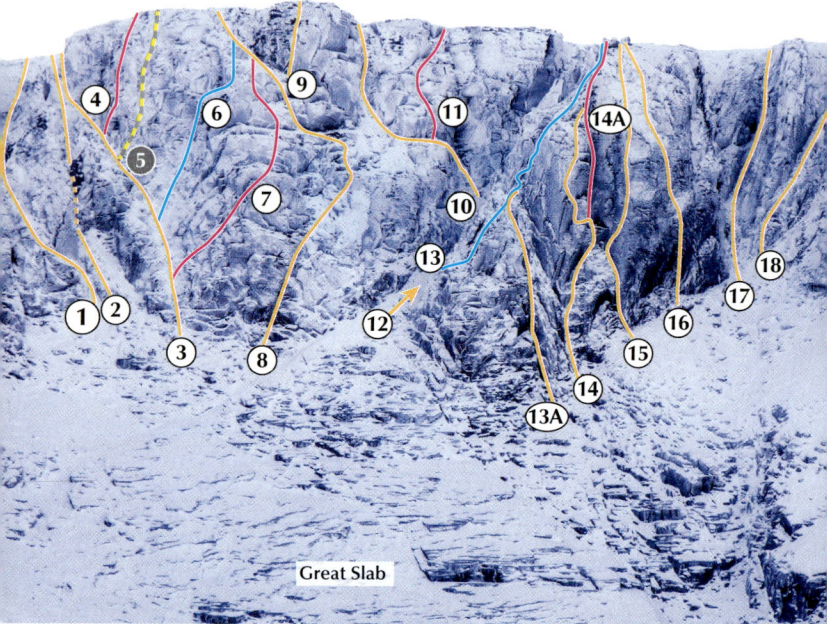

1. Ventilator II/III*
2. Chute Route V,5*
3. The Milky Way III
4. Appetite for Destruction V,6*
5. Demolition Man IV,5
6. Andromeda IV,4**
7. Astroturfer III*
8. Central Crack Route IV,5*
9. The Crack VI,7**
10. Snow Bunting IV,5
11. Crow's Nest Crack III*
12. The Couloir I**
13. Ewen Buttress III**
13A. Ewen Buttress, Direct Start V,6*
14. The Migrant VI,7**
14A. Migrant Direct VII,8
15. The Vicar VIII,8***
16. Happy Tyroleans IX,9**
17. Grumbling Groove VI,6*
18. The Head-hunter VI,6*

Coire an Lochain

The Milky Way 110m III**
T.W. Patey, V.N. Stevenson and I.W. Armitage, February 1959
The obvious left-slanting line on the left of the buttress. Climb this wide, shallow fault over several steps. Continue up and left to finish near the top of The Vent. An alternative start is to climb the wide snow bay on the left of the fault and gain the ramp higher up by a short deep groove.

Appetite for Destruction 110m V,6*
A. Fyffe and J. Hepburn, 14 February 1995
Takes the corner on the right side of the upper tower. Climb The Milky Way to below the tower then slant back right to gain and climb the corner. Continue up the corner and move right at the top. Finish direct.

Andromeda 120m IV,4**
R.D. Barton and J.C. Higham, 30 December 1970
The main corner line on the left of the most prominent part of the buttress. Start up The Milky Way and climb it to the main corner. Climb either the left or the central groove which slants up right to easier ground on the crest and finish on the left of the conspicuous wall as for Central Crack Route.

Astroturfer 120m III*
J. McKeever and I. Dawson, 7 December 1985
Goes diagonally right across the buttress to finish as for Central Crack Route. Start as for Andromeda but take the lowest chimney which leads right onto the front of the buttress. Climb the wall above on the right and continue to finish on the left of the conspicuous wall.

Central Crack Route 120m IV,5*
T.W. Patey, 2 February 1958
A fine route with the first pitch being the crux. It takes the obvious right-slanting corner crack. Start by the lowest rocks and climb this corner crack. The start is hard and the short chimney awkward, both harder in lean or powder conditions. From its top go up mixed ground bearing slightly right to below a great square wall. Go diagonally left below it until a way through the cornice can be found, usually just on the left of the wall. Sometimes a much longer traverse is needed.

The Crack 20m VI,7**
R. Anderson and R. Milne, 12 January 1992
The obvious wide crack in the headwall can be reached from a number of routes.

The Inquisition 90m VI,8**

(no photo topo)

R. Anderson, G. Ettle and R. Milne, January 1992

Starts up the obvious right-facing corner on the wall some way up The Couloir. Climb the superb corner then ledges to below a steep prow just left of a cul-de-sac (50m). Slant up left to cracks on the right, leading to the higher of two platforms (25m). Climb the overhanging crack on the left and flake to the top, crux (15m).

Snow Bunting 90m IV,5

R. Anderson and G. Ettle, 26 January 1992

This lies on the right side of the buttress starting well up The Couloir just below the dead-end of its left branch. Go up this branch, left to a ledge and along it to its end. Step left and ascend a snow bay to reach a stepped crack on the left. Climb this then go right below a roof (with ice here the climb is much easier) then up broken ground to the top.

Crow's Nest Crack 60m III*

S. Kennedy and C. McLeod, 18 December 1983

Takes a prominent chokestone chimney left of dead-end left branch of The Couloir. Climb this branch and move left, as for Snow Bunting, then climb the chimney to a ledge. Work up and right by easier ground to finish.

The Couloir 150m I**

The wide slanting gully is normally straightforward with no pitches. The cornice can be large but there is a way through above the col.

Number 3 Buttress

NH 984 026 Crag base altitude 1150m North facing

This is also known as Ewen Buttress. It consists of a slanting rib on the left then a huge steep recess bounding a sheer section of cliff. The right side, where the cliff swings round to overlook the Left Branch of Y Gully, is seamed with corner and crack lines.

Ewen Buttress 90m III**

T.W. Patey and V.N. Stevenson, February 1959

Follows the edge overlooking The Couloir. Go up The Couloir for about a pitch until the buttress can be gained and followed to a saddle. Move right and up a short, steep step (crux) leading to a gully which is followed to the top of the buttress and The Couloir.

Coire an Lochain – Number 3 Buttress

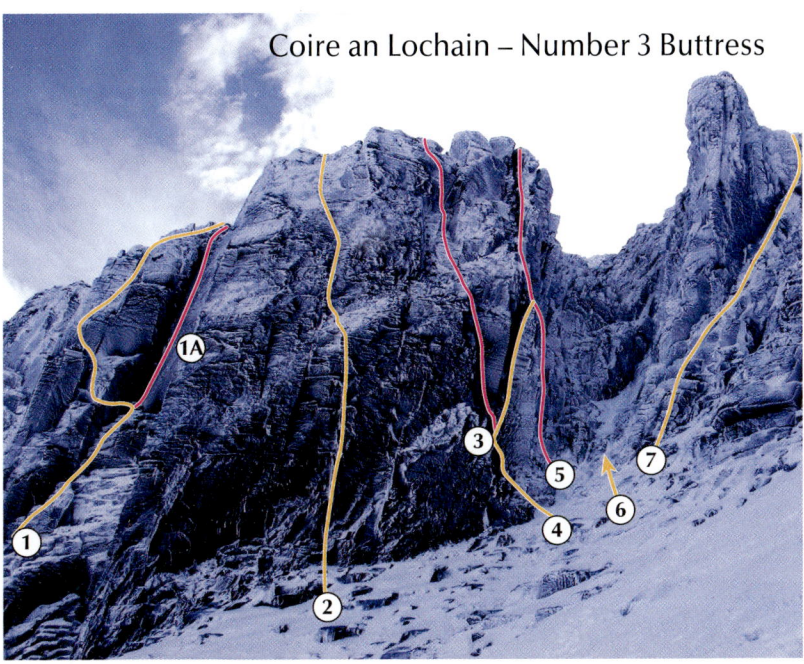

1. The Migrant VI,7**
1A. Migrant Direct VII,8
2. Happy Tyroleans IX,9**
3. The Overseer Direct V,6*
4. The Hoarmaster VI,6***
5. Hooker's Corner VI,6**
6. Left Branch of Y Gully III
7. The Head-hunter VI,6*

Ewen Buttress, Direct Start 50m V,6*

The obvious corner fault to the right of the toe of the buttress is climbed to join the normal route. There is a hard move to gain the easier ground, particularly if the build-up is poor.

The Migrant 100m VI,7**
A. Cunningham and A. Nisbet, 13 March 1986
In the left side of the buttress is a huge alcove. This fine route climbs into this then out on the left side. Start in a groove 5m right of Ewen Buttress Direct Start and climb this (deceptive), then make a step right to a belay (20m). Go up right under the overhanging wall and at the first possible place go into the alcove (20m). Descend a short way and break out left on to a ledge on the arête. Follow this left then go up over a chokestone to the top of a pinnacle. Move left to a rib leading to easier ground (40m). Go right and finish up Ewen Buttress (20m).

Migrant Direct 90m VII,8
W. Garrett and A. Coull, 13 December 1996
This takes the challenge of the huge hanging groove on the left of the buttress. Start up The Migrant to gain the groove which is climbed direct. It is sustained with adequate but hard-to-place protection.

The Vicar 70m VIII,8***
G. Ettle and A. Nisbet, 20 December 1992
A magnificent climb taking the arête right of the huge recess. The first pitch can be split. Start up an overhanging groove then go left towards the back of the recess. Under an overhanging groove traverse right and gain a ledge with large blocks. Climb up to a second ledge directly above the first (35m). Climb the shallow corner, moving left and climbing wall cracks where the crack becomes blind. Move onto the left wall which leads close to the flake crack. Move back right (thin) onto the arête and follow this to the top.

Happy Tyroleans 60m IX,9**
F. Schranz, H. Zak and E. Netzer, 1 March 2001
A test-piece originally climbed redpoint style. Characterised by three roofs, it takes the right-hand crack line up the steepest part of the wall. Start below a left-facing corner with a roof at about 10m. Climb the shallow corner with increasing difficulty to a poor stopping place just below the second roof. Beyond the third roof the corner becomes a thin overhanging crack. Climb this by powerful moves to a desperate final rockover onto the slabby ledge (30m). Directly above the belay, an obvious groove follows a natural fault up the slightly bulging wall. Follow this turfy crack/groove to the top of the headwall and a series of blocky steps which lead to easy ground (30m).

The Overseer Direct 60m V,6*
A. Nisbet and N. Main, 20 November 1992
This takes a line up the right side of the buttress. Start at the right corner of the buttress and traverse left on a ledge to gain and climb two consecutively steep corners.

The Hoarmaster (photo: Guy Steven)

Continue direct to the base of a capped chimney. Pull out left and climb a vertical corner to easier ground.

The Hoarmaster 60m VI,6***
R. Anderson, G. Nicol and R. Milne, 19 November 1988
This steep and strenuous but well-protected climb takes a chimney and crack line on the right edge of the buttress. Start at the right corner of the buttress and gain a ledge then pull into and climb the square-cut chimney, hard to start and sustained. Continue up the wide crack above for the second pitch.

Hooker's Corner 60m VI,6**
R. Anderson and C. Greaves, 26 November 1988
This climbs the obvious open corner right of the edge of the buttress. Start at the toe of the buttress and climb up just right of the corner. Step across, climb the corner to the top and finish up The Hoarmaster.

Left Branch of Y Gully 100m III
T.W. Patey, G. Nicol and A. Wedderburn, 16 November 1952
The wide gully between the right side of No. 3 Buttress and the steep narrow pillar. Climb the gully to belay on the right of the icicle whose presence is essential. Climb the icicle and follow the gully to the top. Rock protection can be hard to find.

Stagefright 50m VI,7**
(no photo topo)
G. Ettle and R. Milne, 25 January 1998
Climbs a fault on the left of the pillar between the branches of Y Gully. Start up and left of the big groove on the left of the pillar (Grumbling Groove). Climb the fine crack on the right wall to a point where it widens (big gear). Step left into a steep leftwards

Coire an Lochain – Number 4 Buttress

1. Deep Throat V,6**
2. Gaffer's Groove Winter Variation V,5*
3. Bulgy VII,7*
4. Savage Slit V,6***
5. Fall-out Corner VI,7***
6. Procrastination VII,6
7. The Third Man IV,6*
8. Sidewinder III,4**
9. Western Route IV,6***

crack to reach a ledge (25m). Climb the wide crack above to reach good ice leading to the plateau (25m).

Grumbling Groove 60m VI,6*
S. Allan and A. Nisbet, 17 December 1983
The big groove on the left side of the pillar which separates the two branches of Y Gully is climbed direct but with some suspect rock.

The Head-hunter 60m VI,6*
A. Fyffe and R. Mansfield, 1 December 1989
Takes the diagonal line which runs up the right side of the pillar. The groove/ramp is climbed to its top. Finish up easier ground.

Right Branch of Y Gully 100m II*
(no photo topo)
R.F. Stobbart, T. Stobbart, Miss Harbinson and E. Thompson, 14 April 1934
The wide, steep gully tucked in the upper-right corner of the corrie on the left of No. 4 Buttress. It is often in condition, being very high and sheltered; it can hold ice or be high-angled snow. The cornice can be large.

Number 4 Buttress NH 983 026 Crag base altitude 1100m North-east facing

This has a steep crack and corner seamed face looking east, and higher front face looking north. In the centre of the side wall is the unmistakable open-book corner of Savage Slit. This is an ideal mixed route venue which comes into condition quickly and is popular.

Oesophagus 70m III,4**
(see overview topo)
W. March and party, 9 April 1971
About 10m right of the Right Branch of Y Gully is a groove leading to a snowy amphitheatre. The groove is often full of ice.

Deep Throat 70m V,6**
R. Anderson, T. Prentice and R. Milne, 2 December 1989
About 20m left of Savage Slit is a pillar with a wide crack in its left side. Climb a wide groove then the crack which is followed over or round three roofs until a delicate traverse left below a large roof leads to a belay on a ledge (30m). Regain the crack and climb it to the top of the pillar (15m). Climb the groove on the right to the top (25m).

Winter Climbs in the Cairngorms

Gaffer's Groove Winter Variation 80m V,5*
J. Cunningham and A. Fyffe, February 1975
The main groove left of Savage Slit may hold lots of ice on occasion, but usually later in the season. Gain the groove direct or by traversing from the right above a rectangular roof. Above the groove climb a wide chimney leading to snow slopes and the top. Without the ice it is VI,7 and instead of the wide chimney, climb the corner running up and rightwards towards Bulgy.

Bulgy 80m VII,7*
A. Nisbet and J. Preston, 27 November 1988
The groove left of the left arête of Savage Slit, finishing up a wide crack through the obvious twin roofs. Start at the foot of Savage Slit and work out left to gain the fault. Traversing out left below the first roof is the crux. Large cams and no verglas are useful.

Savage Slit 90m V,6***
G. Adams, J. White and F. Henderson, 21 April 1957
A classic route up the wide crack in the unmistakable corner. The corner can be climbed inside or out. Above the main corner, finish easily up and left. Bold and superb on the rare occasion that it is fully iced.

Fall-out Corner 90m VI,7***
A. Cunningham and A. Nisbet, 9 December 1985
An excellent climb taking the corner right of Savage Slit. Start below the corner and climb up to below the roof at the foot of the corner. Cross this and continue up the

A team on the second pitch of Fall-out Corner (photo: Kevin Roet)

main corner which is technical and sustained but well protected. Continue in the same line to finish as for Savage Slit.

The Third Man 100m IV,6*
S. Allan and A. Nisbet, 18 December 1983
Right of Fall-out Corner is a set of three corners. Start up the ramp running up right, Sidewinder, then go up to gain the right-hand corner. Climb the corner and the following wall to easier ground where Sidewinder crosses. Climb a shallow corner 10m right of the corner/chimney of Sidewinder and finish up a short wall.

Sidewinder 110m III,4**
A. Nisbet and E. Clark, 11 December 1983
A good route which uses both faces of the buttress. Start under a set of three corners and climb the ramp leading right onto the frontal face. Continue in this line, crossing a short, harder wall, then trend back left on easier ground to climb a corner/chimney onto a big ledge. A short descent down a slot leads to the finish up the top of Savage Slit.

Western Route 120m IV,6***
T.W. Patey, February 1959
A fine route up the front face. Start near the bottom corner of the buttress and climb the obvious right-slanting crack into a large recess. Climb the cracks in the right wall of the recess to easier ground. Continue via a short deep V chimney then into the big upper gully. Climb this and finish out the right wall which can be deceptively difficult. It is also possible to finish on the left side of the capping chokestone.

Torquing Heads 120m VII,7*
(see photo topo on p.80)
W. Todd and A. Cunningham, 20 January 1986
The prominent chimney on the front face is climbed over a chokestone and a leaning wall (crux, bold) to below a wide flake crack. Climb this and the bulging chimney above to easy ground. Finish up right of the steep upper buttress.

Lurcher's Crag (NH 968 032)

Start	Coire Cas (ski centre) car park NH 989 060 or Sugar Bowl car park NH 985 074
Time	2hr–2hr 30min
Crag base altitude	800–900m
Aspect	South-west to west
Route lengths	80–300m
Style	Some good long ice routes in the Northern Section. The Southern Section tends to be shorter and more mixed in character.

Usually referred to as Lurcher's Crag, this large broken cliff lies below the summit of Creag an Leth-Choin and overlooks the northern section of the Lairig Ghru. It is a large, sprawling cliff split by four long but fairly easy-angled gullies separated by ill-defined ribs. Besides the main gullies, which can hold large quantities of ice, several short but good practice ice pitches can be found in this area, particularly to the north of the main cliff.

Approach
From the north, park in the Sugar Bowl car park which is on the left at the first big bend (NH 985 074) on the Coire Cas road. Cross the road and follow the track through the Chalamain Gap then contour round to the cliff or, for a better view and easier walk, descend to the Lairig Ghru and re-ascend. From the Coire Cas car park it is possible to follow the path south-west as for Coire an Lochain, then go to the col south of Creag an Leth-Choin (NH 969 033) and descend to below the cliffs. Alternatively, descend South Gully (NH 969 031). A flatter but longer approach is the Lairig Ghru track from Loch Morlich.

Descent
Descend northwards from the top of Creag an Leth-Choin down the ridge to reach the path leading back to the Sugar Bowl, or retrace approach from Coire Cas.

Conditions
This is the only cliff in this area to face west so conditions here can be different from those found elsewhere. Large amounts of ice can build up and the routes, although

not too steep, can become sheets of continuous ice. It can be relatively sheltered when there are easterly winds. South of the main crag is a set of blocky buttresses which are not so dependent on the build-up of ice.

Lurcher's Crag, Northern End NH 967 033 Crag base altitude 800m West-south-west facing

Although broken and rambling in places, this section of the crag is substantial and long. In good conditions it forms some great icy lines.

North Gully 240m III*
R. Campbell, F. Harper and M.A. Thompson, 23 December 1965
The big gully in the most northerly section of the crag. It usually has a couple of ice pitches. At the top it forks and either can be taken: the left may contain a good ice pitch; the right has a short but steep pitch.

K9 180m IV,4*
A. Fyffe and B. Fyffe, 23 March 1996
Climbs up the lower icefall of Window Gully by the easiest line, then trends left across mixed ground. Ascend easier terrain and go to the foot of the upper icefall running down a corner and climb this to finish.

Central Gully, high on Lurcher's Crag (photo: Alex Riley)

Lurcher's Crag (north)

1. North Gully (left fork) III*
2. K9 IV,4*
3. Window Gully IV,4
4. Arctic Monkey III,4*
5. Central Gully III*
6. Diamond Gully IV,4
7. Eskimo Gully II*
8. South Gully I

Window Gully 180m IV,4 ⓚ
W. March, J. Cleare and J. Bradshaw, 9 March 1972
The icefall between North and Central Gullies. Easy ice leads up to the overhangs where it is often possible to go behind the ice and climb through a window near the left side. Climbing the outside of the icefall or the separate pillar to the right gives harder options. An easy gully then leads to the top, or finish up K9 for more fun.

Arctic Monkey 300m III,4*
S. Allan and A. Nisbet, 6 January 2008
The ridge on the left of Central Gully. Start on the left of the gully and climb easy ground to where it steepens. This is passed by a line of weakness on the right, passing a smooth groove heading left, to a recess below a prominent jutting block. Pull out left through a small cave (crux) and go left up a less well-defined groove to reach the crest. Follow the crest which becomes progressively easier.

Central Gully 300m III*
B. Taplin and O. Ludlow, 4 March 1970
The most obvious gully in the centre of the cliff. It may have several ice pitches low down and either of the two branches can be followed at the top. On occasions it can be a continuous line of ice, when it is worth two stars.

Sunny ice on Central Gully (photo: Alex Riley)

Diamond Gully 240m IV,4
E. Clarke and A. Nisbet, February 1984
Midway between Central and South Gullies is an icefall halfway up the cliff. Follow ice up the lower slabs then climb the short, steep screen and easy snow gully to the top.

Eskimo Gully 240m II*
J. Lyall, B. Cook and J. and K. Penrose, 18 March 2008
The gully left of Doorway Ridge starts as a shallow icy fault up the lower slabs. Climb a steep ice pitch followed by easier ground.

Doorway Ridge 200m IV,5*
J. Lyall and A. Nisbet, 8 December 2007
This is the second ridge left of South Gully. Start on its right and climb a subsidiary buttress to a steep corner which leads onto the crest, then follow this to a slight col (45m). Continue just right of the crest, then over a slight pinnacle and a steeper section to reach easy ground (45m). Finish up this easier crest over the doorway. An easier start on the left of the buttress slants up right to the slight col and gives a more balanced route at Grade III.

South Gully 150m I
The well-defined gully right of where the slabby ground at the base of the cliff disappears. A straightforward descent route.

Pinnacle Ridge 150m II
A. Nisbet, 9 November 2007
The ridge on the right of South Gully. Climb a right-slanting fault, then go left onto the crest. Follow this over the pinnacle (avoidable) to a col and finish by a right-slanting fault.

Lurcher's Crag, Southern End   NH 969 029 Crag base altitude 900m West facing

About 300m right of South Gully is an area of blocky buttresses and ribs with a rocky amphitheatre high up which has the steep Wolfstone Gully on its back wall. The routes here tend to be shorter and more mixed in character.

Drystane Ridge 100m III
A. Nisbet, 14 January 2007
The ridge which bounds the left side of the amphitheatre. The crux is at half-height, a steep blocky section with good flakes.

Winter Climbs in the Cairngorms

Wolfstone Gully 80m VI,7
J. Lyall and A. Nisbet, 24 January 2009
The steep gully in the back of the amphitheatre. A steep start leads directly to the crux pitch (25m). Climb a crack in a shallow corner on the right to below a big chokestone (15m). It may be possible to climb the gully direct here if there is enough ice. Climb past the left corner of the chokestone to reach the easy upper gully (10m). Finish up this (30m).

Quinn 80m III,4*
B. Findlay, R. Ross and G.S. Strange, 10 February 2002
The gully in the right corner of the amphitheatre slanting up rightwards to a through route to join Collie's Ridge.

Collie's Ridge 120m II*
A. Nisbet, 8 January 2007
The ridge bounding the right side of the amphitheatre and joining Quinn near the top.

Deerhound Ridge 180m III
I. Dillon and J. Lyall, 27 December 1994
This is about 150m right of the amphitheatre and this ridge comes down lower than the others. Zig-zag up the lower part of the ridge then go on the left to reach a col. Climb the crux groove on the left side then finish up the crest.

Approaching Wolfstone Gully (centre) with Quinn slanting up to the notch on the right

Sron na Lairige (NH 963 026)

Start	Sugar Bowl car park NH 985 074
Time	2hr 30min
Crag base altitude	850–900m
Aspect	North-east
Route lengths	120–220m
Style	Good quality mixed routes.

These cliffs lie on the flank of Sron na Lairige overlooking the Lairig Ghru. There are several broken buttresses but the most obvious feature, towards the south of the crags, is Lairig Ridge.

Approach
Approach as for Lurcher's Crag but continue south down the Lairig Ghru then walk uphill to the routes. These routes are described from right to left as this is the usual direction of approach.

Descent
The usual descent is north down Sron na Lairige to gain the Lairig Ghru.

Conditions
The routes here come into condition quickly as the rock tends to be fairly vegetated. There can be a substantial cornice with westerly winds but there is usually a way through at the top of Lairig Ridge.

Sron na Lairige, Northern End   NH 962 026, Crag base altitude 850m, North-east facing

About 150 metres to the North-east of the prominent Lairige Ridge is an area of slabby, broken buttresses that provide a pleasant series of alternate buttresses and gullies.

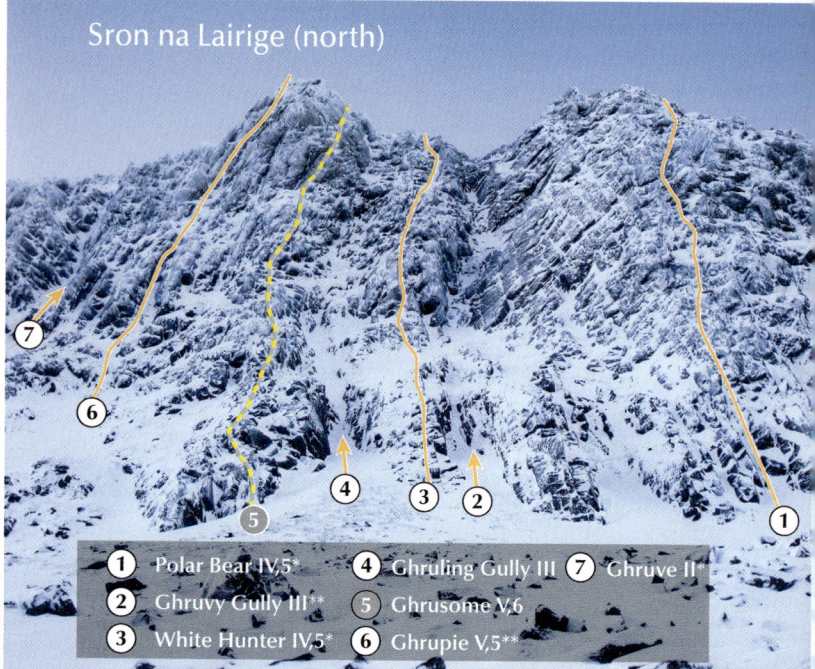

Polar Bear 200m IV,5*

J. Lyall and A. Nisbet, 7 January 2008

This is the first big buttress reached from the north and is the right hand of two which are fairly broad. Climb a turfy grooves system in the crest. The crux is a smooth section which is climbed near the right arête.

Ghruvy Gully 220m III**

J. Lyall, 18 March 2008

The main gully between the buttresses of White Hunter and Polar Bear. A choice of two starts leads to the main gully, with the final ice pitch being the crux and slow to form.

White Hunter 220m IV,5*

H. Burns and J. Lyall, 8 January 2008

The slim pillar between Ghruling and Ghruvy Gullies. Climb the lower, easy-angled crest to a steeper section (90m). Gain and climb the left-hand groove then a cracked wall to pass left of a prominent roof (45m). Easier climbing leads to the top.

Sron na Lairige

Ghruling Gully 220m III

J. Lyall, 18 March 2008

The gully on the left of the White Hunter and right of the left-hand buttress of Ghrupie. It becomes less pronounced with height and has a short mixed crux before the upper slopes.

Ghrupie 200m V,5**

J. Lyall and A. Nisbet, 6 December 2008

Takes a groove on the left side of the buttress. Climb easily up left from the lower crest of the buttress to below the central of five grooves, the one with a right dog-leg. Climb the groove which leads directly into the most prominent groove in the upper buttress (50m). Start up this groove for about 15m (serious) then break right to more cracked terrain and follow this to join the crest at the tower (40m). Gain the top of the tower and finish up the crest.

Ghruve 220m II*

J. Lyall and A. Nisbet, 2 April 2008

The long well-defined groove on the left flank of the left-hand buttress, heading for two pinnacles near the top of the ridge.

Sron na Lairige, Southern End NH 963 025, Crag base altitude 900m, North-east facing

The South Section is dominated by Lairig Ridge. The routes described are found on the right side of this and join Lairig Ridge in its upper reaches. Gormless takes the most prominent line of grooves on the right-hand side.

Braer Rabbit 130m IV,4*

J. Lyall, A. Nisbet and J. Preston, 20 December 2006

The rib right of Gormless. Start up and right from the base of the rib at a steep groove. Climb the groove for 25m then move left onto the rib (45m). Continue up the crest to the top in two pitches.

Idiot Proof 130m IV,6*

J. Lyall and A. Nisbet, 2 April 2008

A line of grooves in the right wall of Gormless. Start just right of Gormless and climb a groove to a steep top which can be climbed direct or passed on the left (50m). Climb another groove, including a short crux overhanging section, until near the crest of the rib (35m). Go diagonally left under the crest, then join the crest beyond its difficulties and follow it to the top (45m).

Sron na Lairige

Gormless 130m III*
K. Geddes and R. Barton, 1982
The furthest right of the bigger faults on this face. Start up open ramps which develop into more defined grooves. At the fork trend right to finish near the top of the ridge.

Pupster 130m III
D. McGimpsey and S. Wood, 22 January 2008
The rightmost of the three grooves, starting about 10m left of Gormless at a turfy groove which is climbed for about 20m into the left side of a snowy bay which is climbed to its top. Belay as for Gormless (50m). Go up and right on easy ground to a large rock fin (Gormless takes the groove right of the fin). Take the groove on the left below the main upper groove (40m). Follow this groove to the top (40m).

Sinclair's Last Stand 150m III
B. Findlay and G.S. Strange, 15 March 1992
The central groove on the large right face of Lairig Ridge. Start at an ice-smear about 30m up from the lowest rocks. Climb the smear and the groove above to a short wall (50m). Turn the wall on the left, go up slightly right and climb the next groove (40m). Traverse left to a big flake on the edge then climb the ridge crest (20m). Follow the crest to the top (40m).

Cerro Norrie Finish 40m V,5
D. McGimpsey and D. Crawford, 9 March 2007
Climbs the thin groove above the traverse to gain the ridge at the top of pitch three.

Lairig Ridge 200m IV,5**
G.S. Strange and B. Ross, 8 December 1985
The largest and best-defined feature. Climb the lower 30m slabby wall by its right edge. Avoid an overhang on the left and go up to easy ground. This can be avoided by a groove on the left of the wall to give an easier and more balanced route (III). Go up to the ridge proper and start up on the right by climbing walls then slabs to a short chimney leading to the crest, which is followed direct over towers to the top.

The Loch Avon basin

This area lies in the beating heart of the Cairngorms, giving the most sublime climbing location in the British Isles. Surrounded by cliffs of varying shapes, aspects and character, with great ice and mixed climbs, this is a place of splendour, far removed from the everyday world. The most common approach is from the ski area car park to the north, but the area can also be approached from the south. The former is shorter but requires confidence in navigation and snow assessment; the latter is longer. Either way requires commitment but the rewards of climbing here are great.

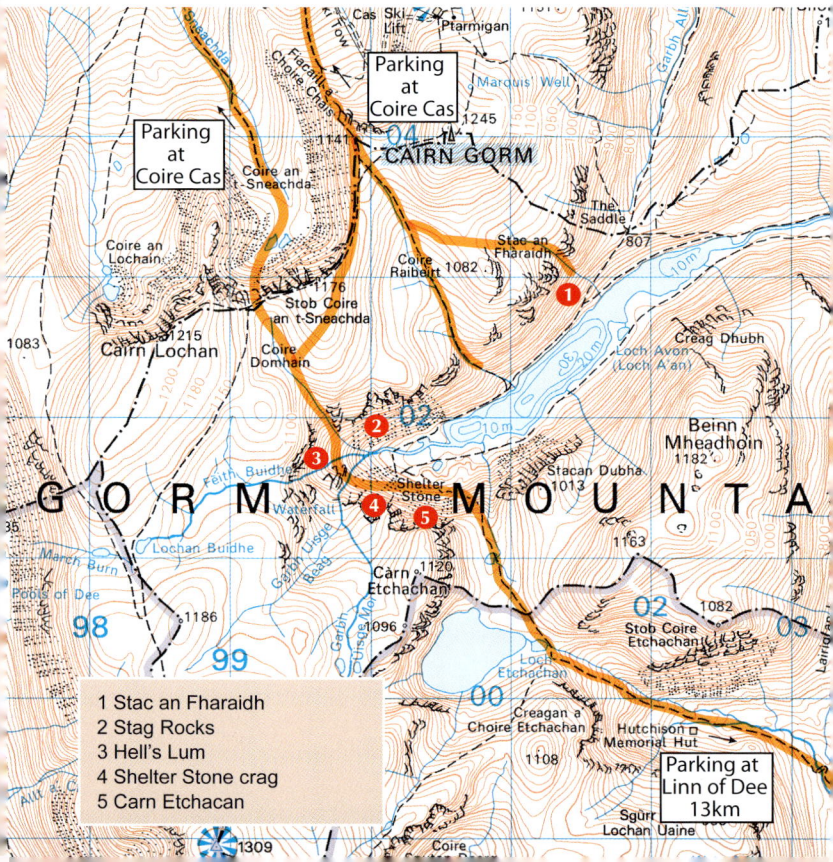

1 Stac an Fharaidh
2 Stag Rocks
3 Hell's Lum
4 Shelter Stone crag
5 Carn Etchacan

Stac an Fharaidh (NJ 013 029)

Start	Coire Cas (ski centre) car park NH 989 060
Time	1hr 45min
Crag base altitude	900m
Aspect	South-east
Route lengths	120–160m
Style	A mix of low grade snow and ice lines, and a few much more technical icy mixed routes.

This cliff lies on the south-east side of Cairn Gorm overlooking Loch Avon and near the saddle at the head of Strath Nethy, and consists of two sections of slabby cliff. The right hand or East Flank may blank out completely but some interesting climbing up thin smears of ice up the slabs may be had in lean conditions. Between the two sections is Rectangular Gully, a broad but shallow Grade I/II. The left-hand sector, the West Flank, is bounded on the left by more broken ground which is split by several other shorter gullies. The West Flank is characterised by a long vertical diagonal wall running across the slabs at about mid-height with the highest and steepest rocks on the left side. The routes are described from right to left as this is the usual direction of approach.

Approach
The usual approach is from the north from the ski-centre car park in Coire Cas. Gain the plateau via the Fiacaill a' Choire Chais and contour the south side of Cairn Gorm to reach the stream flowing south-east to Loch Avon. Descend the line of this stream and contour below the cliff to reach the routes. This bowl can be avalanche prone and other descent lines nearer the saddle may be preferred even if this entails a longer traverse and ascent back up to the climbs.

Descent
To return to the north either retrace the approach route or skirt the summit of Cairn Gorm on the east and descend to the car park through the ski area (also a possible approach route).

Conditions
A very variable cliff. The slabby sections can bank out completely, especially the East Flank. However, on the West Flank ice can form in quantity giving some fine climbs.

The Loch Avon basin in deep freeze

Cascade, Stag Rocks (photo: Rob Brown)

Stac an Fharaidh

Facing south, however, means that this can strip quite quickly so the cliff is best early in the season or in cold, cloudy conditions.

East Flank
NJ 013 030 Crag base altitude 900m South-east facing

This section of cliff can vary enormously from banking out totally to having thin streaks of ice running the height of the cliff. The best of these is taken by Pushover IV,4 (not shown/described) which takes the main line up the centre of the cliff.

1. Rectangular Gully I/II
2. Apres Moi III*
3. Hoity-Toity IV,4*
4. Sermon V,6**
5. Spirit Voices VI,8
6. Not Fade Away V,6**
7. Rectangular Rib III
8. Narrow Gully I/II*

Winter Climbs in the Cairngorms

Rectangular Gully 140m I/II ◇ or ⊗
The shallow open gully between the two flanks may disappear under heavy snow but can give some interesting ice pitches, particularly up the left side of the fault.

West Flank   NJ 012 029 Crag base altitude 900m South-east facing

This flank is slabby on the right and is cut by a long diagonal wall which increases in height leftwards. On the left is a steeper section of cliff. Ice can build up here in large quantities.

Apres Moi 150m III*
K. Spence and R. Anderson, 7 December 1980
This climbs a right-to-left line to gain the big right-facing corner in the upper wall. It can hold ice in quantity. Start near the right side of the lower slabs and climb to the overlap then through it at the main break. Continue up and left to gain the ice in the corner. Climb the corner and continue trending left on the obvious shelf.

Sermon 120m V,6**
A. Fyffe and I. Peter, 28 January 1986
When in condition this is a good route up the left side of the main slab, left of the diagonal wall. Climb thin iced slabs to steeper but thicker ice leading into the main recess in the steep upper wall. Climb the right corner/crack out of the recess to easier ground.

Spirit Voices 120m VI,8
A. Fyffe and R. Mansfield, 12 January 1991
Climbs a gradually steepening line near the left edge of the slabs and is based on the summer line of Speakeasy. The first pitch is up thin iced slabs into a right-facing corner in a long overlap. Traverse right under this roof to gain thicker ice leading up and left into a large recess in the steep upper rocks. Climb up and into a short V chimney (crux). Climb this and exit awkwardly left to a large ledge. A short, deceptive wall leads to easier ground and the top.

Not Fade Away 120m V,6**
S. Blagbrough and A. Fyffe, 14 February 1996
A mixed route which does need some ice. It takes the big open corner left of the vertical wall defining the upper edge of the main section of cliff. Go up a shallow, tapered chimney as for Rectangular Rib until the right wall can be climbed on ice smears to reach a large block (25m). Go up the slabby corner to an easing in angle (45m). Go up right into the main corner and follow this by some short deep cracks to a huge block below a steepening (40m). From the top of the block climb a short crack, going up on the right to finish left of the capping block (10m).

Rectangular Rib 120m III
R. Anderson and A. Russell, 22 February 1981
Right of Narrow Gully is an area of more broken rocks abutting the main slabs. Start up a shallow tapered chimney then follow the slabby rib to the top.

Narrow Gully 160m I/II* or
The obvious gully bounding the left side of rocks. It is narrow and very well defined to start but opens out into easy snow slopes above a short awkward step. (With a poor build-up, this step can approach Grade III.)

The first pitch of Sermon (photo: Scott Frazer)

Stag Rocks (NJ 002 020)

Start	Coire Cas (ski centre) car park NH 989 060
Time	1hr 45min
Crag base altitude	900m
Aspect	South
Route lengths	45–220m
Style	A variety of mixed routes, gullies, and short but steep pure ice routes.

These cliffs, lying between Coire Domhain and Coire Raibeirt, look south over Loch Avon. They are divided into two main sections and one lesser section by a Y-shaped gully (NJ 000 021) and by Diagonal Gully (NJ 002 021), a long fault whose screes nearly reach the head of the loch.

The leftmost section consists of a short but very steep cliff down which ice in quantity can build up: the Cascade area. This is left of the Y-shaped gully. Between that gully and Diagonal Gully is an area of defined ridges. Right of Diagonal Gully is the most substantial section of cliff which is itself cut on the left by the straight and aptly named Amphitheatre Gully. On the left of Amphitheatre Gully is Pine Tree Buttress which has a well-featured wall dropping into Diagonal Gully. Right of Amphitheatre Gully is the flat front face of Longbow Crag.

Approach
From the Coire Cas car park, walk up through the ski area to gain the Fiacaill a'Choire Chais and ascend this to the top (NH 999 039). Descend Coire Raibeirt to the east of the cliff or follow the plateau edge over spot height 1176 and down into Coire Domhain, then follow stream steeply to the west end of the cliff. Alternatively, go to the top of the crag where Diagonal Gully and Y-shaped Gully give quicker descents to the appropriate section of the cliff. The climbs on the right wall of Diagonal Gully, especially those near the top, are best approached from above but the avalanche hazard must always be considered.

Descent
These cliffs are usually approached from the north, and the climbs finish on the plateau. Any of the approach routes can be used as a return to Loch Avon.

Topping out of Stag Rocks, Carn Etchachan and Shelter Stone Crag in the background

Conditions
Conditions vary across the different parts of the cliff. The ice routes need a period of cold weather for them to form from springs above the crags. The mixed routes on Pine Tree Buttress and Longbow Crag only need a little cold weather and snow. Northerly winds are good for this crag. However, the mixed routes strip extremely rapidly in mild weather or with strong sun, and cold weather is essential for the harder climbs. Dry rock climbing can be had on the frontal face in winter while cliffs opposite are still clothed in snow and ice.

Left-hand Section   NJ 001 020 Crag base altitude 900m South facing

This is the section of cliff left of Diagonal Gully. It consists of two parts: the Cascade area which is the short but steep section of cliff that lies in the middle of the hillside on the west of the main rocks, and the higher set of ribs and grooves between Y-shaped Gully and Diagonal Gully.

The Overflow 45m III
A. Fyffe and I. Peter, 1986
The deep groove bounding the left side of the wall, down which cascade forms can give a fine ice-choked pitch.

Stag Rocks (left side)

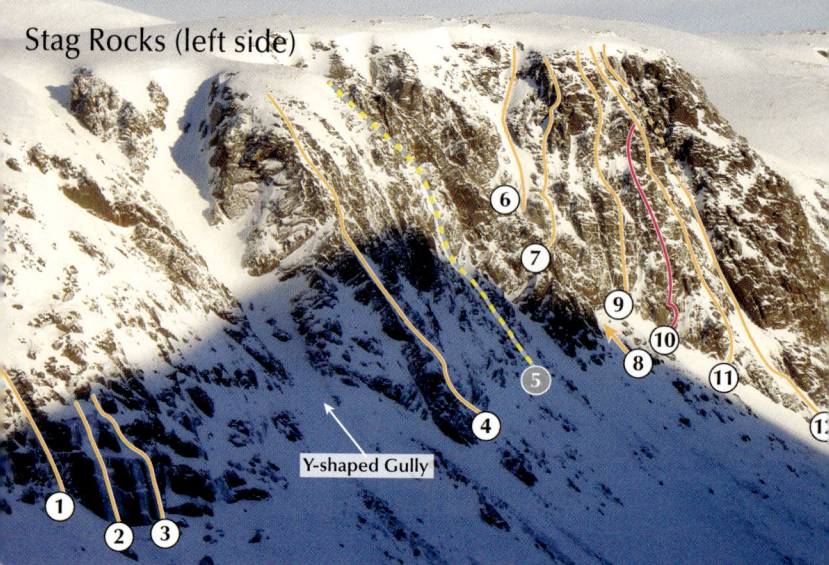

Y-shaped Gully

① The Overflow III
② Cascade V,5***
③ Cascade Right-hand IV,4
④ Afterthought Arête III*
⑤ Stag Route II
⑥ Apex Gully III
⑦ Light Entertainment III,4*
⑧ Diagonal Gully I
⑨ Honest Outlet IV,5*
⑩ Monarch of the Glen VI,7*
⑪ Pine Tree Route IV,4
⑫ Amphitheatre Gully V,6***

Cascade 45m V,5***

W. March and D. Alcock, February 1977

The obvious left-hand icefall gives a pure ice climb; although just less than vertical it gives a sustained and serious pitch, not to be underestimated.

Cascade Right-hand 45m IV,4

The icefall which forms round the corner on the right. Not as steep as its neighbour but can be thicker.

Stag Rocks

Truly, Madly, Chimbley 90m III
S. Fraser, J. Lyall and M. Twomey, 12 February 1996
A mini Deep Cut Chimney, this surprising climb lies on the narrow diagonal buttress on the left wall of the Y-shaped gully right of Cascade. Start a short way up the gully below a large block which sometimes banks out. Climb an icefall left of the block and move left into a bay below the chimney (25m). The back of the icy chimney is climbed until blocked by an overhang. Pull out on to the higher set of chokestones (25m, and an excellent pitch for the grade). Follow the easy gully to the top (40m).

Afterthought Arête 150m III*
W. March, November 1969
This is the rib which bounds the Y-shaped gully on its right and forms a fine narrow arête. Start on the right of the ridge and follow the crest to the plateau. Rarely holds snow.

> Left of Diagonal Gully are two defined ridges, Triple Towers and Serrated Rib, which forms the left side of Diagonal Gully. Both are very vegetated Grade III.

Afterthought Arete (photo: Allen Fyffe)

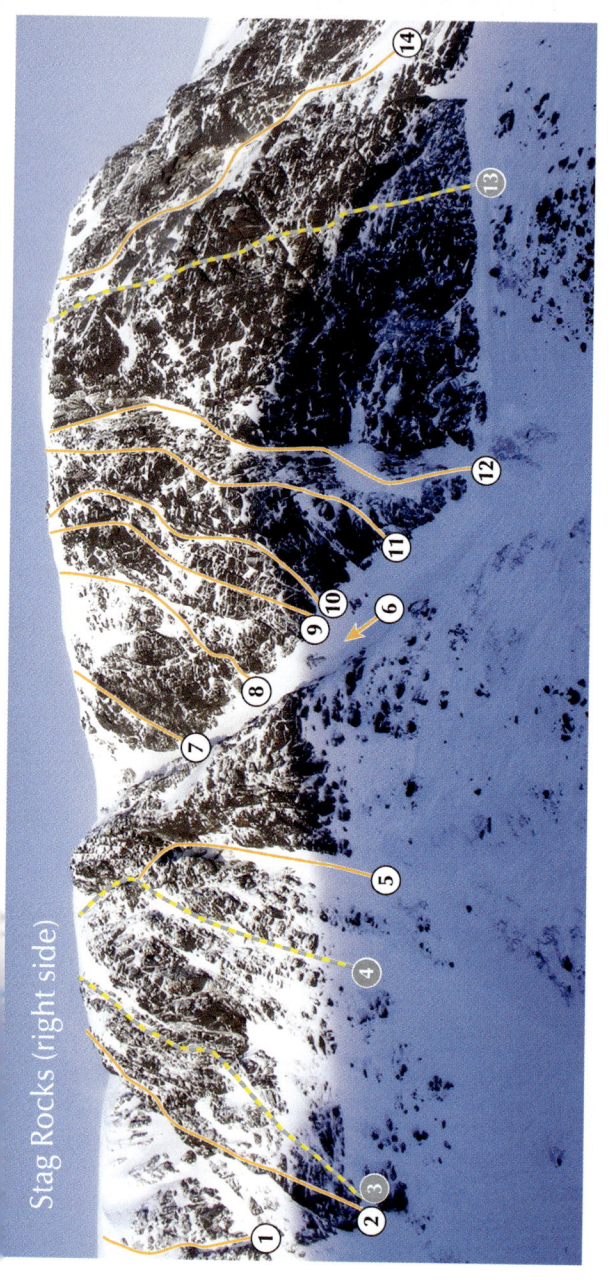

Stag Rocks (right side)

1. Truly, Madly, Chimbley III**
2. Afterthought Arête III*
3. Open Caste III
4. Stag Route II
5. CM Gully II/III
6. Diagonal Gully I
7. Final Groove II/III
8. Apex Gully III
9. Groove and Rib V,6**
10. Deception Inlet IV,5
11. Pine Tree Route IV,4
12. Amphitheatre Gully V,6***
13. Central Route VI,7
14. Stagnant Gully IV,4

CM Gully 140m II/III

J. Cunningham and W. March, Winter 1970

The gully between Triple Towers and Serrated Rib. The gully curves up left and passes below an obvious vertical rock wall to finish up easy snow.

Diagonal Gully 250m I

The long easy-angled gully, which divides the two sections of cliff, is very straightforward and is more often used as a descent to approach routes on its true right wall. There is seldom a cornice although the top section is the steepest.

Right-hand Section   NJ 003 021 Crag base altitude 900m South facing

This is divided into two main sections by Amphitheatre Gully, with Pine Tree Buttress on its left and overlooking Diagonal Gully and Longbow Crag on the right. The climbs on Pine Tree Buttress starting out of Diagonal Gully are usually approached by descending the gully.

Final Groove 70m II/III

J. Lyall and M. Sclater, November 1988

The large right-facing groove near the top of Diagonal Gully is climbed direct.

Bambi 70m IV,5

(no photo topo)

G. Ettle and J. Finlay, 18 December 1995

This takes the large groove immediately right of Final Selection, which is the defined ridge on the right of Final Groove. Climb up a short way then traverse right across a slab to gain the base of the groove. Climb this till it steepens, then climb a thin crack on the slab to the right. A few insecure moves on the rib gain a good ledge (30m). Climb the corner crack on the right, moving right to easier ground (40m).

Purge 80m IV,4*

(no photo topo)

A. Cunningham and A. Nisbet, 12 December 1986

Takes the narrower twin slabby ramps above Albino. Climb the ramps heading right for a full pitch, sparsely protected. Move left then go up into the deep wide groove which has a steep section at the start. Climb the groove to easy ground.

Albino 80m IV,5*
(no photo topo)
J. McKeever and G. Taylor, 13 December 1986
A good route up the corner whose slabby right wall has a distinctive blocky appearance. Climb the corner (delicate) to the steep headwall and go right to a huge flake. Go round the corner then climb onto the crest of the buttress and follow a shallow groove. Alternatively, from round the corner, go rightwards on a steep, blocky line to gain a large groove. Climb the groove and its continuation to finish up a steeper, shallower fault leading to easy ground.

Apex Gully 150m III
W. March and J. Hart, 18 February 1971
This is the large open fault which starts about two-thirds of the way up Diagonal Gully. The lower section is often a fine ice pitch. Above this there is a choice of routes; the left fork may contain a further ice pitch.

Light Entertainment 140m III,4*
J. Lyall and D. Bulmer, 25 November 1989
A good route up a set of grooves in the vague buttress. Start just below Apex Gully where a horizontal ledge goes right. Traverse this ledge, then climb the groove at its end. Continue up grooves and chimneys to finish up a groove in a steeper tower (crux).

Groove and Rib 140m V,6** or
M. Hamilton and R. Anderson, January 1985
The left hand of three big grooves starting in Diagonal Gully at about the level of the lowest rocks on the left. When in condition it is one of the best routes on the cliff. Climb a line of ice into the main left-facing corner. Climb this then continue up the rib above to the top. If there is no ice, the summer start up a corner on the left is technical 8.

Honest Outlet 150m IV,5* or
J. McKeever and N. Green, 15 December 1986
The central, straight groove merges with Deception Inlet at its top. It is very vegetated but can hold ice in quantity.

Deception Inlet 150m IV,5
G. Smith and K. Gasely, 1979
The lower of the three grooves has a distinct curve to it. Climb the groove to its end in an amphitheatre, where there is a choice of finishes either trending back left or going right to finish near the top of Pine Tree Buttress.

Monarch of the Glen 160m VI,7*
J. Lyall and R. Wild, 12 January 1991
Follows a system of grooves on the left flank of Pine Tree Buttress. Excellent when in condition. Start at the base of a steep wall with red streaks. Climb a groove on the right of the wall to a diagonal roof. Move left beneath it, then break through at a notch. Go up the groove above, then right to between two grooves. Climb the left groove for about 7m then swing left into an easier groove to a ledge. Climb a steep crack in a short wall to another groove system which is followed to a ledge overlooking Deception Inlet. Climb the obvious cracks then the easy ridge to the top.

Pine Tree Route 200m IV,4
J. Bower and A. Morgan, 7 February 1970
Follows the buttress crest which forms the edge overlooking Amphitheatre Gully. Start up the broad lower buttress which may be iced from Amphitheatre Gully. Above this there is a choice of lines but the best stays close to the right edge.

Amphitheatre Gully 220m V,6***
W. March and J. Hart, 17 February 1971
The gully defining the left side of Longbow Crag, the flat front face of Stag Rocks. It provides a varied and interesting climb, especially when icy. Climb ice into the amphitheatre then climb the left corner next to the wedge-shaped upper wall. This gives two sustained pitches up the corner.

Right-hand Finish V,7 takes the corner line on the right side of the upper wedge-shaped wall.

Stagnant Gully 180m IV,4
G. Ettle and S. Kitchen, 6 January 1995
Near the right margin of the crag a large, shallow, grassy gully runs up into an amphitheatre. Climb the lower gully into this upper depression then head left into an obvious V-groove. Ascend this groove, go behind a chokestone and continue to the top. By trending left above the main face the climb is Grade II.

Hell's Lum Crag (NH 996 018)

Start	Coire Cas (ski centre) car park NH 989 060
Time	1hr 45min
Crag base altitude	920m
Aspect	South-east
Route lengths	100–160m
Style	A good venue for ice and icy mixed routes. Catches a lot of sunshine, which can strip the crag on a warm spring day.

Hell's Lum Crag is one of the better cliffs in the Cairngorms for pure ice routes. It is a compact straight-fronted crag which takes its name from the huge, deep gully Hell's Lum (*lum* is Scots for 'chimney'), which angles into its left-hand side but is hidden from most angles. The crag consists of two sections. These sections and the routes are described from right to left as they would normally be approached in this direction. These sections are separated by Hell's Lum.

The frontal face has a few large features. The first is the shallow icy trough of The Escalator and then Kiwi Gully, most defined in the upper section, near the right side. Between Kiwi Gully and Deep Cut Chimney is the left-facing corner of The Wee Devil and further left the parallel Hellfire Corner. Deep Cut Chimney is a narrow deep fault with a diagonal lower section.

The slabs left of Hell's Lum are steepest on their right where they angle into the gully and often hold ice in quantity.

Approach
From the Coire Cas car park walk up through the ski area to gain the Fiacaill a'Choire Chais and ascend this to the top (NH 999 040). Follow the plateau edge overlooking Coire an t-Sneachda over spot height 1176m and then go down to the col at the head of Coire Domhain. Alternatively, go into Coire an t-Sneachda and ascend the Goat Track to the same point. Follow the stream heading south and down a steep section, then traverse to below the cliff. This final steep part of the approach can be avalanche prone and should be treated with caution.

Descent
For those returning to the north, retrace your approach and return to Coire Cas that way. To return to the Loch Avon basin, either descend down Coire Domhain or the

Unstable cornice above Hell's Lum

slopes well to the south of the cliff, taking care to avoid the cornice which can extend as far as the Feith Buidhe.

Conditions
Ice is fairly reliable here because of the drainage from springs above, although very cold weather may freeze them at source. Snow build-up can be very extensive, especially when the winds have been from the north, and much of the lower section of cliff can bank out, shortening many of the climbs. However, because of its south-easterly aspect, in warm or sunny weather avalanches and ice fall are a real danger, as are the large cornices which usually develop above the slabs left of the Lum and on the right of the frontal face. Avalanche conditions can also develop quickly with northerly and north-westerly winds when any snowfield can be a risk.

Sneer 120m II/III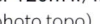
(no photo topo)
D. Haston, B. Robertson and J. Heron, 23 January 1966
The triangular-shaped slabs running up to the right, and right of The Escalator, often become sheathed in ice. The lower slabs usually bank out but the upper section, above a diagonal snow ramp, gives a choice of ice lines which can often be done as individual pitches.

Hell's Lum Crag (right side)

① Auld Nick III
② Kiwi Slabs IV,3*
③ Kiwi Gully IV,4*
④ The Wee Devil IV,5*
⑤ Devil's Delight V,5***
⑥ Hellfire Corner VI,7**
⑦ Salamander V,4**
⑧ Brimstone Groove IV,4**
⑨ Towering Inferno VI,5*
⑩ Nobody's Fault IV,6**
⑪ Deep Cut Chimney IV,4***
⑫ Hell's Lump V,6
⑬ Hell's Lum II/III***
⑭ The Chancer V,6**
⑮ The Gullet III*

The Escalator 150m II/III* ◇ or ❄

(no photo topo)

J.Y.L. Hay and A. Thom, January 1960

The main fault on the right of the cliff. The lower section usually banks out, but the upper fault can be a long, undulating trough of ice leading to the upper snow field and cornice.

Hell's Lum Crag

> The cliff left of The Escalator is slabby and crossed by several bands of overlaps. The lower section of much of this area can bank out with snow, making route identification difficult at times.

Auld Nick 150m III
M. Freeman and G.S. Strange, 20 November 1971
Based on the left-facing corner, parallel to and left of the middle section of The Escalator. It becomes more defined with height. Climb interlinked ice walls and snow slopes, heading towards a steeper grey tower of rock. Climb either side of this to reach the upper snow field. Very variable in terms of difficulty, length and line depending on build-up.

Kiwi Slabs 150m IV,4*
T.W. Patey and V.N. Stevenson, February 1959
Follow Kiwi Gully to its deepest section then break up rightwards on easier angled but continuous ice smears. These lead into a left-slanting corner which in turn leads to the upper snow field. This can be extensive and heavily corniced.

Kiwi Gully 150m IV,4**
W. March and I. Nicolson, 2 January 1972
The obvious gully slanting up and left gives a good ice route. Follow the slanting lower fault into the gully proper and climb this over a steepening at about two-thirds height. Above this, trend left to gain and follow the main corner on the right of the steep upper tower (as for The Wee Devil).

The Wee Devil 150m IV,5*
D. Dinwoodie and J. Mothersele, 17 November 1971
This route takes the well-defined left-facing corner midway up the face. Climb a vague gully system into the corner. Climb the corner to the overhang and traverse left below it. Go up then right on a flake to gain cracks, then continue up to the corner on the right of the steep upper tower. Finish up this corner (common with Kiwi Gully). Sometimes a line of ice leads from the corner into the upper fault which can be followed direct.

Devil's Delight 160m V,5***
J. Cunningham, W. March and R. O'Donovan, February 1973
A superb ice route when in condition. It takes the cascade of ice which forms in the centre of the wall between The Wee Devil and the parallel left-facing Hellfire Corner. Start up the ice which leads into then out of a large triangular recess. Above, the wall is steeper and is climbed by linking narrower ice runnels which form in grooves and

corners. This build-up of ice determines the degree of difficulty, but the top part normally constitutes the crux.

> In the centre of the face near the highest point of the cliff lies the left-facing Hellfire Corner. Between that feature and the next break on its left lies an area of slab topped by a steeper headwall. This often forms a great sheet of ice about 30 metres across, up which three routes find their way. The lower slabs are open to variation but the lines through the steep upper rocks are well defined.

Hellfire Corner 160m VI,7**
J. Grosset and M. Sclater, 13 February 1985
A good route up the right bounding corner of the ice sheet which forms in the centre of the face. It is unlikely to be ice all the way but if it is then it will be a grade easier. Climb ice in the corner to below the steepening. Climb the overhanging corner (steep but well protected) to gain the upper fault and follow this to the top.

Salamander 160m V,4**
J. Cunningham, W. March and R. O'Donovan, February 1973
Takes a line up the centre of the ice sheet starting near the foot of Hellfire Corner. The grade can vary with the condition and build-up of the ice. Climb the ice by the most convenient line to reach a tapered chimney in the upper wall. This is steep to start but develops into an easier chimney leading to the top.

Brimstone Groove 160m IV,4**
S. Docherty and K. Spence, 27 December 1970
Climb the left edge of the ice sheet to go through the upper rocks via the wide break beside the huge beak of rock.

Towering Inferno 160m VI,5*
A. Fyffe and R.D. Barton, 5 February 1986
This route lies on the pillar right of Deep Cut Chimney and Nobody's Fault and is characterised by two large rectangular roofs set one above the other. It is poorly protected in the lower section. Start below the pillar up easy slabs then take a left-facing corner to the lowest roof, then right onto a rib and up into a shallow chimney. Climb to the second roof. Move left and climb up the fault and left-leaning continuation to the top.

Nobody's Fault 160m IV,6**
G. Smith and party, 1979
A fine route which follows the shallower fault parallel to and right of Deep Cut Chimney. The initial recess and the overhanging chimney provide the most difficult sections.

Deep Cut Chimney 160m IV,4*** or
T.W. Patey and D. Holroyd, 19 January 1958
A classic route which takes the narrow, dark fault on the frontal face. Depending on the build-up the upper chimney can be approached by the diagonal introductory fault or directly from below. Once the fault is gained, the way is obvious to the final capping chokestones after which the finish comes with startling suddenness.

Hell's Lum 150m II/III*** or
G. McLeod and I. Brown, March 1956
The obvious deep gully with the overhanging right wall gives a great climb in superb surroundings, although rock protection can be hard to arrange. It can vary from having up to four ice pitches to being very steep snow; in very lean conditions it can be Grade IV. The second pitch is normally the most substantial and the cornice, which may be huge, can normally be outflanked on the right.

The Chancer 90m V,6**
J. Cunningham and W. March, January 1970
A short but sustained route of considerable historic importance up the ice pillar high up the face. Start at the top of the main ice pitch of Hell's Lum and climb ice on the left wall to a cave behind the ice of the steep section. Above is a large icicle which is climbed onto easier ice and the final snow fields and cornice. Occasionally there is a thinner pencil of ice to the right (VI,6); the ice sheet on the left is the easiest.

The Gullet 130m III*
J. Bower and B.S. Findlay, 28 December 1969
This route takes the central and best-defined of the three faults in the slabs left of Hell's Lum. (The other two faults are also Grade III.) Start about 20 metres left of Hell's Lum and climb the fault, very shallow at first, to where it becomes deeper and better defined. Turn the steepest section on the left and continue up the corner above to the upper slopes. The cornice can be large and occasionally impassable.

Garbh Uisge Crag (NH 999 014)

Start	Coire Cas (ski centre) car park NH 989 060
Time	2hr
Crag base altitude	860m
Aspect	North-east
Route lengths	90–150m
Style	Dwarfed by its more famous neighbour, this crag provides some good ice and mixed routes in a spectacular location.

This is the smaller, broken crag on the right of Pinnacle Gully and Shelter Stone Crag. The main feature of the cliff is Garbh Gully, a Y-shaped gully which runs up the centre of the crag.

Approach and Descent
As for Shelter Stone Crag.

Conditions
A much more amenable crag than its bigger neighbour, but still with a long approach. The climbs come into condition quite rapidly and can often withstand a fair thaw. They can contain large quantities of ice, especially on the right flank in the vicinity of Quartz Gully.

Blunderbuss 150m III
J.C. Higham and D. Wright, 4 March 1978
Follows the buttress crest left of Garbh Gully. Start at the lowest rocks left of Garbh Gully and climb a steep chimney. Continue direct via grooves and short walls to the final snow slopes.

Garbh Gully 150m III*
A. Fyffe and E. Fyffe, February 1972
Climb the deep Y-shaped gully in the centre of the cliff, taking the right branch where it forks. The crux is normally a tapered ice corner after the fork. Above, easier ground leads to the plateau. The left branch is a chimney with a chokestone crux (IV,6*).

Garbh Uisge Crag

1. Blunderbuss III
2. Garbh Gully III*
3. Crystal Crack III,4
4. Quartz Gully II*

Garbh Uisge Crag

Quartz Gully 90m II*
A. Fyffe and E. Fyffe, February 1972
The slabby, open gully on the right flank, bounded on its right by a defined rib. The gully is climbed direct. Never very steep, it can contain large quantities of ice which sometimes spill over the right wall giving some fine practice ice pitches.

Approaching the Loch Avon basin via the Cairn Gorm plateau (photo: Allen Fyffe)

Shelter Stone Crag (NJ 001 013)

Start	Coire Cas (ski centre) car park NH 989 060
Time	2hr 15min
Crag base altitude	850m
Aspect	North-east
Route lengths	90–270m
Style	A large and impressive crag with some excellent long mixed and icy mixed routes.

This huge flat-topped crag is the most impressive in the Northern Cairngorms. It is bounded on the left by Castlegates Gully (see Carn Etchachan section for route description) and on the right by Pinnacle Gully with the distinctive Forefinger Pinnacle near its top. The crag consists of the main face looking north-east and two lesser faces overlooking the gullies on either side. On the left of the main face is the narrow tower-like Raeburn's Buttress. The section right of this is the Central Slabs which are massive, high-angle granite slabs defined at bottom and top by the Low and High Ledges. On the right is the Main Bastion, the most continuous rock. Near the right edge of the Main Bastion is the fault of Clach Dhian Chimney, right of which the cliff soon turns into Pinnacle Gully and diminishes in height.

Approach

The normal approach is from the north and is initially the same as the approach for Hell's Lum. From the Coire Cas car park, walk up through the ski area to gain the Fiacaill a'Choire Chais and ascend this to the top (NH 999 039). Follow the plateau edge overlooking Coire an t-Sneachda over spot height 1176m and then go down to the col at the head of Coire Domhain. Alternatively, go into Coire an t-Sneachda and ascend the Goat Track to the same point.

Follow the stream heading south. Go down the steep section and cross the streams below slabby rocks then traverse round below Garbh Uisge to the base of the crag. The section of the approach from the descent of Coire Domhain involves crossing on or below steep avalanche-prone slopes and care should be taken.

It is also possible to approach from the south. The approach is from Creagan a'Choire Etchachan, from where the path is followed to Loch Etchachan and then down to Loch Avon. This would normally only be used by parties staying in the Hutchison Memorial Hut.

Shelter Stone Crag

Descent
Castlegates Gully and Pinnacle Gully are convenient descents to the head of Loch Avon. To return to the north, head west then north, passing above Hell's Lum Crag to reach the upper part of Coire Domhain. Alternatively take a descending traverse west of Garbh Uisge Crag to go below Hell's Lum and ascend into Coire Domhain. From there, follow either the Goat Track or the Fiacaill a'Choire Chais back to the car park in Coire Cas.

Shelter Stone Crag (front face)

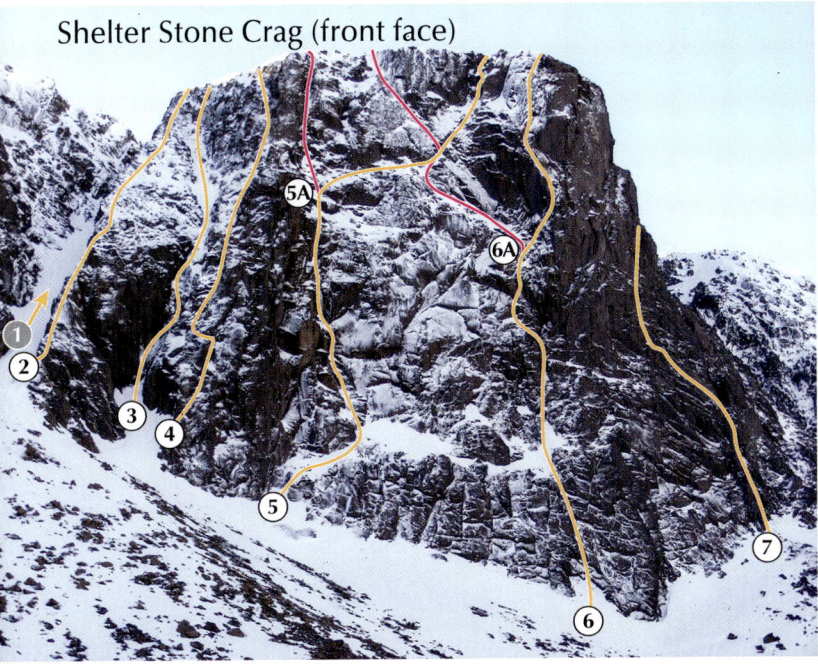

① Castlegates Gully I**
② Castle Wall IV,5
③ Breach Gully IV,5
④ Raeburn's Buttress IV,5*
⑤ Sticil Face V,6***
⑤A Sticil Face Direct Finish V,6*
⑥ Citadel VII,8***
⑥A Citadel Winter Variation VI,8**
⑦ Clach Dhian Chimney V,5*

Castlegates Gully route description is in the Carn Etchacan section

Conditions
Most of the routes here are mixed so cold weather and snow are the main requirements. However, with climbs over 250m in length, conditions can vary considerably over the length of a route. Good conditions low down may mean lots of snow in the upper sections. Many of the features on the harder routes are shallow so snow strips quite quickly in warmer conditions. Some routes such as Sticil Face depend on ice. Most climbs here, however, are long and the cliff's remote location, like that of Carn Etchachan, means that the climbs are always serious, especially if the weather turns bad.

Castle Wall 210m IV,5
B.S. Findlay and G.S. Strange, 31 January 1970
The well-defined arête on the face overlooking Castlegates Gully. Start some way up the gully near the foot of the arête and traverse right onto the crest. This is then followed to the top. The first two pitches are the most defined and difficult.

Breach Gully 240m IV,5
M. Freeman and G.S. Strange, 12 March 1977
The obvious gully between Castle Wall and Raeburn's Buttress. The first pitch can be bold. The steep blank section is turned on the right and the gully gained higher up. A through route and another right traverse then lead into the easier upper couloir. Sometimes the gully can be climbed direct on ice in which case the grade will be IV,4.

Raeburn's Buttress 240m IV,5*
W. March and J. Hart, February 1971
Takes the left side of the tower-like buttress. Start in the big bay on the left, at the foot of Breach Gully, and traverse right onto the front face and climb up until a line goes diagonally left to the main fault. Climb this fault to a deep, tapered chimney which is climbed on its right edge. Above, continue to the top of the buttress and then by the easy line slanting up on the left side of the upper rocks.

Sticil Face 260m V,6***
K.A. Grassick and A.G. Nicol, 27 December 1957
A superb classic route up the slabby corner between Raeburn's Buttress and the Central Slabs. Start below and left of the huge corner and climb diagonally up right onto the Low Ledge. Trend back up left into the main corner below a steep wall. Climb the open corner by ice on its right wall (ice required here for the climb to be the given grade). Continue up the awkward chimney to the High Ledge then go up diagonally right in a very exposed situation until a wide fault is reached. Climb this fault until it is possible to move left into another fault and so to the top.

Icy mixed climbing on the crux of Sticil Face, Shelter Stone Crag

Direct Finish V,6* 100m Above the awkward chimney, climb up to a corner directly above. Climb this and a short wall to easier ground and the top. This finish needs ice.

Citadel 270m VII,8***
M. Hamilton and K. Spence, 23 February 1980
A hard but superb route which takes the fault on the right of the Central Slabs then a line of weakness up the left side of the nose above. Good conditions all the way are hard to find, and many ascents have required at least one point of aid at the lower crux but this is becoming less common. Start at the shallow chimney fault on the left of the main bastion and climb this for two pitches to the Low Ledge, then for a further two pitches up the fault until overhangs force an exit to ledges on the left. Trend right over slabs (ice here is a great help) to a corner with a crack in the right wall. Go up this (lower crux), then right again to gain the slab above. Climb the fault till a right traverse leads into an open corner. Climb this corner and the following one to gain a ridge. Go up the ridge then left to a huge flake. Hand traverse this then climb the crack and chimney above (upper crux). Continue up the crack above, then traverse right with a step down to ledges. Climb the right-slanting fault until the left of two short chimneys leads to the plateau.

Winter Climbs in the Cairngorms

Citadel Winter Variation 130m VI,8**
A. Rouse and B. Hall, 1975
A fine variation taking a natural line. From above the lower crux, go up and left to Sticil Face. Climb that for 10m to below an obvious thin ramp trending slightly left. Climb this up the headwall to finish.

Clach Dhian Chimney 220m V,5*
C. Butterworth and A. Frost, 4 January 1972
The obvious wide chimney line which has its crux right at the start. Climb the fault over a steep section and continue for a couple of pitches to a steepening when an exit on the left of the chimney is taken. Go diagonally up and left (not always obvious) to gain the Slanting Crack, a fault which leads up and right. Follow this till a sensational ledge leads right to the lower step on the horizon. Continue up to below the final wall and go diagonally right to finish.

Postern Variations 240m VI,6**
M. Hamilton, K. Spence and A. Taylor, 5/6 January 1980 (original line)
The way described has now become the usual way to do the route and the one which is most likely to be in condition. There are other, harder starts. Start just right of Clach Dhian Chimney and climb the fault a short way till the chimney can be crossed and a left-slanting ramp followed to the terrace. Climb the Slanting Crack which runs

Enjoying the sunshine on the upper section of Clach Dhian Chimney (photo: Giles Trussell)

Shelter Stone Crag (right side)

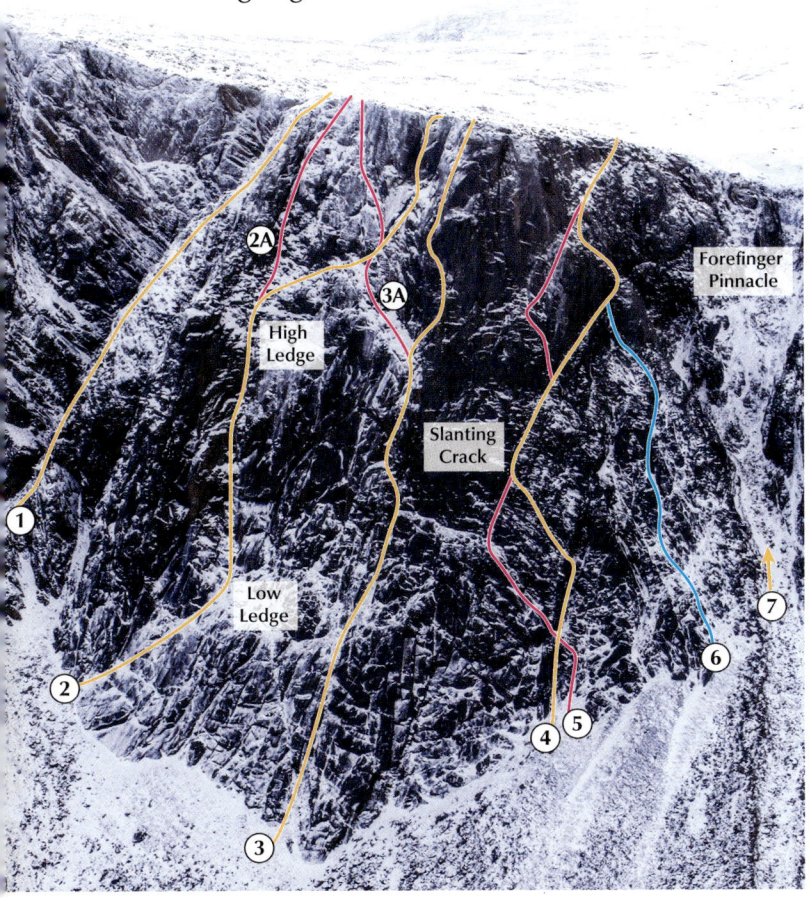

1. Castle Wall IV,5
2. Sticil Face V,6***
2A. Sticil Face Direct Finish V,6*
3. Citadel VII,8***
3A. Citadel Winter Variation VI,8**
4. Clach Dhian Chimney V,5*
5. Postern Variations VI,6**
6. Western Grooves IV,5*
7. Pinnacle Gully I

diagonally right to where it becomes a deep chimney. Climb this chimney until unlikely moves left gain a short corner which is climbed, followed by a traverse left with one step down into a gully. Continue left until possible to gain a higher ledge system. Gain and climb the obvious right-trending line to the Second Step, the large platform on the skyline. Finish diagonally out right as for Clach Dhian Chimney or climb the open groove directly above the platform (VII,7).

Western Grooves 220m IV,5*
A. Fyffe and R.D. Barton, March 1978
Takes a line of grooves right of Clach Dhian Chimney to finish up the top section of that route. Start about halfway between the chimney and the buttress edge and follow grooves heading for a short, deep, red chimney. Climb this and its continuation groove till a ramp leads left into Clach Dhian Chimney and so to the first step. Finish up Clach Dhian Chimney.

Unknown Gully 150m III*
(no photo topo)
A. Fyffe and party, 1979
Lies on the wall overlooking Pinnacle Gully and starts about halfway up that route. Climb the open gully which runs up left to the first step on the horizon and gives a chance to sample the exposure of routes on the frontal face. Finish diagonally right as for Clach Dhian Chimney.

Games of Chance 90m VI,7*
(no photo topo)
A. Fyffe and R. Mansfield, February 1991
A steep and varied climb which takes the wide, shallow chimney in the upper part of the face between Unknown and Pinnacle Gullies. It needs ice in the upper section. Start in the big snow bay up from Unknown Gully and climb up and left to below the upper wall. Climb the steep crack over bulges to gain the main fault. Climb this wide chimney, mostly on the right side on ice to the top.

Pinnacle Gully 250m I
The wide straightforward gully on the right of the crag has the unique Forefinger Pinnacle at its head.

Carn Etchachan (NJ 004 012)

Start	Coire Cas (ski centre) car park NH 989 060
Time	2hr 30min (from the north)
Crag base altitude	850–900m
Aspect	North
Route lengths	75–290m
Style	A big complex cliff with a selection of fine mixed routes of various lengths.

This is the large pointed crag lying below the top of the same name. It is a complex cliff with two distinct sections: the Main Face overlooking the head of Loch Avon (pronounced A'an) and the Gully Face which rises out of Castlegates Gully, the huge fault which separates Carn Etchachan from the flat-topped Shelter Stone Crag on its right.

The Main Face is cut at mid-height by the Great Terrace, a series of big grassy ledges starting on the left and fading out near the junction with the Gully Face. Above the Great Terrace is the Upper Cliff which is steep and complex; below is the more open and slabby Lower Face. Routes on the Lower Face can be used as access to the Upper Cliff or finished on the Great Terrace. The Gully Face in particular gives fine winter routes which can hold more ice than routes on the Main Face. Near the left margin on the Gully Face is a huge, complex vertical fault which is taken by Scorpion, and near the right side, starting well up Castlegates Gully, is the distinctive wide ramp of Sideslip which is often a uniform snow slope slanting leftwards. Near the foot of Castlegates Gully is a vertical triangular rock wall about 15m high. This is the Sentinel and is a useful landmark. Below the Sentinel and running up leftwards to near the left end of the Great Terrace is the wide snow ramp of the Diagonal Shelf, the easiest means of access to the Great Terrace from the west side of the cliff.

Approach
From the north: The normal approach. As for Shelter Stone Crag, then continue traversing round to the base of the Lower Cliff. For climbs on the Upper Cliff either do a route on the Lower Cliff, ascend to the Beinn Mheadhoin-Carn Etchachan col and traverse the Great Terrace, or go up the Diagonal Shelf near the right end of the lower face.

From the south: The approach is from Creagan a'Choire Etchachan, from where the path is followed to Loch Etchachan and then down to Loch Avon or along the Great Terrace.

Descent

Castlegates Gully is usually a quick and convenient return to the loch side. To return to the Coire Cas car park, either descend to the base of the crag and then retrace the approach route, or alternatively continue across the top of Shelter Stone Crag to gain the approach via Coire Domhain by traversing round the plateau passing above Hell's Lum Crag. Another way is to take a descending traverse west of Garbh Uisge Crag to go below Hell's Lum and then ascend into Coire Domhain. From there, follow either the Goat Track or the Fiacaill a'Choire Chais back to the car park in Coire Cas. The descent down the slopes above Loch Etchachan is awkward because of the outcrops, unless conditions are good.

Conditions

This cliff has its base at around 850m and faces north. It is a big, complex face but the buttress and chimney routes on the Main Cliff come into condition quickly with snow and cold weather. The Gully Face is much icier and the build up here does depend to some extent on freeze/thaw action. Consequently, the latter part of the season may be the best time for these climbs, which can hold their conditions until late into the spring. The Lower Cliff is slabbier and lower than elsewhere and so tends to lose its snow cover more rapidly.

The Lower Cliff, Main Face   NJ 004 013 Crag base altitude 900m North facing

This lower slabby face is cut by several left-trending ramps and bounded on the right by the Diagonal Shelf. Climbs here can be used to approach routes on the Upper Cliff.

Eastern Approach Route 100m IV,5*
A. Fyffe and A. Liddell, 4 February 1979
Near the left side of the face is a right-slanting broken fault which ends at the Great Terrace. This is the line of the route.

The Silent Approach 110m IV,6*
J. Lyall and A. Nisbet, 28 December 1989
Parallel to Eastern Approach Route and starting near the centre of the cliff. It slants right and crosses Western Approach Route then finishes up a trough to below The Guillotine on the upper cliff.

Carn Etchachan – Main and Gully Faces

1. Eastern Approach Route IV,5*
2. The Silent Approach IV,6*
3. Western Approach Route III*
4. Crystal Groove IV,6
5. Crevasse Route V,6*
6. Equinox VI,6**
7. Nathrach Dubh VI,6**
8. The Guillotine V,6***
9. Nom-de-Plume VI,6**
10. Pagan Slit V,6**
11. Route Major IV,5***
12. Red Guard VI,6**
13. Scorpion V,5***
14. The Sword V,5**
15. Siberia IV,5
16. Sideslip III*
17. Castle Gully III
18. Castlegates Gully I**

Western Approach Route 110m III*

A. Nisbet and D. McCutcheon, 19 December 1989

Follows a series of left-slanting ramps which reach the Great Terrace below Equinox. Start at the lowest point of the face, left of some huge blocks, and climb three narrow ramps and a short chimney to the terrace.

The Upper Cliff, Main Face NJ 004 012 Crag base altitude 1000m North facing

This is a complex face consisting of several buttresses and amphitheatres. About halfway along the Great Terrace a pink rib is distinctive; a second and larger but less steep pink area of rock is just to the left of the Battlements Groove. Routes here may still be in condition when the Lower Cliff is not.

Crevasse Route 75m V,6*

S. Kennedy and A. Nisbet, 13 January 1981

A technical and varied route up the leftmost buttress, which is characterised by a rock window above half-height and a big diagonal ramp on the left. The route takes a line roughly up the centre of the buttress. Start at the lowest rocks just right of centre and climb to a corner on the right (40m). Climb a large leaning block then an overhanging curving crack (crux), then step left and ascend huge flakes to a crevasse. A contorted chimney on the right leads to a fine perch. Take the crack above for about 25m then trend right to finish up the nose of the buttress.

Equinox 90m VI,6**

S. Kennedy, A. Nisbet and N. Morrison, 14 February 1981

The gully line right of the buttress of Crevasse Route is the first major fault encountered when moving right. Climb the left side of the fault for two pitches, then go right to a chimney with a constricted top which is tucked under a square-cut tower on the right. Climb this or the line on the left to finish.

Nathrach Dubh 100m VI,6**

G. Ettle, J. Lyall and J. Preston, 16 December 1996

A good, direct route up the crack line which runs straight up the amphitheatre right of Equinox and just left of The Guillotine. From the terrace the finish can be seen as a W-shaped notch on the skyline. Start just left of The Guillotine and follow a ramp left until it is possible to break out right and climb cracks up into the central right-facing corners (35m). Follow the three-tiered corners, the last being the hardest, to below the headwall (30m). Follow the groove, crack and chimney to finish just left of big roofs at the W-shaped notch (35m).

Carn Etchachan – Upper and Lower Cliffs

1. Eastern Approach Route IV,5*
2. The Silent Approach IV,6*
3. Western Approach Route III*
4. Inside Edge V,6
5. Crevasse Route V,6*
6. Equinox VI,6**
7. Nathrach Dubh VI,6**
8. The Guillotine V,6***
9. Nom-de-Plume VI,6**
10. Pagan Slit V,6**
11. Route Major IV,5***

Good snow cover on the second pitch of Nathrach Dubh

Carn Etchachan

Snake Charmer 90m V,6**
(no photo topo)
J. Lyall, A. Nisbet and E. Pirie, 23 December 1996
Takes the back left corner of the upper amphitheatre, right of the prominent wide crack of Boa (VI,6). Start as for The Guillotine then trend left crossing Nathrach Dubh at its middle corner to below the final crack of Boa (55m). Climb a turfy crack just right of the corner right of Boa for about 10m then make a short traverse left into the corner and follow it to the top – a fantastic pitch.

The Guillotine 100m V,6***
A. Fyffe and A. Liddell, 4 February 1979
Lies in the right of the bay, left of the pink spur. Start below the upper amphitheatre and climb a groove and shallow chimney to a wide chimney (30m). Climb this to the amphitheatre (20m). Climb the second chimney on the right, passing under the huge rock guillotine blade to exit on the crest of the spur (20m). Finish up the chimney with an overhang at its top (30m, crux).

Nom-de-Plume 90m VI,6**
A. Nisbet and P. Langhorne, 23 December 1982
The chimney-crack in the corner on the right side of the pink spur is steep and strenuous. Climb a series of chimneys in the corner to a huge diamond-shaped block. Pass this on the left and go onto the crest of the spur. Finish up the thin groove right of the chimney of The Guillotine or climb the last pitch of that route.

Pagan Slit 90m V,6**
M. Fowler and A. Strapcans, 27 January 1980
The right-slanting chimney right of the last route. Initially climb on the right of the chimney, which is broken by several ledges, then finish by the fault.

The Gully Face   NJ 002 012 Crag base altitude 950m North facing

This overlooks Castlegates Gully and may stay in condition well into the spring. The routes are generally long and interesting, but some depend on a good build-up of ice. Some of the rock on this part of the cliff is somewhat suspect.

Route Major 290m IV,5***
T.W. Patey and M. Smith, 10 February 1957
A Cairngorm classic, long, complex and with awkward route finding. Usually climbable under most conditions and in condition longer than most routes here. Although

it starts on the Gully Face, it finishes on the Main Face of the Upper Cliff. Start up the Diagonal Shelf, climb about 60m, then take a ramp line going up and right to reach a snow basin. Alternatively, start at the foot of Red Guard and climb groove/ramps parallel to and above Diagonal Shelf directly into the snow basin. Climb the left-slanting tapered chimney and, from a ledge on its right, exit on the left where it narrows (often the crux). A ramp leads to broken ground. Go about 70m trending up rightwards below pink rock to reach the Battlements Groove. This is difficult to see from below but is just right of the second pink rib on the Upper Cliff. Follow this groove, perhaps with a detour on the right at a steepening, to gain the main groove with its distinctive right wall with stepped ledges. At its top go up and left to gain a snow bay. Finish up the wide chimney with a couple of steep steps.

Red Guard 250m VI,6**
N.D. Keir and M. Freeman, 24 March 1978
A fine route which is continually interesting. Initially it takes a huge chimney which cuts left into the cliff, and above mid-height it follows a wide ramp sloping left. Start just above the start of the Diagonal Shelf and climb a groove for a pitch into the main bay. Climb the partly subterranean deep and block-filled chimney. Above this, climb up and right into the continuation groove (crux) and follow this to ledges and easier ground. Go rightwards about 10m to gain and climb the big left-slanting ramp, the lower of two. At its top continue up and left till a line of weakness going back right allows an open groove to be gained and followed to the top.

Scorpion 240m V,5***
T.W. Patey, J.M. Taylor, A.G. Nicol and K.A. Grassick, 6 December 1952
A great route which finishes up the huge square-cut fault with the obligatory sting in the tail. Start about 15m below the Sentinel and climb a steep corner then go left to a

Emerging from the subterranean crack of Scorpion (photo: James Thacker)

ledge below a steep wall. Climb this by a subterranean slanting crack (difficult to locate, and a grade harder if climbed on the outside). Above this, ascend an overhanging wall then go round the corner and climb a left-slanting line. Cross a slab leftward then go up to below the upper fault. Climb a long wide chimney with a leaning left wall which goes into the main fault. This is climbed on its right side to the top and may have lots of ice and a big cornice. Sometimes it may be necessary to exit on the left.

The Sword 250m V,5**
J.C. Higham and D. Wright, 5 March 1978
Takes a long diagonal to finish up the higher ramp on the upper buttress left of the huge fault of Scorpion. Start at an open groove immediately left of the Sentinel. Climb this, then a long open groove, then short walls. Work leftwards by ramps and short walls to an area of ledges. Climb Scorpion's chimney for a short way to gain a ramp (above the Red Guard ramp). Climb the ramp and finish up steps and corners, as for Red Guard.

Siberia 210m IV,5
A. Fyffe and T. Walker, 28 February 1979
Takes the large funnel-shaped fault in the upper cliff right of Scorpion. Needs a good build-up of snow. Climb snow ramps, following the bottom edge of the buttress with the ramp of Sideslip, for two pitches. Where it steepens, go right and climb ramps overlooking the main gully. Where progress is halted (level with two big blocks on the right skyline) go onto the rib on the right, descend, then gain a groove which is climbed into the main funnel which leads to the top. The cornice can be large.

Sideslip 150m III*
A. Fyffe and R. O'Donovan, 14 March 1975
The huge ramp is climbed to its top edge. Go round the corner, and a short steep traverse left leads into the main hanging funnel-shaped gully which is climbed to finish. The cornice can be large.

Castle Gully 150m III
K.A. Grassick and D. Burnett, 5 January 1964
The gully on the right of the pink scarred buttress. Either climb the open fault leading to the better-defined upper fault or take the fault further right and traverse left into the upper section.

Castlegates Gully 210m I**
J. McCoss, W.B. Meff and R. Clarke, Easter 1914
The wide snow corridor between Carn Etchachan and Shelter Stone Crag is straightforward in ascent and descent.

The Ben MacDui crags

A wild and remote pair of crags which can be approached from the north or the south. Both approaches are long, and it is unlikely you will meet many other climbers on these crags. Being on the east side of Ben MacDui, the highest peak in the Cairngorms, these crags can catch lots of snow blown across its bulk. Coire Sputan Dearg lies high up but feels open and friendly, while Creagan a'Choire Etchachan is more compact and offers fewer easy lines.

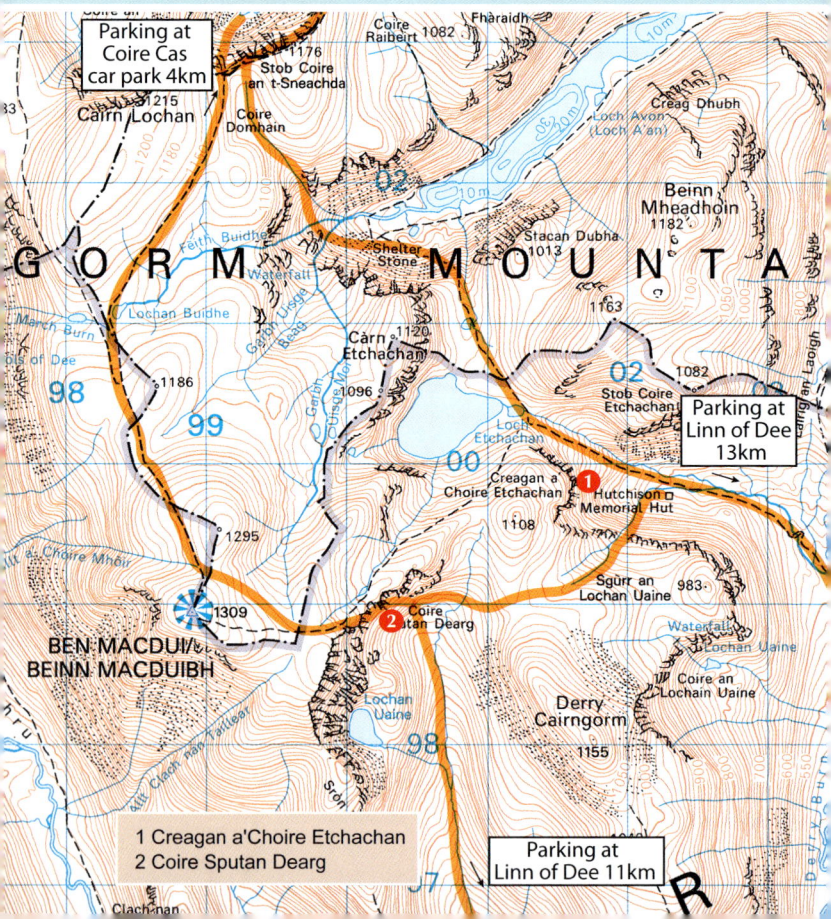

1 Creagan a'Choire Etchachan
2 Coire Sputan Dearg

Creagan a'Choire Etchachan (NO 016 998)

Start	Coire Cas (ski centre) car park NH 989 060 or Linn of Dee NO 063 897
Time	3hr 30min
Crag base altitude	850m
Aspect	East
Route lengths	100–160m
Style	Some great mixed and ice routes in a wild and remote location.

An excellent winter cliff where the long approach is rewarded by the quality of the routes. In places the rock is wet and vegetated, and consequently many routes carry ice in quantity. Although there is a long approach from any direction, the Hutchison hut at its foot does provide accessible if spartan accommodation.

The cliff itself is split into several buttresses but the two main features which aid route location are the wide gash of The Corridor, left of centre, and the narrow fault of Red Chimney towards the right side. The Corridor bounds the Bastion, the left-hand buttress, and Red Chimney marks the left edge of the distinctive Crimson Slabs. At the top of much of the cliff is a large snow apron which may have a big cornice well back from the top rocks. This should be treated with caution as it can present a severe avalanche risk.

Approach

From the north: As for Shelter Stone Crag but drop lower towards Loch Avon. Continue round the loch to reach, then follow, the obvious path leading up to Loch Etchachan. Walk along the east shore of the loch then follow the path by the stream draining the loch. Contour to below the cliff.

From the south: If approaching from Braemar, drive to the Linn of Dee then cross the river and go back towards Braemar a short way to the car park. From here go to Derry Lodge and about 200m further turn right, cross a bridge and take the good path up Glen Derry. Take the left fork in the path at NO 035 990 which leads to the Hutchison Memorial Hut NO 023 998 then onto the cliff. This fork in the path can be difficult to find in bad weather.

The expanse of the Ben MacDui plateau stretches beyond Carn Etchachan and Shelter Stone Crag in the foreground

Descent
The cliff can be descended at either end, the northern one being the most obvious.

Conditions
The cliff faces east and gets the morning sun so it can suffer later in the season, especially as it is not a particularly high crag. Early in the season is generally the best time for climbing here, although some of the deeper faults such as The Corridor can hold their ice till later in the year.

Quartzvein Edge 120m III*
J.Y.L. Hay, G. Adams and A. Thom, 29 December 1956
Climbs the left edge of the Bastion overlooking Forked Gully. Start at the foot of Forked Gully past a huge block. Follow the buttress edge for a pitch then climb slabs. These develop into a shelf which leads round a false tower. An open chimney leads to the top.

Bastion Wall 150m IV,4
J. McArtney and D. Pyper, 23 February 1963
A good route although open to much variation; in good conditions it may be Grade III. Start about 60m below and right of the buttress edge. Climb the easiest line to long iced grooves and a 30m chimney up near the top of the buttress.

Original Route Direct 150m V,6*

J. Ashbridge and S. Richardson, 29 November 1992

Takes a line of grooves just right of the buttress crest. Start to the right of the lowest rocks and go left up an easy depression leading to a deep V-groove, best located from directly below. Climb this groove (crux) to a depression. Go out from the right of this then come back left to gain another large V-groove which leads to easier ground.

The Corridor 120m IV,5**

F.R. Malcolm and A. Thom, 20 March 1954

Something of a classic route, going up the left corner of the huge open gully. There are usually two main ice pitches, one going into and one leaving a cave. The cornice can be large but is usually easiest on the left.

Architrave 120m IV,4*

A. Fyffe and J. McArtney, 29 December 1969

A fine companion route to The Corridor, climbing the right corner of the gully. Usually more sustained but less steep than The Corridor. Climb an ice groove directly to below the chimney continuation. Either go straight up or go left across a ramp to join The Corridor.

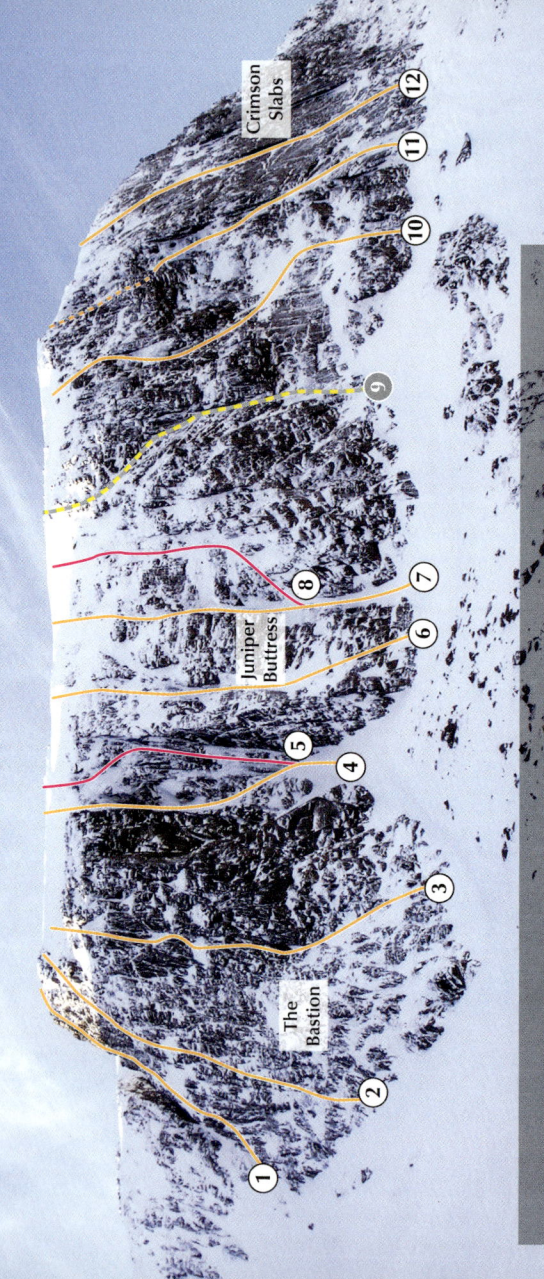

Central Chimney 120m III*

T.W. Patey, A.O'F Will, G. Adams and M. Smith, 27 February 1955

Right of The Corridor is Juniper Buttress which is split into two ribs by the line of this route. An obvious V cleft gives access to the chimney which is climbed direct over several ice pitches. Finish via a right-sloping ramp then the upper snow apron. If a sloping line starting from the foot of Square-cut Gully is used to avoid the initial V cleft, the route is Grade II.

Square-cut Gully 150m V,6**

M. Forbes and M. Low, March 1966

The obvious gully right of the twin ribs cut by Central Chimney. The gully is straightforward to the ice pillar at the big overhang. Climb the pillar (or icicle) and continue up the gully. The final slab may also be difficult.

Winter Route 150m III

W.D. Brooker, J.W. Morgan and D.A. Sutherland, 2 January 1949

A good natural line. Start up Square-cut Gully and take the obvious line leading up rightwards. Mixed climbing and an ice pitch lead to the top.

Carmine Groove 150m IV,5*

R.A. Smith and G. Stephens, November 1974

A good climb taking as its main feature the obvious red groove on the upper cliff, left of the big overhang. Start below a rock scar and climb rightwards to the Meadows, the upper snowfield below the overhangs. From here, follow the groove from its left corner, mostly on ice, to the top.

Flanking Ribs 150m IV,4 or

J. McArtney and A. Fyffe, 6 January 1967

This first gains the Meadows, the large snowfield under the overhangs, then finishes up the rib right of Red Chimney. Start left of Red Chimney and climb the rib to cross Red Chimney at its easier mid-section. Pull onto the right rib and follow this to the top. Can be an escape from Red Chimney.

Red Chimney 150m V,5**

I.A. Paterson and S.P. Hepburn, January 1967

An extremely fine ice climb. Start up twin corners right of the chimney and, higher up, gain the chimney by iced slabs. The chimney is then followed with another difficult section above the amphitheatre crossed by Flanking Ribs, where a way up and left through ice bulges must be found to gain the final corner. Above this, the climbing eases to the top.

Creagan a'Choire Etchachan (right side)

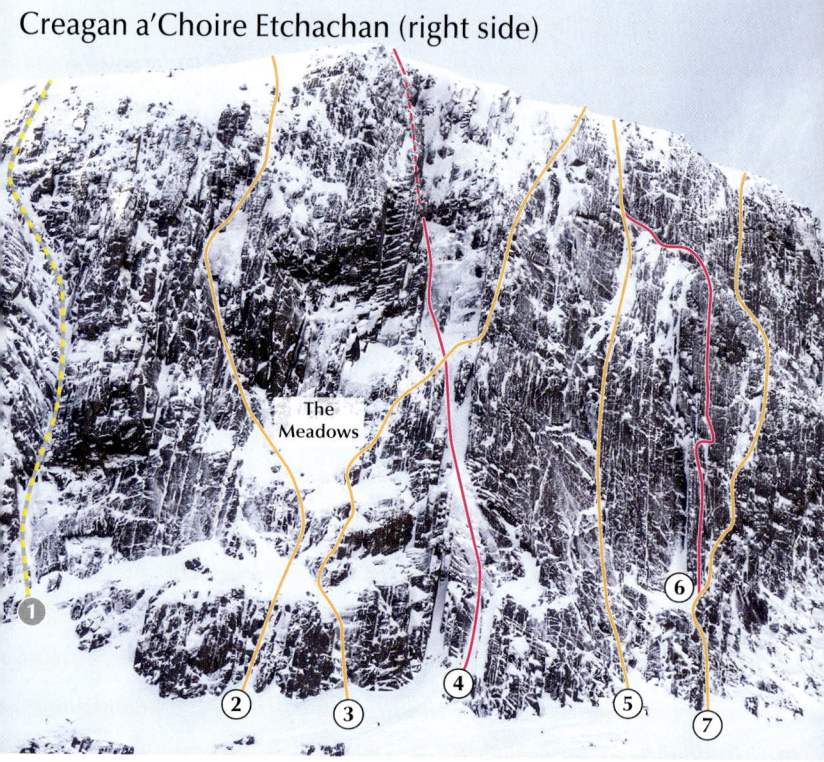

1. Avalanche Gully VI,6*
2. Carmine Groove IV,5*
3. Flanking Ribs IV,4
4. Red Chimney V,5**
5. Djibangi V,4***
6. Scabbard VI,7**
7. Switchblade VI,7**

Djibangi 140m V,4***

J. McArtney and W.J. Barclay, 31 January 1965

A superb ice climb when formed. It follows the leftmost corner running up the Crimson Slabs. Start directly below the corner and climb iced slabs into the corner

Creagan a'Choire Etchachan

Ice and sunshine on Djibangi (photo: Pete Davis)

itself. Continue up the corner to the top (the overlap may prove to be the crux). Go on up via grooves and iced slabs trending left to reach straightforward snow leading to the cornice.

Scabbard 140m VI,7**
C. MacLean and A. Nisbet, 10 January 1985
The right corner on the Crimson Slabs is Dagger V,5, but slow to come into condition. Scabbard takes cracks in the right rib of this corner. Start in a right-facing corner below the rib. Climb this corner, hopefully on ice but with limited protection, then move left to a stance. Climb the sustained but well-protected cracks in the rib above to a huge spike at the top of Dagger corner. Move right, descend a short way and go right to an edge. Climb blocks and cracks to reach the broken ramp-like terrace. Finish up this.

Switchblade 160m VI,7**
J. Lyall and A. Nisbet, 2 February 1991
A very good technical route which takes the line of turfy cracks that trend right, right of Scabbard. Start up a vegetated line slanting up left from the bay on the right and belay just right of Scabbard (20m). Climb the right-facing corner that bounds the right side of Scabbard, then follow a wide crack to slabs. Make a thin traverse right into a turfy left-facing corner and follow it to a turfy bay (40m). Go over an overhang at the top right corner, climb cracks, then go diagonally left to the terrace just below its top (45m). Climb a thin turfy crack left of the arête (35m). Easy ground leads to the top.

Topping out in wild conditions (photo: Calum Musket)

Coire Sputan Dearg (NO 004 988)

Start	Coire Cas (ski centre) car park NH 989 060 or Linn of Dee Parking NO 063 897
Time	3hr 30min
Crag base altitude	1100m
Aspect	South to south-east
Route lengths	70–130m
Style	A variety of snow, ice and mixed routes, with the focus in the lower grades.

This corrie lies high on Ben MacDui, looking southwards down Glen Luibeg. It is an open bowl with a rim of defined buttresses and several large, easy-angled gullies. The routes tend to be quite short but very enjoyable, and the descent back into the corrie floor is generally easy. There is not a wealth of hard climbing here, but there is a good range of fine, easier routes. Although a more light-hearted place to climb than many of the Cairngorm cliffs, it is still a long walk in, especially in poor conditions.

Approach

From the north: A long approach which goes over Ben MacDui to the corrie rim, then goes down by Glissade Gully, Main Spout or by the col at the north-east corner.

From the south: From Braemar, go to the Linn of Dee and continue right on the north of the river to a car park where a path leads to the track to Derry Lodge, as for Creagan a'Choire Etchachan. Follow the Lairig Ghru path for about 3 kilometres until a lesser path cuts off before the Luibeg Burn. This can be followed into the corrie.

From the Hutchison Memorial Hut: Approach the hut as for Creagan a'Choire Etchachan then go up the slope by the stream behind the hut. This leads south-west over the col north of Derry Cairngorm and into the corrie.

Descent

Two main descent gullies lead back to the corrie floor. These are Glissade Gully, in the centre of the cliff and right of Grey Man's Crag (the largest buttress), and the Main Spout, on the extreme right of the cliff but left of Terminal Buttress. The last is the easiest to locate and descend.

Winter Climbs in the Cairngorms

Coire Sputan Dearg – Grey Man's Crag area

1. Pinnacle Buttress III**
2. Red Gully I
3. Crystal Ridge IV,4*
4. Slab Chimney II/III**
5. Hanging Dyke V,5
6. Ardath Chimney III**
7. Anchor Gully I*
8. Anchor Route III*

Coire Sputan Dearg

Conditions

The base of these cliffs lies at 1100m above sea level. Because of the corrie's situation snow accumulations can be large, banking out many lower and slabbier features. However, the southerly aspect also means that the buttresses can lose their cover rapidly in thawing or sunny weather, especially later in the season. Conditions here and at nearby Creagan a'Choire Etchachan can be very different. However, some buttress routes come into condition quickly with cold weather and fresh snow.

Grey Man's Crag   NO 001 988 Crag base altitude 1100m South-east facing

This is the largest and best defined of the buttresses. On its left is Slab Chimney above which is a very steep wall. The front face is cut by a series of grooves and the right side is defined by Anchor Gully, so named for the shape of the spring snow at its foot.

Pinnacle Buttress 120m III**

W.D. Brooker and J.W. Morgan, 5 January 1950

The leftmost buttress provides an enjoyable route. Start at its foot and climb into and up a long groove left of the buttress crest. This may contain ice. Above, easier ground leads to the top.

Red Gully 120m I

The gully between Pinnacle Buttress and Crystal Ridge.

Crystal Ridge 90m IV,4*

W.D. Brooker and M. Smith, 5 January 1949

The next buttress on the right, separated from Pinnacle Buttress by Red Gully. The main feature is a large slab on the right whose left edge forms a very narrow crest. Start at the buttress foot, climb to the narrow crest and follow it to its top. Above, climb an arête to a shelf and then another pitch on the right to easier ground.

Slab Chimney 120m II/III**

A. Parker and J. Young, 17 March 1949

The best gully in the corrie. It is Y-shaped and the left branch, running up the right side of Crystal Ridge, is Grade I. The right branch, this route, cuts into the side of Grey Man's Crag. The gully is climbed direct, the difficulties depending on the build-up on the two chokestone pitches.

Ardath Chimney 120m III**

J.Y.L. Hay, 2 April 1955

This lies on the right flank of Grey Man's Crag. Start near Anchor Gully and climb the chimney which is steep and defined for the first 45m. Above, the upper depression contains a short iced slab which can be difficult. Best early in the season and when there is ice in the chimney.

Anchor Gully 120m I*

The gully on the right of Grey Man's Crag. There may be a pitch at the narrows of the gully. Above it is easy, and the cornice is usually turned on the right.

Anchor Route 120m III*

G. Adams and R.W.P. Barclay, 25 December 1955

Lies on the two-tiered buttress right of Anchor Gully. Climb the lowest tier by the easiest line to a terrace below the upper tier (this may bank out). Follow the left edge overlooking Anchor Gully to a steepening which is avoided by a short steep corner on the gully wall. An overhang high up is turned on the right, and above the buttress splits into two. The left-hand ridge is climbed, or can be avoided to the right of the buttress.

Snake Ridge Area   NO 002 989 Crag base altitude 1080m South-east facing

Lying near the centre of the cliff is a broad easy gully: **Glissade Gully** (the cornice is usually avoidable on the left). This area lies between Glissade and Narrow Gullies and consists of twin ridges, Snake Ridge being the right hand and longer of the two.

Snake Gully 130m II*

J. McArtney, T. Mackie and B.T. Lawrie, 2 March 1963

A good route up the gully separating the two long ridges. Start up steep snow and curve left up an ice pitch. Climb this to easier ground. A short ridge and ice groove then leads to where the gully follows the right side of the upper buttress.

The Ladders 120m II*

(no photo topo)
G.R. Simpson and K. Menmuir, 21 February 1971
The slim gully on the immediate right of Snake Ridge.

Narrow Gully 130m I ◇
A well-defined but straightforward snow climb which lies right of Snake Gully and left of a trio of buttresses.

The Central Buttresses   NO 003 990 Crag base altitude 1100m South-east facing

Right of Narrow Gully is a set of three buttresses – Cherub's Buttress, the more spectacular Black Tower and Flake Buttress. They are separated by wet slabby depressions which give the Left and Right-hand Icefalls.

Cherub's Buttress 130m III
G.S. Strange and D. Stuart, 21 November 1970
The buttress right of Narrow Gully consists of two ridges leading into an upper amphitheatre. Start at the foot of the left ridge by Narrow Gully. Climb a flake crack and slab to below a nose. Go right into a depression and climb this to regain the crest. A chimney and arête lead into the upper amphitheatre. A level arête forms here, and above it a snow ramp going right leads to a corner on the crest and then easier ground.

Flying Ridge 130m II
M.D.Y. Mowat and A. Fyffe, 4 January 1966
The right-hand ridge is climbed into the upper amphitheatre where the route continues as for Cherub's Buttress.

Left-hand Icefall 90m IV,4
R.J. Archbold and D.M. Nichols, 6 March 1974
The icefall between Cherub's Buttress and the impressive Black Tower. The ice groove close against the Black Tower is the crux, and above easier snow leads to a col then an arête leads to the top.

Right-hand Icefall 90m II/IV*
A. Fyffe, P. Williams, M. McArthur and I. McLean, 3 January 1967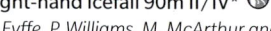
Between the Black Tower and Flake Buttress is a depression full of ice. Depending on the build-up and the line taken, the grade can vary considerably.

Flake Buttress 120m III**
W.D. Brooker and S. McPherson, 10 April 1950
The right-hand buttress. Start just right of the lowest rocks and follow a depression right onto the crest. Continue in the same line until a crack leads back left to a short

Heavy snow cover on Flake Buttress

corner. Go up left then climb a chimney and then follow ledges to the crest. Climb a crack behind a huge flake and go up to the gap. Climb the arête to the top.

Terminal Buttress   NO 005 991 Crag base altitude 1080m South facing

The Main Spout is the broad easy gully which lies on the left of Terminal Buttress, the last major rocks on the right. It is very straightforward and a convenient descent.

Terminal Buttress 70m IV,5
D. Reid and D. Pyper, 4 February 1963
Takes the prominent curved groove. Start in a short gully and climb it till a traverse round a rib gives access to a deep groove and a belay. Follow the groove until forced left round a corner onto a ledge. Go up to a broad shelf and climb the broken rib on the right to finish. The lower section can bank out late in the season.

The Cairn Toul/Braeriach amphitheatre

This is a huge area of remote cliffs and corries shared by Cairn Toul and Braeriach, two of the four Cairngorm summits over 4,000ft in height. Because of the height of this amphitheatre and its situation, cutting back into a huge high-level plateau, the cliffs share some features in common, the main one being the vast amounts of snow that accumulates here. In fact, the Garbh Choire Mor, the innermost corrie of An Garbh Choire, has snowfields which rarely disappear, even in summer. Another feature is the huge cornices which can stretch unbroken round the complete corrie

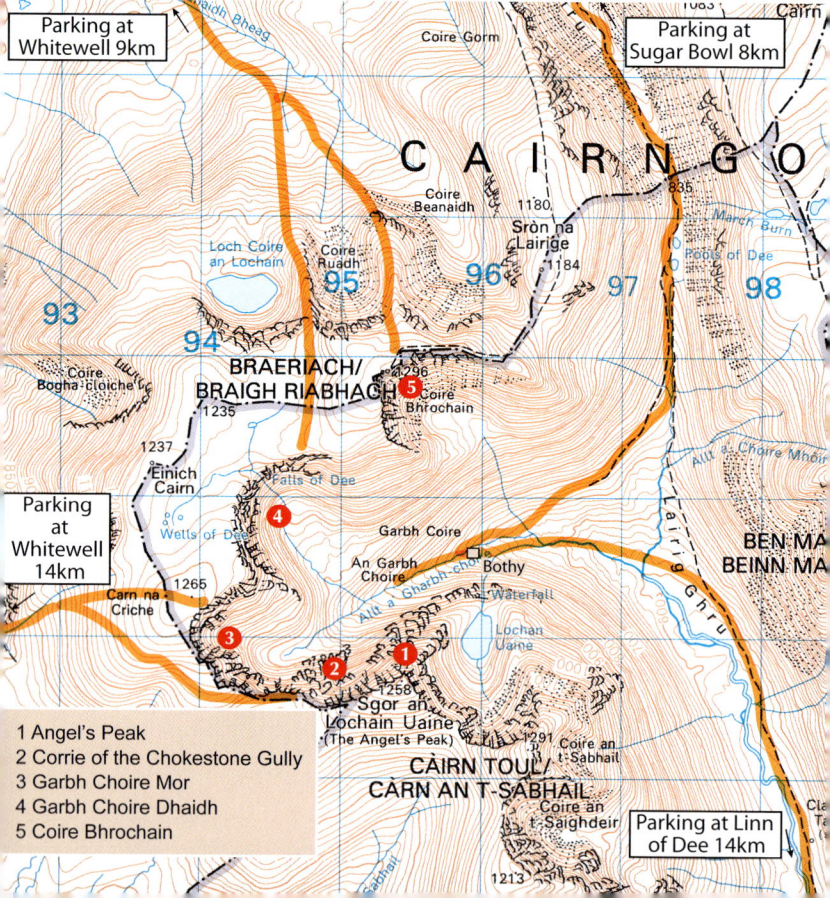

1 Angel's Peak
2 Corrie of the Chokestone Gully
3 Garbh Choire Mor
4 Garbh Choire Dhaidh
5 Coire Bhrochain

rim. This can make the exit from some climbs difficult or even impossible and force retreats or descent down suitable routes, or long traverses below the cornices to find weaknesses through them.

All the approaches to these corries are long and arduous. The use of skis at certain times will make the approach easier but single-day visits, especially early in the year, will usually involve much travel in the dark. The recently rebuilt Garbh Choire bothy (NN 959 986) provides weatherproof but basic accommodation for four (possibly more if comfort is not important). However, at busy times of the year it cannot be relied upon to be empty. From the bothy, access the climbs by walking uphill into the corries. Corrour Bothy (NN 981 958) in the Lairig Ghru can also be used as a base to climb from. It is larger so there is more chance of having floor space, but the daily approach is longer. However, it does get very busy during holiday periods.

From the north: From Aviemore go up the ski road towards Coire Cas to the Sugar Bowl car park (NH 985 074), which is on the left by the big bend at the upper edge of the Glenmore forest. From the car park cross the road and follow a good path down and over the bridge then round and through the Chalamain Gap and so into the Lairig Ghru. Alternatively, from the west end of Loch Morlich cross the river and continue south past Rothiemurchus Lodge and so into the Lairig Ghru. Continue past the Pools of Dee then contour south-west to Garbh Choire bothy.

From the south: Go to Derry Lodge (see Coire Sputan Dearg) then follow the path into the Lairig Ghru. Continue past Corrour Bothy to where a vague path by the Allt a Gharbh Choire heads off into the main amphitheatre and so to the bothy.

From the west: From Achlean in Glen Feshie ascend Carn Ban Mor and cross the north end of the Moine Mor. Ascend Einich Cairn then use one of the descents into the appropriate corrie. Mostly used as a ski approach. The ability to navigate accurately is essential if using this approach.

From Glen Einich: This approach benefits from the use of a mountain bike, so if the Glen Einich track is clear of snow and you have use of a bike, this tends to be the quickest approach. For the actual descents, see the individual corrie descriptions. From the end of the public road at Whitewell (NH 915 086) go down to the main track and follow it into the glen. For Coire Bhrochain leave the track where it crosses the Beanaidh Bheag (can be difficult to cross if the stream is high) and follow the path till it ends. Cross the stream then climb the ridge between Coire Beanaidh and Coire Ruadh to the top, then go down into the corrie. For Garbh Coire Dhaidh climb the ridge between Coire an Lochain and Coire Ruadh and navigate to the north-east corner of the corrie. For Garbh Choire Mor leave the main track about 400 metres before the loch and follow the track up Coire Dhondail. When the plateau is reached go over spot height 1265 to reach the top of the corrie. For Corrie of the Chokestone Gully head for the col west of Sgor an Lochain Uaine.

Sgor an Lochain Uaine, Angel's Ridge on the right

Winter Climbs in the Cairngorms

Angel's Peak (NN 954 976)

Start	Various options; see notes on approach at start of this section.
Time	4hr
Crag base altitude	Ill-defined
Aspect	North-east
Route lengths	100–300m
Style	A lovely, wild peak with a couple of great easy mountaineering routes.

Sgor an Lochain Uaine, also known as Angel's Peak (to balance up Devil's Point), is an attractive peak, particularly when seen from the north or the east. It provides limited climbing but the routes are of Alpine length and appearance.

Approach
Various options, most likely through the Lairig Ghru from either the north or south. See start of section for more discussion on the approach.

Angel's Peak

Descent
Various options; see start of section for more discussion.

Conditions
The Lochain Uaine waterfall needs cold weather to form but the upper ridge is usually climbable.

Lochan Uaine Waterfall 100m II
(no photo topo)
A fine way of approaching the Cairn Toul/Braeriach plateau if combined with Angel's Ridge. Start at the foot of the waterfall coming from Lochain Uaine, the corrie between Angel's Peak and Cairn Toul. Climb the waterfall direct. The route is a little artificial as it is possible to escape in several places. It does, however, lead to the foot of Angel's Ridge.

Angel's Ridge 300m I***
(no photo topo)
The north-east ridge between Coire an Lochain Uaine and the Corrie of the Chokestone Gully is followed throughout, with a narrowing at the top. A very fine way to ascend Sgor an Lochain Uaine. There is seldom a cornice and this route can be used as a descent.

Cairn Toul, Angel's Peak and Garbh Choire Mhor

Corrie of the Chokestone Gully (NN 949 979)

Start	Various options; see notes on approach at start of this section.
Time	4hr
Crag base altitude	1100m
Aspect	North
Route lengths	120–160m
Style	A wild, snowy corrie with a number of moderate mixed routes.

This corrie, the only one on Cairn Toul to give major climbs, lies west of Sgor an Lochain Uaine or Angel's Peak, and some way right of its shapely north-east ridge. The most prominent feature is the great gash of Chokestone Gully in the centre of the corrie's back wall. To its left the ground is more broken; on its right is a massive and well-defined buttress whose edge is taken by Bugaboo Rib. On much of the rest of the cliff, the climbs are less well defined and open to variation.

Approach
Various options for approach from either above or below the crag. If approaching from above, the descent described below will be necessary to gain the base of the routes. See start of section for more discussion on the approach.

Descent
Below the cliff and slanting up to the right or south-west is a large diagonal slope which gives one of the easier ways onto and off the plateau. Cornices in this area tend to be a bit smaller than elsewhere. The start can be difficult to locate in bad weather, but it slants down from a small promontory about 300m west of the top of Chokestone Gully (NN 947 976). Angel's Ridge can be used as a descent; although longer it is easier to locate and is unlikely to have a big cornice.

Conditions
A high north-facing corrie which, in common with the other corries in the area, can have huge, extensive cornices. Because of the corrie's northerly aspect, conditions here can persist well into the spring when the routes can have an Alpine character. Unfortunately, the rock in this corrie is generally poor.

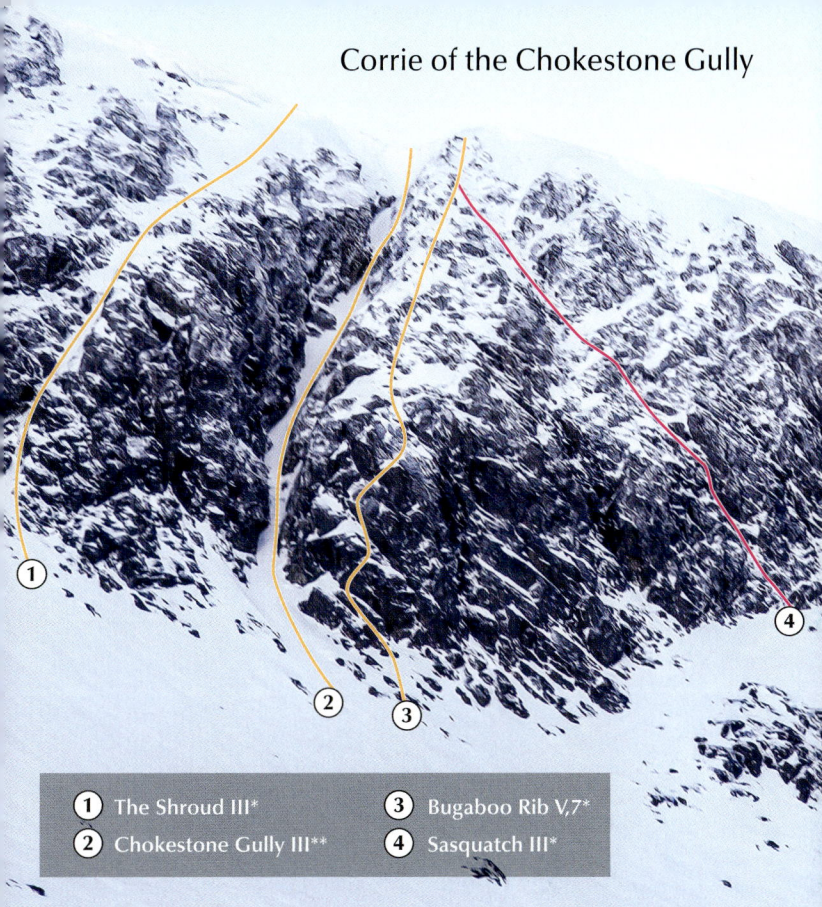

Corrie of the Chokestone Gully

1. The Shroud III*
2. Chokestone Gully III**
3. Bugaboo Rib V,7*
4. Sasquatch III*

The Shroud 160m III*

J. Knight and I. MacEacheran, 9 February 1964

The narrow gully parallel to, and just left of, Chokestone Gully. It may be necessary to climb icy rocks to gain the gully which can contain some ice pitches.

Chokestone Gully 150m III**

A.H. Hendry and party, March 1937

A remote but classic climb up the twisting fault in the steepest buttress. Can be a grade harder in lean conditions. Start near the lowest rocks in the centre of the main

Winter Climbs in the Cairngorms

face. The first half of the gully is usually steep but straightforward then it curves, narrows and steepens, and there may be an ice pitch. Above a snow basin is the chokestone, which gives an ice pitch of variable size depending on the build-up. If insufficiently built up, an escape on the right is possible. The cornice is usually easiest on the right.

Bugaboo Rib 150m V,7*
B.S. Findlay and G.S. Strange, 13 April 1970
The buttress on the right of Chokestone Gully which forms a vague rib in its upper section. Start between the gully and the centre of the face and climb to a grass platform (probably banked out). Climb a steep slanting crack to an obvious block, traverse round the block and under an overhang and go up to a large platform. Climb a crack heading right to below an overhang then go right round a corner and along a tapering shelf to a belay. Follow the much easier ridge to the top.

Sasquatch 120m III*
R.J. Archbold, D. King, G.R. Simpson and G.S. Strange, 31 March 1974
Start right of the lowest rocks where they descend lower into the corrie at a horizontal ledge going left onto the face (can bank out). Traverse this to gain and climb a shallow icy depression. Continue direct or go diagonally left across another depression to finish at the top of Bugaboo Rib, where the cornice may be less imposing.

Breaking through the cloud to reach the summit of Corrie of the Chokestone Gully

Garbh Choire Mor (NN 940 980)

Start	Various options; see notes on approach at start of this section.
Time	4hr
Crag base altitude	1130m
Aspect	North to east
Route lengths	100–120m
Style	Probably the snowiest corrie in the UK, provides a range of grades. Lower pitches can bank out and cornices can be huge.

The innermost of the two subsidiary corries that make up An Garbh Choire. It is separated from its neighbour, Garbh Choire Dhaidh, by a spur extending east from the plateau. The corrie itself consists of two sections, the Lower and Upper Corries – the latter being the more important.

Approach
Various options for approach from either above or below the crag. If approaching from above, the descent described below will be necessary to gain the base of the routes. See start of section for more discussion on the approach.

Descent
Descent back into the corrie floor may be difficult because of the cornices. These are often huge and can overhang a considerable distance. Pinnacle Gully provides the most likely break in the cornice, as Pinnacle Buttress protrudes and can give access to the gully. The spur running east between Garbh Choire Mor and Garbh Choire Dhaidh is one possible descent. The slope between Garbh Choire Dhaidh and Coire Bhrochain is further away but less likely to be corniced. The descent down the shelf into Corrie of the Chokestone Gully is also convenient. Any descent is best checked out before starting a climb and it must be remembered that an abseil descent or a retreat from below an insurmountable cornice may be required. When on the plateau accurate navigation is mandatory, especially in bad weather. In such circumstances it may be better to keep the rope on.

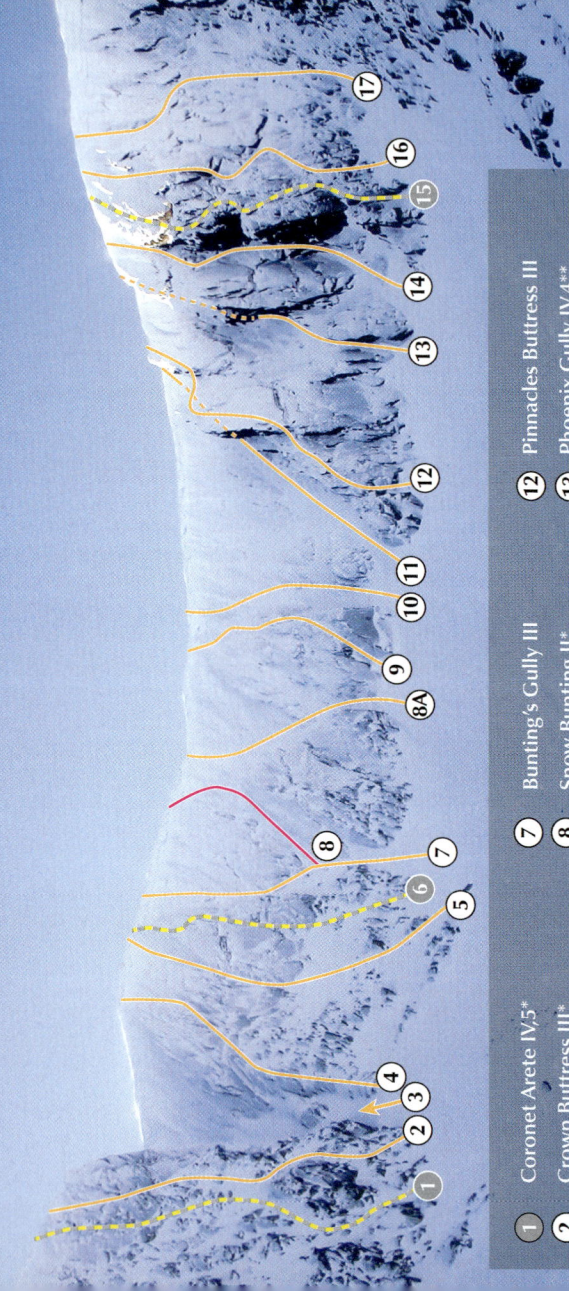

Garbh Choire Mor

Conditions
This is probably the greatest snow-holding corrie in the Cairngorms; immense depths can accumulate, and the snow fields here often last all year. They only disappeared a few times last century but have been less extensive in recent years. This amount of snow means that many of the lower features or easy-angled slopes simply disappear and identification of routes can be difficult. Some of the easier gullies may become straightforward snow slopes. There is usually a huge and often insurmountable cornice, which can be up to 10m in height. Possible routes may be determined by breaches in this cornice, and long traverses or abseil retreats from below the cornice are not uncommon.

The Upper Corrie NH 940 980 Crag base altitude 1130m North facing

This corrie consists of several compact well-defined buttresses lying high under the plateau rim. Depending on the build-up here, some features may be obliterated or at least shortened. At times the cliff between Sphinx Ridge and Pinnacles Buttress can be a snow slope. However, the main features are the narrow well-defined Great Gully on the left, Sphinx Ridge, a narrow, crested buttress in the centre of the cliff, and a trio of buttresses on the right. The leftmost of these is Pinnacles Buttress and between it and Sphinx Ridge is a large slabby recess. Any of the climbs in this corrie can have impassable cornices and this goes for the easier climbs as well. Try to check the cornice's condition before starting on a climb.

Crown Buttress 120m III*
J. Bower and P. Kale, 26 January 1967
This is the buttress on the left of the corrie which flanks the left side of Great Gully. The Crown is a rock flake on top of the arête. The route takes the big V-groove between two arêtes at the top of the buttress. Start at the bottom left corner of Great Gully and climb iced slabs and ribs to a large block, keeping close to the gully edge. Continue up to the big groove which starts as an icy chimney (crux). Easier ground leads to the plateau.

Great Gully 120m I
The well-defined gully on the left is a snow climb which can be heavily corniced.

She-Devil's Corner 120m IV,5**
G. Boyd, B.S. Findlay, G.R. Simpson and G.S. Strange, 19 April 1969
The buttress on the right of Great Gully. On the right of the crest are two corners. This route takes the left of these twin corners. Climb iced grooves and snow arêtes on the

edge overlooking Great Gully (60m). Traverse right over a flake to gain the leftmost of the twin corners. Climb this to the top and, hopefully, a snow prow breaking the cornice line.

Vulcan 100m V,4***

J. Bower, J. Ingram and K. Turnbull, 1 March 1975

The rightmost of the twin corners gives a very fine, icy climb. Start in the bay right of the lowest rocks and climb the prominent V-groove over a series of ice pitches. The lower section constitutes the crux, and the upper part may be a snow arête on the right, forming a break in the cornice.

> The shallow gully right of Great Gully is Bunting's Gully, which has on its right a buttress consisting of twin ribs which meet at a col near the top. The initial gully is easy to the fork below mid-height, after which there is a choice.

Bunting's Gully 100m III

J.J. Light and O.J. Ludlow, 9 January 1964

This is the left fork; climb it to about 15m below the overhang, then go on to the right wall and go up and right till near the right crest. Traverse left into an upper corner which leads to the cornice.

Snow Bunting 100m II*

J.J. Light and J. Vigrow, 15 March 1966

This is the right fork which runs up to the col where the twin ribs meet. Above is a shallow gully and probably a giant cornice.

Solo Gully 100m I*

J.J. Light and O.J. Ludlow, 8 January 1964

Right of Bunting's Gully and left of the shapely Sphinx Ridge is Solo Gully. It is narrow at the bottom and straightforward but it does, however, offer a descent from other routes which may have impassable cornices.

Sphinx Ridge 100m III**

J.J. Light and J. Vigrow, 14 March 1966

A shapely, well-defined buttress in the centre of the cliffs, rising between Solo Gully and a snowfield. There is a steep triangular wall at the foot of it. Start in Solo Gully and climb a small gully to reach the knife-edge at the top of the lower wall. This leads delicately to a shallow groove then a short chimney (crux) on the left. Follow the arête

Garbh Choire Mor

Climber high on Sphinx Gully (photo: Lawrie Brand)

above, often with a double cornice, to a platform and a col. Climb steep snow and the usual cornice to the plateau.

Sphinx Gully 100m II ◇
A. Watson and P.D. Baird, 31 October 1954
Between Sphinx Ridge and Pinnacles Buttress is a recessed area. This is the gully right of Sphinx Ridge. Climb the gully; the main pitch is climbed by a short groove and ridge on the right.

Pinnacle Gully 100m I* ◇
The gully on the right of the recess, left of Pinnacles Buttress. It curves right and steepens behind Pinnacle Buttress. This route has the most reliable break in the cornice, so is a possible descent.

Pinnacles Buttress 100m III
J. Bower, G.R. Simpson and G.S. Strange, 12 April 1968
On the right of the corrie is a trio of buttresses. The route climbs the leftmost one which consists of two distinct pinnacles. Start just left of centre and climb to blocks near Pinnacle Gully. Climb a crack in a slab to more blocks and at their top climb a short wall to a broad ledge. Go to its right end then to the top of the first pinnacle. Ascend the second pinnacle, above which a snow arête leads to the top.

Phoenix Gully looking steeper than it actually is (photo: Allen Fyffe)

Phoenix Gully 100m IV,4**

J.J. Light, G. McGregor, M. McArthur and D. Halliday, 19 March 1967

This is the steep icy gully between Pinnacles Buttress and the Tower of Babel, the first and second of the trio of buttresses. It is climbed direct to the usual problematic finish.

White Nile 100m V,5**

R.J. Archbold and M. Hillman, 12 March 1977

The classic route of the corrie up the steep ice between the second and third of the buttresses. Climb the ice, with a deviation left and back right at about two-thirds height to turn an iced wall. Tends to be produced by freeze/thaw and may be better in March, but by April it catches the sun.

Phoenix Buttress 120m IV,4**

M.G. Geddes and J.S. Robinson, 21 December 1971

The large rightmost buttress of the three gives a fine climb. From the base of the buttress crest, go up and right to a steep nose. Traverse left round this to a good ledge. Go up the groove above and go to piled blocks under a steep wall which is climbed by a short, steep corner on the right. Above, go up and right into a groove leading to the plateau.

Forked Lightning Route 100m III*

R.J. Archbold, D. King, G.R. Simpson and G.S. Strange, 30 March 1974

The grooves on the right edge of Phoenix Buttress are often icy late in the season. Start at the top right corner of the snow bay right of the buttress and climb ice in the second groove to the right of the buttress. Climb a left-slanting groove to gain the nearest groove to the buttress which leads to the top.

Garbh Choire Dhaidh (NN 943 986)

Start	Various options; see approach notes at the start of this section.
Time	4hr
Crag base altitude	1100m
Aspect	South
Route lengths	130–150m
Style	Generally slabby rock where ice can build up but, being south-facing, has a shorter season than other crags in the area. A mix of styles.

This is the right-hand corrie of An Garbh Choire, separated from its companion by a spur running roughly eastwards. The Dee waterfall divides Garbh Choire Dhaidh (pronounced 'yay') into two sections. The left section, running round to the dividing spur, is undistinguished. In fact, this whole section can bank out into a long, steep snow wall easily climbable anywhere. However, in leaner conditions there are some long gullies of Grade I and II standard.

Right of the Falls of Dee are the main rocks, which are divided centrally by The Great Rift, only seen well from the left side of the corrie. Near the right margin where the rocks are less massive is the obvious fault of The Chimney Pot. The leaning buttress of Pisa next to it marks the end of the cliff proper.

Approach
Various options for approach from either above or below the crag. If approaching from above, the descent described below will be necessary to gain the base of the routes. See start of section for more discussion on the approach.

Descent
The slope between Garbh Choire Dhaidh and Coire Bhrochain is straightforward and rarely corniced all the way round. The spur between the two Garbh Choires is less easy and normally corniced.

Conditions
Although some fine routes are to be found here, its south-facing aspect makes conditions less reliable than elsewhere as the sun can rapidly strip the rocks of their cover of snow and ice. The ice routes are best early in the season or on cloudy days.

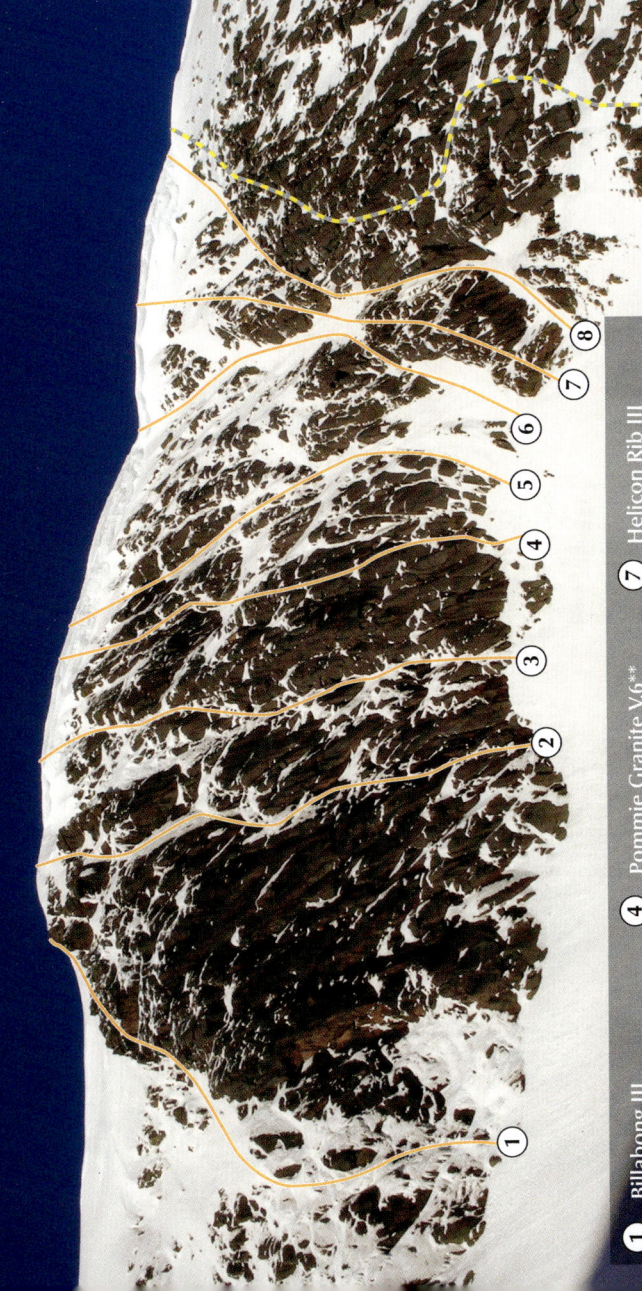

Winter Climbs in the Cairngorms

Billabong 150m III
G. Boyd, B.S. Findlay, G.R. Simpson and G.S. Strange, 18 April 1969
This climbs the obvious icefall near the left margin of the main face and is based on the leftmost corner. This may, in heavy snow years, virtually disappear. Start below a corner well left of The Great Rift. Climb the icefall to reach a platform. Continue up the ridge crest to finish via a narrow chimney in the final wall.

The Culvert 130m V,4*
A. Nisbet and P. Barass, 17 December 1981
Left of The Great Rift is a series of ramps and corners which can form a fine icefall. The ice is climbed by the best line.

From shade to light on Twilight Gully

The Great Rift 140m V,5**
J.J. Light and A.G. Nicol, 21 February 1965
This defined chimney in the centre of the face is the classic climb of the corrie. Once committed to the rift, the route is obvious. Best early in the season before it is too affected by the sun.

Pommie Granite 130m V,6**
G. Ettle and J. Lyall, 13 February 2007
Takes the rib on the right of the prominent corner of Koala, VI,6*. Start at the base of the rib and climb cracks on the right to gain the crest, then step right and follow wider cracks (35m). Continue up steps with wide cracks and blocks to the top of the rib (45m). Head up to a left-facing corner in the upper wall, move right into a groove and follow this curving back left to rejoin the main corner (50m). Sustained.

Boomerang 150m IV,4*
D. Pyper and D. Reid, 23 February 1962
Lies on the right side of the main cliff, right of The Great Rift. This route starts behind a small arête and curves up left. It can contain several ice pitches, but these may shorten and bank out at times.

Twilight Gully 150m II** ◇ or ✱
J. Bower, B.S. Findlay, G.S. Strange and D. Stuart, 11 April 1971
The bow-shaped gully left of Helicon Rib and right of the main mass. It may contain ice and have a huge cornice but is the climb most likely to be continuous in marginal conditions. A better climb when in lean conditions.

Helicon Rib 140m III
D.W. Duncan and A.J.D. Smith, March 1964
The next main break right of The Great Rift is The Chimney Pot, a deep, dark fault. Helicon Rib climbs the rib on its left. Start at the foot of the well-defined rib and climb its crest for about 100m to a small col where the difficulties end.

The Chimney Pot 140m II/III
R.H. Sellars and K.A. Grassick, February 1959
The deep chimney is climbed direct. There is usually an ice pitch at the great chokestone. Above, the chimney widens to an amphitheatre which may have a huge cornice.

Coire Bhrochain (NN 954 998)

Start	Various options; see approach notes at the start of this section.
Time	4hr
Crag base altitude	1100m
Aspect	South to south-east
Route lengths	80–200m
Style	A variety of styles and lengths. A very snowy corrie but, being south-facing, best early season.

This is the huge south-facing corrie lying directly below the summit of Braeriach. For convenience it is divided into three main sections between West Gully, the widest fault, and East Gully, which begins narrow and funnels out. This gives, from left to right, West, Central and East Buttresses.

Approach
Various options for approach from either above or below the crag. If approaching from above, the descent described below will be necessary to gain the base of the routes. See start of section for more discussion on the approach.

Descent
The easiest descent back to the corrie floor is down the slope between Coire Bhrochain and Garbh Choire Dhaidh. The ridge on the east of the corrie leading back to the Lairig Ghru also gives a descent. Depending on the cornice, West Gully can also provide a way back down to the corrie floor.

Conditions
This corrie is remote and isolated, and can hold huge amounts of snow and have big cornices, although probably not so much as Garbh Choire Mor. The more easterly and southerly aspect makes it better as an early season corrie before the sun can strip the buttresses.

Coire Bhrochain

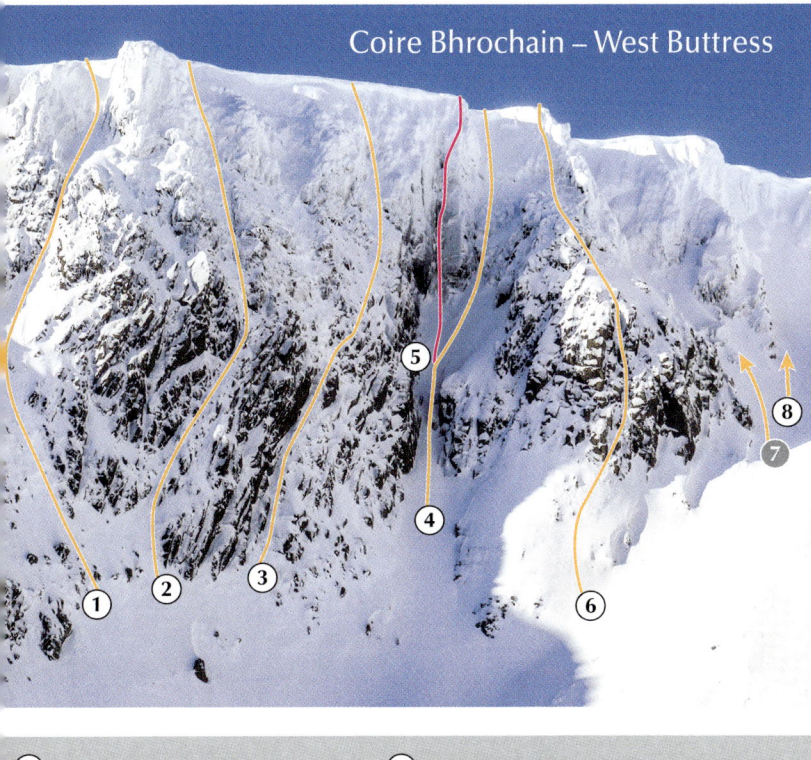

Coire Bhrochain – West Buttress

1. Pioneers' Recess Route III
2. Direct Route IV,5*
3. Vanishing Shelf III
4. The Great Couloir III**
5. Ebony Chimney VI,6***
6. Domed Ridge III*
7. Campion Gully II
8. West Gully I

West Buttress NNN 953 996 Crag base altitude 1100m South-east facing

This is the area between the left or southern end of the cliff and West Gully, the largest gully in the corrie. The main mass is slabby low down but steepens and develops more features with height. On the right side of the main mass is the long, defined Great Couloir. Between that and West Gully are several more ridges and gullies. This buttress holds snow very well but can have large cornices.

Pioneers' Recess Route 200m III

G.R. Simpson and G.S. Strange, 20 April 1969

Gains, then climbs, the open chimney on the left. It passes between a square tower and detached buttress characterised by a hooked fang. Start at the lowest point of the left-hand rocks and climb up iced slabs and snow to gain the main fault. Once in the chimney, short, steep pitches lead to steep snow where the chimney widens. This leads to the cornice which can be large; the usual exit is on the left.

Direct Route 200m IV,5*

J. Bower, G.R. Simpson and G.S. Strange, 13 April 1969

Takes the line of the most obvious grooves on the main rock mass. Start up the left hand of the two ramps and climb up right to a short chimney. Continue up by a choice of lines towards the right side of the large square-topped tower at the top of the buttress. Finish by the right of the two chimneys and the rib on its right.

Vanishing Shelf 200m III

R.H. Sellars and K. Grassick, February 1959

The right hand of the two ramp lines is followed to a platform overlooking The Great Couloir. Go to the end of the platform, go left on a ledge then trend up and left to a scoop leading to the top and perhaps a huge cornice.

The Great Couloir 200m III**

J.Y.L. Hay and H. Ross, 28 December 1957

The defined gully on the right of the main rocks. Climb the gully. The difficulty depends on the build-up on the chokestones, and the cornice can also be a problem.

Ebony Chimney 80m VI,6***

A. Nisbet and C. McLeod, February 1982

A superb short route, steep and varied, following the deep chimney which forms the left branch of The Great Couloir. Climb the chimney to above the first chokestone where a right traverse is taken. Above, a through route may be available which leads to big roofs. Go right along a ledge and climb a wall and corner to a rib. Go up the crest, then right, then up a steep groove overlooking The Great Couloir to the top.

Coire Bhrochain

Domed Ridge 200m III*
A.G. Mitchell and W.P.L. Thomson, 9 April 1955
The broad ridge between the foot of West Gully and The Great Couloir. It is climbed direct. Start up easy slabs and grooves leading to a tower which is climbed by a chimney (crux). Go over the tower and continue directly to the top.

West Gully 150m I
The wide gully in the left corner of the corrie. This easy-angled gully provides the easiest way from the corrie floor to the summit plateau. Although the cornice can be continuous, it is usually smallest on the right.

Central Buttress   NN 955 998 Crag base altitude 1100m South facing

This lies at the back of the corrie below the summit of Braeriach and between West and East Gullies. It consists of several facets. In the centre above mid-height is the Black Pinnacle, whose base is easily reached by a line slanting in from the right. This is the Slab Terrace. To the left of the Black Pinnacle are the Bhrochain Slabs, and to the right is the Braeriach Pinnacle with its top near plateau level. Braeriach Pinnacle is actually a buttress, only appearing as a pinnacle from the plateau.

A wild day on Bhrochain Slabs

Bhrochain Slabs 200m III*
W. Gault, D. Bruce and A. Milne, February 1960
Lies on the left of the Black Pinnacle. Start about 30m up and left of the lowest rocks. Climb corners and slabs for about three pitches to a platform. Here a chimney line running from West Gully to the col by the Black Pinnacle is reached. Follow the chimney to the col, then trend up and left to finish. Different lines are available, and much can bank out in some years.

Braeriach Direct 200m IV,3
D. King and R. Simpson, 31 March 1974
A direct line from the lowest rocks to the Black Pinnacle and the top. Start near the lowest rocks and climb an icefall to reach the Slab Terrace. Continue up the slab corner on the left of the Black Pinnacle to the saddle behind it. Finish direct.

Braeriach Pinnacle South Face 130m III
J. Campbell and G.R. Simpson, 18 April 1970
An obvious line left of centre on the Braeriach Pinnacle. Climb a snowy rib to gain an icy chimney then two steep diagonal ramps on the right. A gully finally leads to the top.

Braeriach Pinnacle Eastern Route 130m II
J. Bower, J. Buchanan and A. Sproul, 16 February 1969
Follows the right edge of the Pinnacle overlooking East Gully then goes diagonally left at the top.

East Gully 130m I*
J. Drummond, T. Gibson and A.W. Russell, 5 April 1901
The well-defined gully right of Central Buttress. It starts narrow but widens out into a funnel in the upper half.

East Buttress   NN 956 999 Crag base altitude 1100m South facing

Stretching from East Gully to the right end of the cliff, this group is composed of a set of defined buttresses separated by gullies. These gullies, from left to right, are Tigris Chimney, Pyramus and Thisbe.

Near East Buttress 110m II
P.C.D. Kale and C.A. MacIntyre, 3 February 1969
The buttress right of East Gully. The crest is followed with no special difficulty.

Tigris Chimney 100m II
P.C.D. Kale and C.A. MacIntyre, 19 April 1969
This is the chimney between Near East Buttress and Babylon Rib (Grade II), a ridge in two parts. After the first pitch it opens out into a shallow scoop. If the chokestone is showing it can be turned on the right.

Coire Bhrochain – Central and East Buttress

1. Bhrochain Slabs III*
2. Braeriach Direct IV,3
3. Braeriach Pinnacle South Face III
4. Braeriach Pinnacle Eastern Route II
5. East Gully I*
6. Near East Buttress II
7. Tigris Chimney II
8. Pyramus I
9. Thisbe III*
10. Ninus III

Pyramus 110m I ◇

W.D. Brooker and S. McPherson, 12 April 1950
The next gully is characterised by a rib at its foot giving two starts. It is straightforward and its left branch gives a narrower start.

Thisbe 110m III**

G.H. Leslie and M. Smith, 3 January 1955
One of the best gullies in the corrie, deep and with high walls. The gully is climbed direct and can have up to four pitches, although some can bank out. The last pitch can be turned on the right.

Walking into Coire Bhrochain via the Lairig Ghru

Beinn a'Bhuird

This massive mountain, with its huge, high-level plateau, holds four corries which give winter climbing. However, only the most accessible, Coire na Ciche, and the outstanding Garbh Choire are included. The Garbh Choire routes rank with the best in the Cairngorms, in one of the more remote settings to be found in the area.

The corries are accessible from Deeside and are usually approached from the south. Garbh Choire, however, is some considerable distance away and can also be approached from the north, but this is a long approach.

1 Coire na Ciche
2 Garbh Coire

Parking at Keiloch 7km

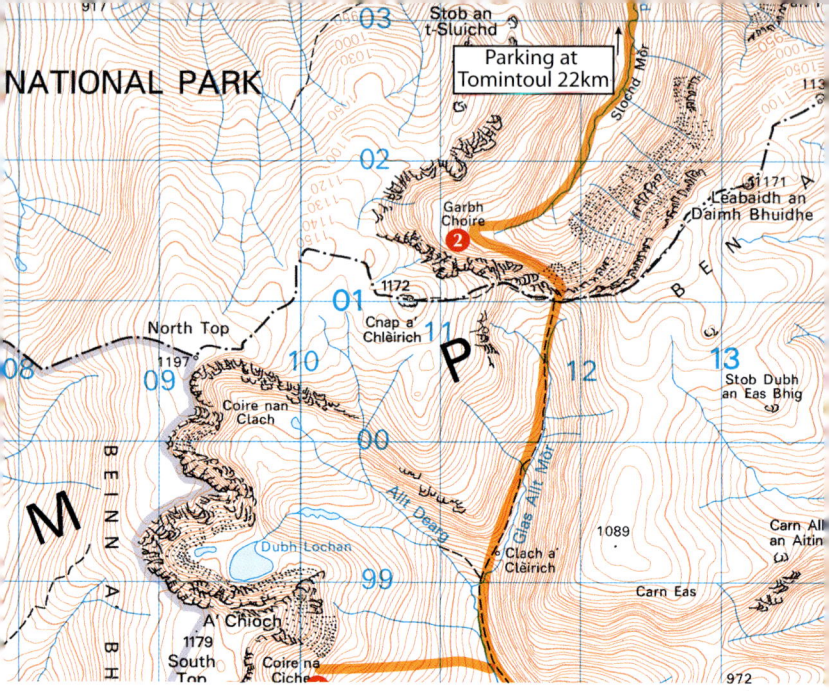

Approach

From Deeside go on the A93 to the Invercauld Bridge about 4km east of Braemar. Take the track about 100m east of the gates to Invercauld House (signposted Keiloch) to the car park on the right (NO 188 913). Follow the road to just before a farm then take a signposted track on the right and descend to gain the original road past the farm. Take the second road on the right, signposted Glen Slugain, and follow it through the forest and a gate into the glen. Continue on this track past Slugain Lodge, a ruin, to where the track becomes a path, then swing north and continue up upper Glen Quoich. It is possible to cycle most of the way.

Conditions

The corries of Beinn a'Bhuird are high and backed by an extensive snow-collecting plateau. The mountain itself is situated to the east of the main Cairn Gorm plateau and often experiences conditions similar to Lochnagar. The buttresses come into condition quickly but the gullies and those climbs dependent on ice tend to be better in the latter part of the season. Another important consideration here is the walking conditions, as with long approaches, particularly to Garbh Choire, any deep or difficult snow or bad weather can make remote climbing extremely serious.

Mitre Ridge, Garbh Choire (photo: Sam Simpson)

Coire na Ciche (NO 098 985)

Start	Keiloch parking, Invercauld Bridge NO 188 913
Time	3hr 30min
Crag base altitude	1000m
Aspect	East
Route lengths	100–130m
Style	A variety of good mixed routes.

A pleasant bowl-shaped corrie lying below the South Top of Beinn a'Bhuird. Because of its relatively easy access, this is probably the most popular corrie with relatively short but technical climbs. Most of the climbing lies on the south wall. On the extreme left is a slabby rib which defines that end of the cliff. Some distance to its right is the huge slab taken by The Carpet. Moving right from this is the more broken Slugain Buttress with its triangular bottom, then Twisting Gully and then the distinctive Hourglass Buttress. Right of Hourglass Buttress are three chimney faults and in the corner of the corrie lies South Corner Gully with the steep Grey Tower high on its left. The back wall of the corrie, right of South Corner Gully, consists of Slab Buttress which may disappear under snow.

Approach, descent and conditions
See start of section for approach notes from Deeside to upper Glen Quoich. Leave this path when opposite the corrie and head uphill into it.

Descent
From Coire na Ciche either descend the ridge running east from A'Chioch or the easy shoulder running south-east.

Conditions
See start of section for information about conditions.

Neptune's Groove 100m IV,6
A. Nisbet and G.S. Strange, February 1982
To the right of the slabby rib on the extreme left of the cliff is an obvious 20m V chimney with an overhung top. Climb the chimney and move out left to gain a line of ice (or grass) in the slab. Climb this, then a corner, then go left to finish up a large corner.

Coire na Ciche
(photo: Greg Strange)

1. Neptune's Groove IV,6
2. The Carpet V,5
3. Slugain Buttress III
4. Twisting Gully II
5. Hourglass Buttress V,6*
6. Jason's Chimney V,6**

The Carpet 110m VI,5* or
J. Bower and G. Boyd, 19 March 1970
A serious route up the huge slab right of the cliff edge. The great slab faces south-east and catches the sun, so it thaws easily. Start below and right of a large rock alcove in a vertical wall. Climb a depression up and right to below the Great Slab. Go up this on thin ice to shelves which go up and right to below an overhanging corner. Climb this (combined tactics may be required) then a short chimney then a right traverse to a rock crevasse. Finish more easily. Above the Great Slab, an ice groove on the left may provide a more natural winter finish.

Slugain Buttress 130m III*
G. Adams and D. Macrae, 10 February 1957
The buttress left of Twisting Gully which has a slanting groove on its left. Start on the right of the buttress and climb a chimney, avoiding the steepest rocks. Traverse left to the edge of the buttress and follow the crest to a huge block. Go up its right side, then by a diagonal chimney to easier ground. The slanting groove itself can be good at the same grade, especially if icy.

Twisting Gully 130m II** or
K. Milne, J. Davidson and J. Reid, 28 February 1948
The best of the easier climbs, lying between Slugain Buttress and the much steeper and defined Hourglass Buttress. It has a short dead-end right branch. The gully is followed throughout, the lower section being steepest, and it may contain ice, although it can bank out late in the season.

Hourglass Buttress 120m V,6*
J. Bower and G. Boyd, 29 March 1970
A steep climb which starts from the foot of Twisting Gully and follows a long chimney to the neck (50m). From there climb up to a big block below a steep wall (15m). Go up this wall on flakes then go right to gain and climb a deep crack to a ledge overlooking Sickle. Take a thin crack leading left to a large platform (35m). Climb the wall above by a crack slanting left then go left to a block. Continue left to finish up a short chimney (20m).

Sickle 110m IV,5*
(no photo topo)
A. Thom and R. Wiseman, March 1959
On the right side of Hourglass Buttress are three chimneys. Sickle is the leftmost and bounds the right side of Hourglass Buttress. It gives a sustained climb which initially follows shallow chimneys and grooves and finishes by a series of chimneys.

Jason's Chimney 100m V,6**

M. Freeman and N.D. Keir, 31 March 1974

The central of the three chimneys. Sustained and can be icy in late season. Start just right of Sickle and climb a shallow groove into a deep chimney. Go up this and turn an overhanging block on its right, above which the angle eases. Finish below a chokestone.

South Corner Gully 120m I

(no photo topo)

The gully on the right of the main cliff and left of Slab Buttress can also be used as a descent.

A narrow gully cuts the left wall and gives **Little Tower Gully, II**.

Ptarmigan, at home on the high tops

Garbh Choire (NJ 110 015)

Start	Invercauld Bridge NO 188 913 or Tomintoul NJ 165 177
Time	4hr 30min
Crag base altitude	950m
Aspect	North-west to north-east
Route lengths	150–250m
Style	A very remote corrie with some magnificent long mixed and ice routes.

This is the magnificent and remote corrie lying at the head of the Slochd Mor. Routes here are very isolated, and deep snow and/or bad weather can make climbing here a very serious proposition. However, in good conditions a visit is well worth the effort.

The main area of cliff is defined by its two finest features at either end. Firstly the Sneck, the col between Ben Avon and Beinn a Bhuird, and further north the unmistakable Mitre Ridge stands proud. Between the two is an area of lesser buttresses and gullies down which the Allt an t-Sluichd pours.

On the north face, near its left end, is a large basin known as the Crucible which can be the origin of much ice. The cornices in this area can be huge. Mitre Ridge itself is one of the finest rock features in the Cairngorms. It has a vertical, featured West Face and a slabbier, less steep but more vegetated, East Face and is topped by three towers. All the faces contain notable climbs.

Approach

See start of section for approach notes from Deeside to upper Glen Quoich. Once there, continue past Clach a'Clèirich (NO 114 992) and go to the Sneck, the obvious col between Ben Avon and Beinn a'Bhuird, then descend and contour left into the corrie.

Garbh Choire can also be reached from the north by going into Glen Avon from Tomintoul and following it upstream to Inchrory and then to a small tin bothy at NJ 129 061. There is a wire bridge over the River Avon here and a track goes part of the way into the corrie. For this approach, the bothy at Faindouran Lodge (NJ 082 062) can be used as a convenient base. Cycling the first part is best for this approach.

Descent

From Garbh Choire either follow the cliff edge round to the Sneck to go south, or take the broad shoulder over Stob an t-Sluichd for a northerly descent.

Garbh Choire (overview)

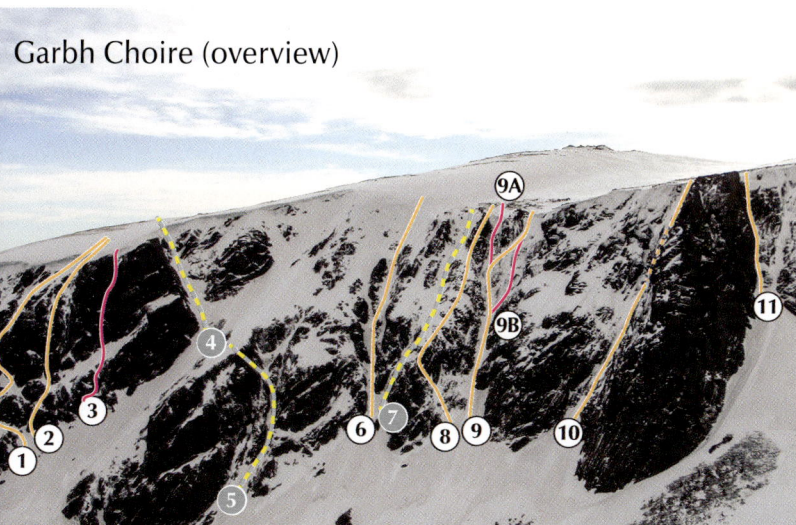

① Alchemist's Route III
② Gold Coast Direct V,5***
③ Crucible Route VI,5**
④ Back Bay Gully II
⑤ Approach Gully II*
⑥ Consolation Gully II
⑦ Nomad's Gully II
⑧ Comala's Ridge II*
⑨ The Flume II**
⑨A Left Hand Finish IV,4*
⑨B The Flume Direct IV,4**
⑩ South-East Gully V,4*
⑪ North-West Gully III*

Conditions
See start of section for information about conditions.

Alchemist's Route 230m III ◇ or ⊛
R.J. Archbold and D.M. Nichols, 2 March 1980
Lies near the left end of the north face, right of the Sneck, starting at an obvious ice gully. Slant up left from the foot of the ice gully to gain a snow slope. Go up

this till a branch leads right and up to an obvious chimney. Climb a ramp on the left wall then go to the top of the chimney. Follow a shallow gully above to steep snow slopes. The cornice can be huge, and it may be necessary to go right into the Crucible and exit right.

Gold Coast Direct 180m V,5***
A. Nisbet and C. McLeod, 11 February 1982; as described: B. Davison, A. Nisbet 10 March 1997
A fine route which climbs the left-hand icefall. Climb a short ice gully below The Crucible then go up to the icefall. Climb this direct in two pitches with a big block belay on the right below the steepest section. Climb into The Crucible and find a way out, most likely to the right. Needs a good build-up of ice.

Crucible Route 210m VI,5**
R.J. Archbold and D. Dinwoodie, 7 April 1978
A route based on the right-hand icefall but which does not need so much ice build-up as the previous climb. Start up the ice gully of the Gold Coast to the icefalls. Go slightly left then back right on a ramp. Go back up onto the ice and gain a pedestal on the rock separating the two icefalls. Traverse left on the left icefall. Climb this into the basin and exit right.

Consolation Gully 200m II
T.W. Patey, R.H. Sellars and R. Harper, 15 April 1956
This is the first full-length gully right of the easy rake from High Bay. It starts well defined then opens out above. The gully is climbed direct and may contain one ice pitch.

Comala's Ridge 200m II* or
G.R. Simpson and G. Boyd, 27 March 1971
Start at the foot of The Flume and climb grooves left to the crest. Climb this to the final tower which is the crux but can be avoided by taking Nomad's Gully on the left.

The Flume 200m II**
J.M. Taylor and G.B. Leslie, 31 March 1954
A good climb which is in fact the bed of a stream, the Allt an t-Sluichd. It lies in about the centre of the cliffs. It is straightforward to near the top, where it may be awkward working between the ice pitches formed by the waterfall.
Left-hand Finish IV,4* An icefall draining from a bowl below the plateau.
The Flume Direct IV,4** The icefall direct that the normal route weaves around.

Garbh Choire (right side)

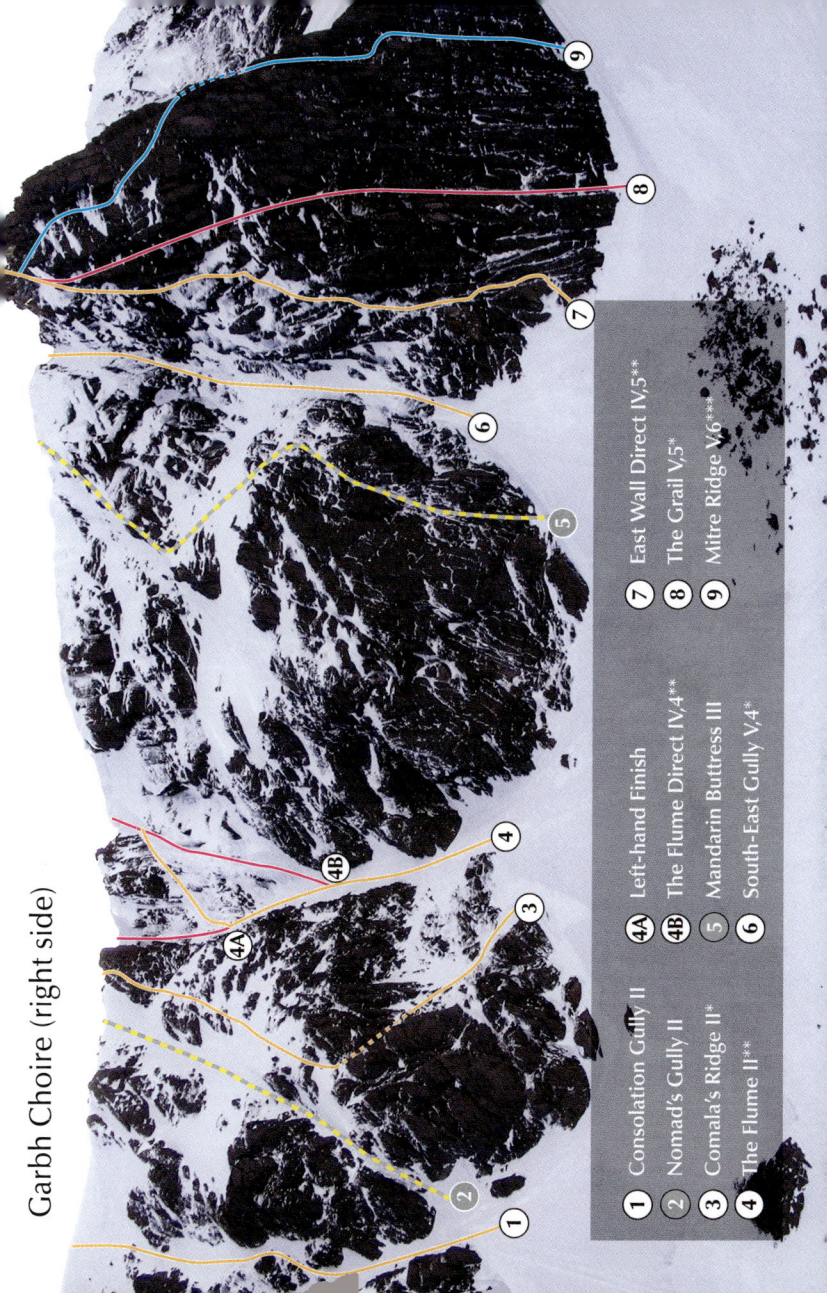

1. Consolation Gully II
2. Nomad's Gully II
3. Comala's Ridge II*
4. The Flume II**
4A. Left-hand Finish
4B. The Flume Direct IV,4**
5. Mandarin Buttress III
6. South-East Gully V,4*
7. East Wall Direct IV,5**
8. The Grail V,5*
9. Mitre Ridge VI,6***

South-East Gully 200m V,4*

R.H. Sellars and G. Annand, February 1959

The shallow gully bordering the left side of Mitre Ridge gives a fine winter route, although protection is poor when the snow is unconsolidated. It climbs a series of ice pitches, the crux being the narrows about mid-height.

East Wall Direct 220m IV,5**

N.D. Keir, J. Mothersele and R.A. Smith, 23 February 1974

A fine sustained climb. Start about 20m left of the lowest point of the slabs. Climb up for 30m then traverse left into a chimney system which leads to about mid-height. Follow a series of ramps below a vertical wall to gain an ice couloir. Climb this and at its top overhangs exit left to finish up the final tower from the col.

The Grail 250m V,5*

A. Nisbet and A. Clifford, 15 February 1984

A direct line up the middle of the East Wall, starting just left of the lowest rocks. Go up the vegetated fault to reach a terrace after three pitches. Climb up to the steep wall and go left to gain a ramp overlooking the ice couloir of East Wall Direct. Climb the ramp for two pitches (crux) to reach the col between the First and Second Towers.

Mitre Ridge 220m V,6***

W.D. Brooker and T.W. Patey, 2 April 1953

A classic winter climb up the crest of the ridge and then via the towers to the plateau. Start on the right of the East Face and climb the largest groove if there is ice. Alternatively climb a weakness at the right corner of the ridge. Above the groove, continue by a shelf running round to the West Face. Here a deep chimney followed by a shallow gully leads to a shoulder on the ridge. Above is a short wall. Traverse right and climb the wall (crux). A platform on the left is then gained by going left across a slab and up a splintered chimney. Climb the wall above and go to the col between the First and Second Towers. Turn the latter on the left and finish over an impressive arête.

Cumming-Crofton Route 160m VI,6***

R. Renshaw and G.S. Strange, 26 February 1977

A superb route up the left corner which defines the cuneiform buttress on the West Face. Start below this right-slanting fault which is parallel to the ridge crest. Climb a prominent chimney, passing a flake on its right, to a cleft at its top. Traverse right for 10m via a groove to a vertical wall, then return left by a traverse across a wall and over a bulge into the main corner. Climb this to a platform. Climb a crack in its left wall then traverse right and go up a sloping ledge to a short wall. A gully then leads to the ridge between the First and Second Towers, the latter being turned on the left to gain the final arête.

North-West Gully 150m III*
R.H. Sellars and G. Adams, 16 December 1956
The gully in the corner between the West Face and the back wall, North-West Buttress. It gives a good climb which may have a very fine ice pitch. If the ice has not formed, then the climb will be much harder.

Cumming-Crofton Route
(photo: Steve Elliot)

Southern Cairngorms

The top pitch of B Gully Chimney, Corrie Fee (photo: James Lamont)

The Loch Muick crags

Loch Muick car park is the starting point for two of the finest crags in the country, Lochnagar and Creag an Dubh Loch. The 'big fridge', as Andy Nisbet called Lochnagar, collects snow from the high plateau to the south-west, creating large

cornices and maintaining snow at depth through many a thaw. Good navigation is required to make a safe descent from the top of Lochnagar. Creag an Dubh Loch at the head of the glen has a lower-level approach but is a big cliff which produces vast amounts of ice at times, with routes that live long in the memory. Eagles Rock and Broad Cairn Bluffs offer some fine but shorter ice routes in cold conditions.

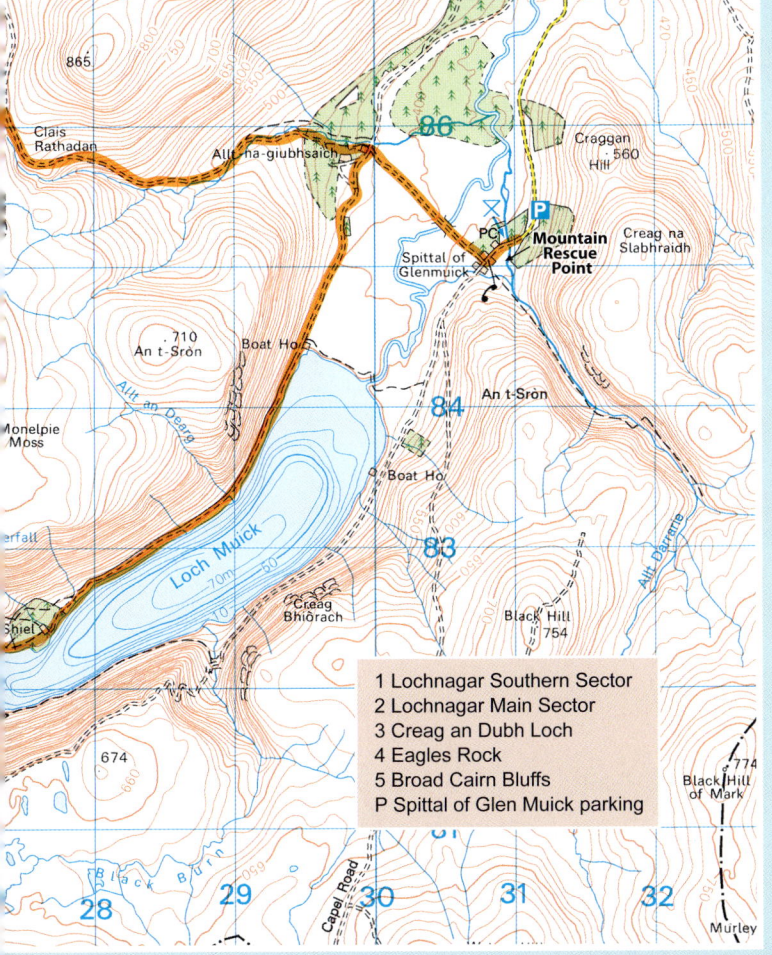

1 Lochnagar Southern Sector
2 Lochnagar Main Sector
3 Creag an Dubh Loch
4 Eagles Rock
5 Broad Cairn Bluffs
P Spittal of Glen Muick parking

The Lochnagar col (photo: Paul Noble)

Lochnagar (NO 244 861)

Start	Spittal of Glen Muick car park NO 310 851
Time	2hr 30min
Crag base altitude	900–950m
Aspect	North to east
Route lengths	60–300m
Style	One of the finest crags in Scotland with a great range of different styles and difficulties. The crucible of modern mixed climbing.

The north-east corrie of Lochnagar is one of the finest in Scotland. The cliffs extend in an arc overlooking the loch from which the mountain takes its name and consist of a series of well-defined and shapely buttresses separated by major gullies. Classic routes of all grades and types are found here, combining quality, line, history and mountain scenery. It is one of Scotland's premier winter climbing areas.

The main corrie is divided naturally into two sections. The southern section consists of a large bay containing two main buttresses, Perseverance Wall and The Cathedral. These come into conditions quickly and are often good early season. Due to the quicker approach and shorter route lengths, they are also a useful option for a short day. The northern section has cliffs that are continuous for about 1km and reach up to 230m in height. These cliffs are generally considered to be four groups of buttresses separated by three important gullies. These are, from left to right; Douglas-Gibson Gully which is a big, straight gully ascending between high walls, Raeburn's Gully which slants upwards in the corner of the corrie and cannot be seen from some angles, and the Black Spout, which is an obvious, wide fault.

When approaching from the Meikle Pap col, the usual stopping and gearing-up point is the first aid box which sits on a flat platform below the main snow slope, roughly below Central Buttress. In bad visibility, it may be necessary to use a compass from here to locate the bottom of the climbs. The magnetic bearings from here to some of the main features are:

Central Buttress – 190 degrees
Shadow Buttress A – 214 degrees
Parallel Gully A – 258 degrees
Parallel Gully B – 260 degrees
Raeburn's Gully – 278 degrees
The Black Spout – 290 degrees
West Gully – 314 degrees

Lochnagar (overview)

1. Central Buttress II
2. Eagle Ridge VI,6
3. Parallel Gully A III*
4. Parallel Gully B VI,5**
5. Raeburn's Gully II***
6. Pinnacle Gully 1 III
7. The Black Spout I**
8. West Gully IV,4*
9. Gelder Gully II

Drifting snow off Meikle Pap (photo: Paul Noble)

Approach

From Ballater go up Glen Muick to the car park at the Spittal of Glen Muick. The last 4 kilometres of this road is across open moor and can be badly affected by drifting snow, and the car park can be crowded at peak periods. Walk through the woods past the visitor centre, then turn right and follow the unsurfaced road across the glen to reach a building by a junction. Take the path by the fence (signposted) and follow this through the woods to reach a track which leads up to the Muick/Gelder col. From this bulldozed track branch off left on the well-marked and obvious track leading to the summit. Leave this beyond the Fox's Well and go over the col between the Meikle Pap and the Cuidhe Crom, the main mountain, then traverse round to below the cliffs.

Descent

To return to Glen Muick, it is usual to follow the cliff edge round and go down the tourist path. In bad weather this may not be straightforward and map and compass work may be required. It is also possible to go down the Glas Allt to Loch Muick which is longer but avoids the cornice danger of following the cliff edge. The shoulder above the West Buttress also provides a way down into Glen Gelder or even back into the corrie. The descent back into the corrie is down the main branch of the Black Spout. The cornice is usually passable on the left, but care is needed on this way down.

Conditions

Because of the variety of routes, there is usually some good climbing to be had in any winter conditions. However, ice routes normally take longer to develop. Avalanche conditions can, unfortunately, build up very rapidly as huge amounts of snow can pour over the edge of the plateau from a variety of wind directions. Cornices can be huge and spindrift avalanches are common. The decision as to which route to attempt should be made in light of the conditions, which may only be discovered on close acquaintance. Beware of avalanches coming down main and side gullies which may affect the approach to neighbouring routes, particularly when traversing across from the first aid box.

Perseverance Wall
NO 253 854 Crag base altitude 950m North facing

This easy-angled wall to the left of The Cathedral contains a number of ribs and grooves, which make fine winter routes. These routes can also be a good choice early in the season as they require little build-up of ice and tend to come into condition readily. To reach these routes, turn uphill before the first aid box on the normal approach.

Perseverance Rib 80m III
C. Cartwright and S.M. Richardson, 7 January 1996
The well-defined rib at the left end of the crag. Climb a shallow groove to the left of a small tower. Continue up the right side of the crest to the top.

Gale Force Groove 70m III*
P. Mather and S. Muir, 15 December 1999
Takes the slightly right-slanting groove which leads to the apex of the next rib to the right. Climb the groove to a square block roof and then step right to belay (30m). Continue up the groove over bulges and up the crest to the top (40m).

Lunar Eclipse 85m III*
P. Mather, S. Muir and H. Watson, January 2001
The next rib to the right. Start at the base of a short deep gully to the right of a slab. Climb a leftward-leading ramp to the middle of the slab and continue up two short corners to belay on the right of a steep wall (35m). Traverse left below this wall until the upper gully can be accessed and continue to a good belay at a cracked block (40m). Continue up snow to the top.

The Gift 80m II*
S.M. Richardson, 18 November 2005
The slightly left-trending gully gives a fine route. There is a bulge at about one-third height, and then finish to the right of the final tower.

Temptress 80m III*
S.M. Richardson, 18 November 2005
Good mixed climbing up the obvious groove to the right of The Gift. Climb over three bulges to finish as for The Gift.

Lochnagar – Perseverance Wall

1. Perseverance Rib III
2. Gale Force Groove III*
3. Lunar Eclipse III
4. The Gift II*
5. Temptress III*
6. Windfall III*

Windfall 80m III*

S.M. Richardson and C. Cartwright, 3 January 1999

The gully/groove line up the right-hand side of the buttress. Climb the gully to a stance on the right (30m). Continue to a short snow slope, then climb two short chimneys to a platform (40m). Steep snow leads to the top.

The Cathedral   NO 252 854 Crag base altitude 950m North facing

The largest and most obvious buttress in the southern sector, The Cathedral has an impressive mummy-shaped tower on its left and a trio of grooves right of this. These lead to a prominent left-slanting terrace. Like Perseverance Wall, this buttress is often good early season or for shorter days and is reached by turning uphill before the first aid box on the normal approach.

Transept Groove 90m IV,5**

R.J. Archbold and G.S. Strange, January 1983

A good route for a short day. Climb the broken groove immediately left of the mummy-shaped tower, then finish up the leftmost and deepest of the two chimneys at the top left end of the terrace.

Transept Route 100m V,6*

S.M. Richardson and R. Everett, 22 January 1994

This fine sustained turfy mixed route takes the groove on the right of the steep mummy-shaped tower. Climb the groove, with some technical moves to surmount an overhang, to a recess and large block belay (40m). Continue in the same line up to a small snowfield. Exit this by the wall on the right to gain a terrace (35m). Finish up the leftmost chimney at the top of the terrace, as for Transept Groove (25m).

Sepulchre 100m V,6**

B.F. Findlay and G.S. Strange, 13 December 1987

Takes the central groove starting from a slight bay. Climb a narrow groove going up right to ledges. Above are twin slabby grooves. Gain the right-hand groove from the right, and climb this for 6m, then transfer and climb the left-hand groove. Trend left and finish as for the previous routes.

Judas Priest 100m V,6*

B.S. Findlay and G.S. Strange, 14 December 1986

The large groove line in the centre of the buttress provides a fine and popular route. Start below the groove, climb a corner on the right and step back into the main

Lochnagar – The Cathedral

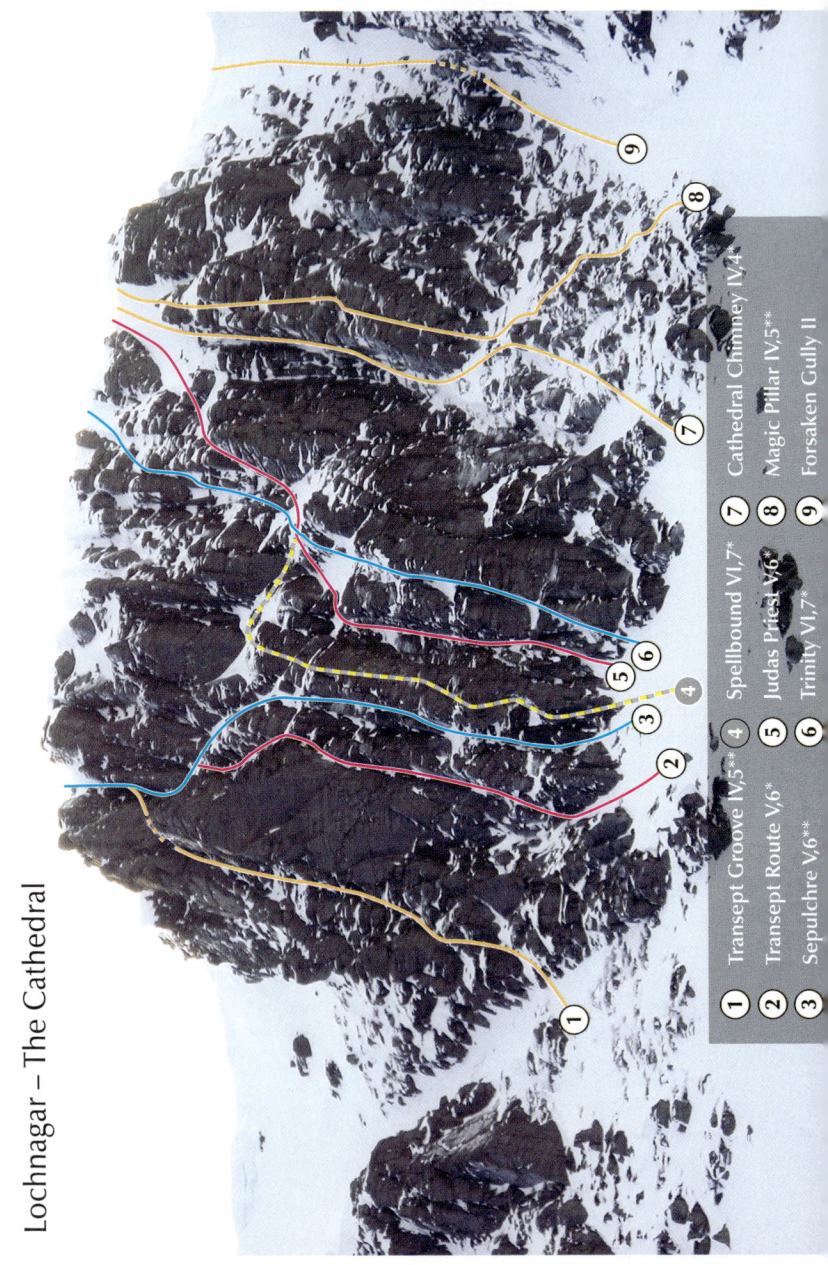

1. Transept Groove IV,5**
2. Transept Route V,6*
3. Sepulchre V,6**
4. Spellbound VI,7*
5. Judas Priest V,6*
6. Trinity VI,7*
7. Cathedral Chimney IV,4*
8. Magic Pillar IV,5**
9. Forsaken Gully II

groove. Continue up this to ledges. Trend up and right through a slot to finish in the snow bay of Cathedral Chimney.

Trinity 100m VI,7*

B.S. Findlay and G.S. Strange, 27 December 1994

This route follows the stepped corner system to the right of Judas Priest. Climb the stepped corner to easier ground. Continue up, crossing Judas Priest, and climb into an alcove. Climb out of this via the right-hand corner. Easier ground leads to the top.

Cathedral Chimney 80m IV,4* or

M. Freeman and G.S. Strange, 12 December 1977

This fine route climbs the obvious deep and narrow chimney left of the rightmost buttress.

Magic Pillar 80m IV,5**

C. Cartwright, S.M. Richardson, 15 November 1998

This route takes the well-defined pillar to the right of Cathedral Chimney. It is easier than its appearance suggests. Start at the base of the pillar. Climb a crack in the crest to a niche (20m). Step right round the roof and continue up the chimney-crack to the top of the pillar (40m). Finish easily up Cathedral Chimney (20m).

Forsaken Gully 90m II

E. Lawrence, R.L. Mitchell, 11 March 1950

This is the narrow and generally straightforward gully between The Cathedral and the next buttress, Sinister Buttress.

Central and Shadow Buttress Group   NO 249 856 Crag base altitude 900m North to North-east facing

This consists of three buttresses on the left of the northern sector of the corrie. First is Central Buttress, with broken ground on its left and the poorly defined Shallow Gully on its right. Next comes Shadow Buttress A with its great overhangs, and then Shadow Buttress B. Between Shadow Buttress A and B is Shadow Couloir, from which rises Shadow Chimney, Giant's Head Chimney and Polyphemus Gully, which separates the two buttresses. Right of Shadow B is the great gash of Douglas-Gibson Gully, defining the right side of the group.

Lochnagar

Central Buttress 300m II*
S.R. Tewnion and J. Tewnion, January 1948
The leftmost buttress gives a good introduction to this type of climbing. Start up an introductory left-trending gully below a very steep right wall at the foot of the buttress proper. At its top traverse right above it as soon as possible to gain the crest which is followed to a level section with two pinnacles. Above this, easier ground leads to the top.

Manticore 60m VII,7*
(no photo topo)
W. Moir and N. Ritchie, 7 February 1998
A fine sustained mixed route. Start just within the initial gully of Central Buttress below a steep rippled slab. Climb an easy ramp to gain a small groove in the slab. Continue up to the top of the slab then step down to a belay ledge (25m). Move up and right to climb a tapering slab into a groove. Climb this then step left and continue to below a square roof. Continue up and left to easy ground (25m). Finish up or down Central Buttress.

Central Buttress Direct 90m IV,6*
M. Geddes and N.D. Keir, 23 March 1975 (3PA); A. Nisbet and D. Wright (FFA), December 1979
To the right of the initial gully of Central Buttress is a steep wall containing several harder routes. Above and to the right of this wall, a line of grooves leads up to join Central Buttress on the crest.

Centrist 140m V,6**
M. Freeman and N. Keir, 3 February 1974
Climbs the right side of Central Buttress to gain that route at the pinnacles. This can then be followed to the top or a descent to the left taken back to the corrie. Start just

Centrist, first pitch (photo: Findlay Cranston)

Winter Climbs in the Cairngorms

Lochnagar – Shadow Buttress

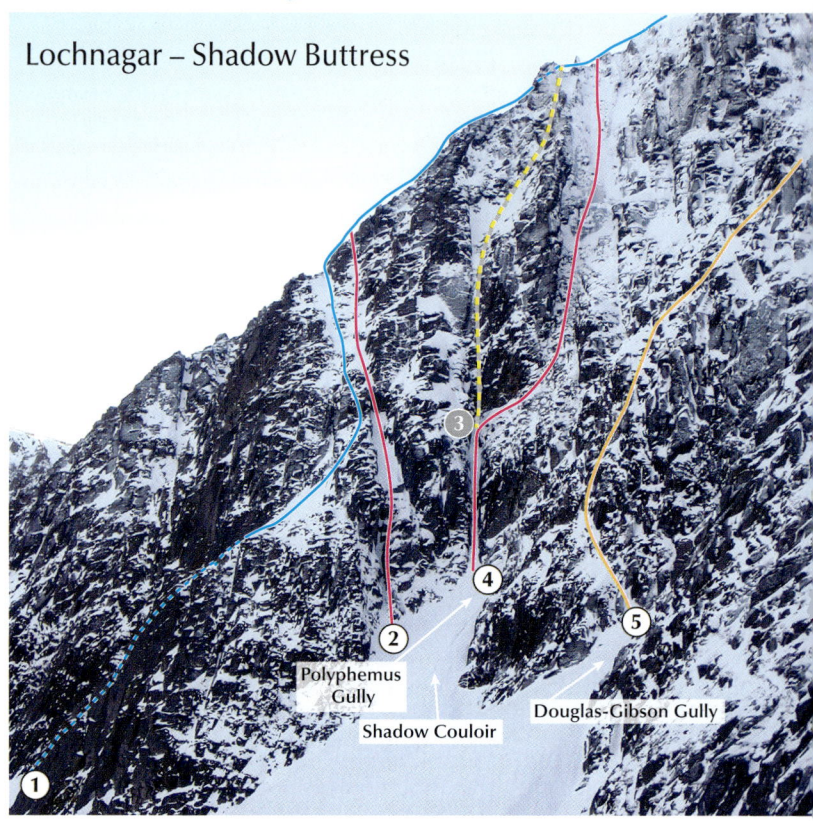

1. Shadow Buttress A IV,5***
2. Shadow Chimney IV,4
3. Giant's Head Chimney Direct V,5*
4. Giant's Head Chimney IV,4*
5. Shadow Buttress B, Bell's Route V,6**

right of the lowest rocks and about 20m left of Shallow Gully. Climb an open groove slightly right and up into a big groove that has overhangs at its top. Turn the overhang on the left (crux) then curve left up ramps until an easier groove leads right to the crest just before the pinnacles.

Lochnagar

Shallow Gully 300m IV,4
D.L. Macrae and F.G. Henderson, 8 February 1959
The depression between Central Buttress and Shadow Buttress A. It is graded assuming the lower section is iced up; this can take a while to occur. Start in the gully up from the foot of Central Buttress and climb it direct, with the lower 60m being the crux. Rock protection can be difficult to find. Above, either continue up the fault or slant left to gain the crest of Central Buttress.

Shadowlands 250m VI,7**
A.D. Robertson and S.M. Richardson, 19 March 1995
A superb and popular mixed route. Start at a cave up and left of the introductory gully of Shadow Buttress A. Climb up and left to a good stance (30m). Trend right over short steep walls until an awkward step down leads to the base of an imposing left-trending fault which cuts through the headwall (25m). Gain this fault from the right and climb it for 15m until it's possible to gain an overhung niche on the right. Pull over this to reach another fine belay stance (20m). A tricky step left regains the fault which is followed to its end (25m). Move up and right to the crest to join and follow the top section of Shadow Buttress A to the top (150m).

Shadow Buttress A 300m IV,5***
W.D. Brooker and J.W. Morgan, 27 December 1949
A great mountaineering route but unfortunately made a bit unbalanced by a recent rock fall. Start in the bay below large overhangs near the foot of Shallow Gully. Climb the gully to reach the prominent Spiral Terrace which is followed to its upper-right end. Climb a vague narrow rib overlooking Shadow Chimney to its top (crux). This can be made a more amenable technical grade with a point of aid. Alternatively, climb the narrow Shadow Chimney on the right to by-pass this section. Above, trend left and climb a shallow gully to regain the crest. Follow this, passing the small tower by a descent on the right, and continue to the plateau.

Shadow Chimney 220m IV,4
F.R. Malcolm and D.J. Ritchie, 22 November 1952
This is the prominent chimney on the left side of Shadow Couloir and left of Giant's Head Chimney. The chimney is followed throughout to finish up Shadow Buttress A.

Moonshadow 220m V,5**
(no photo topo)
S.M. Richardson and J. Ashbridge, 21 November 1992
This fine turfy route takes the well-defined buttress between Shadow Chimney and Giant's Head Chimney. Start as for Giant's Head Chimney and climb diagonally up and left to enter a steep right-facing corner. Climb this and step left to belay in

Shadow Chimney (40m). Climb a wall on the right to gain a hidden ramp which cuts back right to the crest. Pull over a small roof to reach a ledge (25m). Continue easily to a wall cut by parallel cracks. Climb the right side of this to easier ground and a ledge (40m). Climb a short corner above to gain a right-trending weakness (35m). Continue more easily to gain Shadow Buttress A and then the top (80m).

Giant's Head Chimney 220m IV,4*
W.D. Brooker and J.W. Morgan, 29 January 1950
Another fine route. Climb the lower chimney for about 60m to the overhang. Go right on a terrace into a prominent trough which may contain much ice. Climb the trough to easier ground leading to the plateau. Where the trough eases, more difficult climbing may be found by following the Feathered Arête on the right.

Polyphemus Gully 200m V,5***
K. Grassick and H.S.M. Bates, 24 January 1953
One of the classic Lochnagar gullies. It lies between Shadow Buttresses A and B and is not obvious from most angles. In good conditions it is easy for the grade. The gully is reached by traversing steep snow from the base of Giant's Head Chimney. The route contains two pitches separated by 60m of steep snow. The initial pitch is often the crux. Easier climbing leads to a steepening above a cave. This can be climbed direct, or on the left or the right depending on the build-up. Continue up to the cornice which is usually passed on the right.

Shadow Buttress B, Bell's Route 200m V,6**
T.W. Patey and A.O'F. Will, 23 February 1955
A very fine winter buttress route. Start just inside Douglas-Gibson Gully at a shelf which leads left to the centre of the buttress. Climb a crack to reach two teeth below a steep wall. From the left tooth, gain the shaky flake handrail after which a groove leads to the top of the steep section. Finish up the crest where the cornice can be difficult.

Penumbra 110m V,5*
C. Butterworth and P. Arnold, 18 March 1972
A delicate climb up the line of the left-slanting corners high on Shadow Buttress B. Start at the narrowing in Douglas-Gibson Gully and follow the obvious corners and slabs running to the top of the buttress.

Douglas-Gibson Gully 200m V,4**
T.W. Patey and G.B. Leslie, 28 December 1950
The obvious large gully with imposing walls is a climb with a wealth of history to its name. The gully is climbed direct, with a line on the left of the headwall being taken to finish. The cornice can be immense. There is a choice of harder finishes.

Polyphemus Gully with perfect snow-ice conditions (photo: Giles Trussell)

Winter Climbs in the Cairngorms

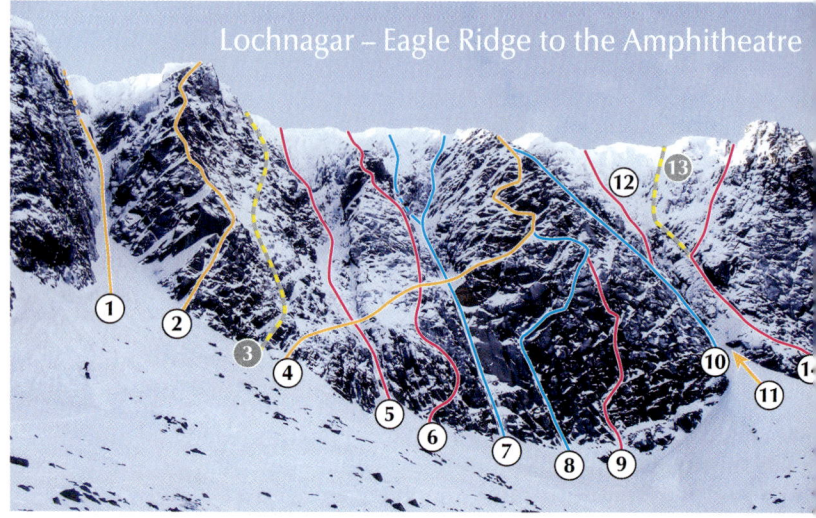

Lochnagar – Eagle Ridge to the Amphitheatre

1. Douglas-Gibson Gully V,4**
2. Eagle Ridge VI,6***
3. Eagle Buttress IV,3
4. Tough-Brown Traverse IV,3**
5. Parallel Gully A III**
6. Parallel Buttress VI,6***
7. Parallel Gully B VI,5***
8. Trail of Tears VII,8***
9. Mort IX,9***
10. Tough-Brown Ridge Direct V,6**
11. Raeburn's Gully II***
12. Scarface V,4*
13. Amphitheatre Route III
14. Pinnacle Gully 1 III

Eagle Ridge and the Parallel Buttress Group

NO 247 856 Crag base altitude
900m North-east facing

This forms the main back wall of the corrie and lies between the straight Douglas-Gibson Gully and Raeburn's Gully, which slants up leftwards behind Tough-Brown Ridge and is hidden from most viewpoints. On the left overlooking Douglas-Gibson Gully is the narrow crest of Eagle Ridge, then Parallel Gullies A and B bracketing Parallel Buttress. Huge rock falls in 1995 and then again in 2000 altered the area between Parallel Gully B, which lost its narrow lower chimney, and the left of Trail of

Tears. Between this and Raeburn's Gully is the huge Tough-Brown Buttress with its steep, compact lower wall.

Eagle Ridge 250m VI,6***

T.W. Patey, J.M. Taylor and W.D. Brooker, 25 January 1953

The narrow soaring crest whose left wall plunges into Douglas-Gibson Gully. Often called the Queen of Lochnagar's winter climbs and is one of Scotland's great winter routes. In lean conditions or under powder it can be hard and should not be underestimated; conversely in good conditions it can be considerably easier. Start just inside Douglas-Gibson Gully and climb the first obvious groove. Continue in the same groove line which is almost a chimney in places. A pitch of easier ground then leads to one of several groove lines. Follow this back left onto the crest at the base of the first Tower. This is an extremely well-scratched but sustained pitch, climbed via a recess on the right then into a sentry box near the top. This is usually considered to be the winter crux. Go along the narrow crest of the whaleback till a ledge leads right to a stance in a corner with a slabby left wall. Climb this to the knife-edge crest and climb the short vertical wall via the crack on the left, which can be very hard but is well protected. Continue along the short ridge then go up to a square-cut overhang and traverse right to gain a corner system slanting up and right to finish.

Tough-Brown Traverse 300m IV,3**

T.W. Patey and D.A. Aitken, 20 January 1952

A classic mountaineering route crossing this impressive face. It takes the diagonal line of weakness cutting the face above the lower overlapping slabs of Tough-Brown Buttress. Start left of Parallel Gully A and go diagonally right to cross it above its initial ice pitch. Cross Parallel Buttress by the obvious line to arrive in Parallel Gully B in the bowl above the lower fault. From the right side of the bowl climb a short chimney onto the Great Terrace. Follow this and before it ends go up, then right on a ramp, then left on a ledge. Zig-zag obviously to the crest leading to the top. Finding the correct point at which to leave the Great Terrace can be a problem, especially in poor visibility.

Going up from the far end of the Terrace gives a pitch and a half of harder climbing.

Parallel Gully A 270m III**

G.W. Ross and R. Still, 28 March 1948

A good climb, although it can vary from having several ice pitches to banking out. Start up the initial pitch, which may be full of ice and is often the crux although it can be avoided on the left. Continue up the gully which may contain other ice pitches. At the junction take the left fork to the top. The right fork, which is much steeper, can be climbed at IV,4**.

Parallel Buttress 280m VI,6***
T.W. Patey, J. Smith and W.D. Brooker, 4 March 1956
Another superb climb up the narrow, elegant buttress which tapers to a tower near the top. Start up a wide groove right of Parallel Gully A, then traverse right into a defined chimney. Climb this to a ledge on the right and go up corners on the right to a flake, then back left to easier ground above the steep base of the buttress. Work upwards until forced to trend right to the buttress edge. Continue very close to the gully by a shelf and then grooves to the Tower. Climb this by a shallow groove (crux) then a shelf on the left until the crest behind the Tower is regained. Continue more easily to the plateau via a narrow ridge.

Parallel Gully B 280m VI,5***
J.R. Marshall and G. Tiso, 22 February 1958
This was a magnificent climb up the fault which started as a narrow chimney before opening out in its upper section. Unfortunately, large rock falls in 1995 and 2000 removed the right-hand side of the lower chimney leaving only a smooth right-facing corner. Ice sometimes forms all the way down this corner. The difficulty and seriousness of the route will very much depend on the build-up of this ice. However, conditions should be easily assessable from the ground. Climb a bulging wall to a belay below the corner (25m). Follow the corner, and at the top either continue directly up steep ice or step right onto an airy snow ramp and go left higher up (55m). The upper gully is followed until blocked by a bulge. This can be climbed on the left or by-passed by a groove on the right. Either way leads to the end of the difficulties, although the cornice can be huge.

If there is insufficient ice in the lower corner, the upper gully can still be accessed from the Tough-Brown Traverse and provides a worthwhile Grade IV,5.

Trail of Tears 130m VII,8***
D. Dinwoodie and A. Nisbet, 7 March 1986
A magnificent hard route using various parts of several summer lines. Start below the right-facing corner right of the rock-fall scar and climb this grassy corner to a ledge on the left (30m). Continue straight up the corner, over a bulge and up to some huge flakes (possible belay). Continue up the groove to a ledge. Move right then up a ramp to a good stance (30m). Climb the big ramp going right to a grassy niche (10m). Climb the ramp to a break, descend right to a lower ramp, and make hard moves round the corner then up to the continuation of the main ramp. Climb cracks in the ramp to its top then go up round a block (40m). Flakes now lead up and left (20m) to the Tough-Brown Traverse, which can used to finish up or down.

Mort 130m IX,9***

B. Davidson, A. Nisbet and D. McGimpsey, 15 January 2000

Another magnificent and very difficult winter route. After numerous attempts spread over 15 years, Davidson took advantage of unusually icy conditions to make the first ascent. Start below the obvious groove to the right of Trail of Tears. Climb this and move right along a ledge (35m). Climb up, passing to the right of a downward pointing tooth, and pull through the obvious roof at twin cracks. To the left is a well-defined rib. Climb to the top of this rib either on the left, if sufficiently iced, or on the right. Continue to a ramp and move 5m along this to belay (35m). Traverse left to the continuation groove and continue over a bulge to a bay and block belay (40m). Follow Trail of Tears left to join the Tough-Brown Traverse (20m) and either continue up this to the top or descend it back to the ground.

Tough Guy 120m VII,7*

(no photo topo)

A. Nisbet and B. Davison, 18 December 1984

Another fine and difficult mixed route based on the right-hand intermittent crack line located at the right side of the face before it bends round to the Tough-Brown Ridge Direct. Start from a shelf which is usually gained by traversing leftwards from the base of Tough-Brown Ridge Direct. Climb up and left to gain and follow a crack, which passes a roof, and continue to a large block belay (30m). Climb a few moves up a corner behind the block, then traverse left round a rib and under a rock-fall scar and climb up to gain a long ledge. Belay at the right end of this (30m). Move up and left to gain and climb a thin left-slanting crack to reach a ledge (possible escape out rightwards along this). Continue diagonally left past some large flakes and cracked blocks to a ledge (35m). Continue up to gain and finish via the crest of the Tough-Brown Ridge (25m).

Tough-Brown Ridge Direct 250m V,6**

M. Rennie and N.D. Keir, 23 December 1969

This route takes a line on the extreme right of the Tough-Brown Face then follows the crest above. Start just inside Raeburn's Gully and climb a groove line slightly left with a difficult section exiting a short deep groove to gain easier ground. Slant right under a steep wall to a little arête above the gully. Either climb the groove above the arête or descend right beyond the arête and climb the wall. These both lead to easier ground and a finish up grooves left of the more prominent groove of Backdoor Route.

Backdoor Route 220m IV,4*

(no photo topo)

T.W. Patey, A.O'F. Will, G. McLeod and A. Thom, 20 March 1954

The big obvious left-facing corner right of the crest of Tough-Brown Ridge. Start before the bend in Raeburn's Gully. Climb the big corner for about 10m, traverse left, then slant back right to its top. Alternatively, climb the corner direct (harder). Both alternatives can be poorly protected. Follow the groove above to reach the crest a pitch below the top.

Raeburn's Gully 200m II*** ◇ or ❄
G.R. Symers, A.W. Clark and W.A. Ewan, 27 December 1932
The large gully which slants up leftwards. It gives a good climb, particularly when not banked out, but then it will be harder. This climb is noted for its avalanche danger, particularly from the large cornices which overlook it. The gully is climbed direct, and the crux is normally an ice pitch at the jammed boulder above the cave.

The Gutter 80m III ❄
(no photo topo)
T.W. Patey and A.O'F. Will, 23 January 1955
A variation finish to Raeburn's Gully, taking the fault in the right wall about 80m from the top of that climb.

Scarface 170m V,4* ❄
D. Stuart and G.S. Strange, 12 February 1972
Climbs directly into the Amphitheatre, a large bowl overlooking Raeburn's Gully on the right. At times the lower section can be very icy. Start just above the bend in Raeburn's Gully. Climb ice as directly as possible into the Amphitheatre then go up its left edge to finish up the leftmost of three faults, an icy groove.

Black Spout Pinnacle   NO 246 858 Crag base altitude 900m North-east facing

This group, lying between Raeburn's Gully and the massive and unmistakable Black Spout, is dominated by the superb Black Spout Pinnacle. This is isolated by its attendant gullies and connected to the plateau by a narrow ridge and col. To the left of the Pinnacle the face overlooking Raeburn's Gully is more broken and faulted. The right side, however, plunges steeply into the Black Spout whose left-hand branch curves up behind it. Between the two branches of the Black Spout is the Stack. For routes which finish on the top of the Black Spout Pinnacle it may be necessary to abseil down to the col from a large spike to gain the ridge, narrow and exposed in places, running up to the plateau.

Lochnagar – Black Spout Pinnacle and West Buttress

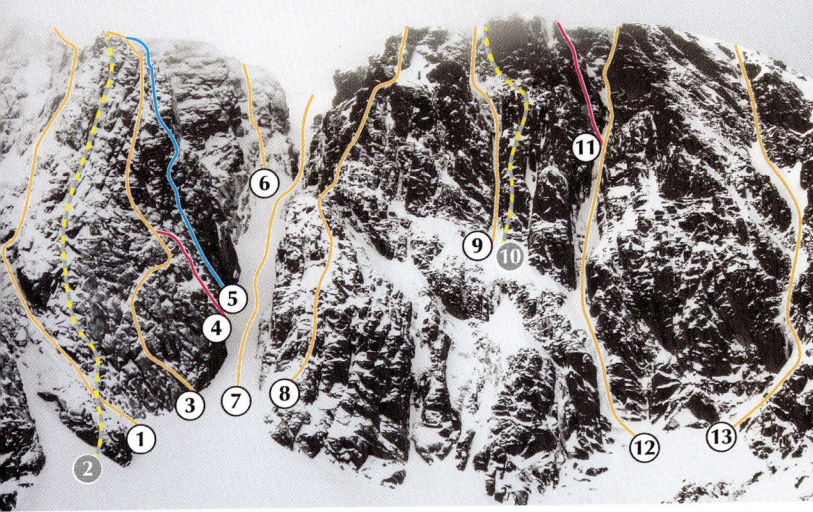

1. Pinnacle Gully 1 III
2. Grovel Wall V,5
3. Pinnacle Face VI,7**
4. Route 1 V,6**
5. The Link Direct VII,7***
6. The White Spout IV,4
7. The Black Spout I**
8. Black Spout Buttress III,5**
9. Gargoyle Chimney IV,4**
10. Bells Pillar V,5*
11. Prince of Darkness VI,7**
12. West Gully IV,4*
13. Gelder Gully II

Pinnacle Gully 1 200m III
T.W. Patey and C. Morrison, 27 January 1951
This runs up to the col behind the Black Spout Pinnacle. Start at the Mound, a subsidiary buttress at the bottom left corner of the Black Spout Pinnacle. Climb from the lowest rocks to the top of the Mound, then go left and follow a chimney slanting left

then broken ground. Traverse right across a slab above a cave. Go up a short chimney then go right to easier ground leading to the col. A pleasant ridge leads to the plateau. To gain the summit of the Pinnacle, go right just before the col then follow slabs to its top.

Pinnacle Face 200m VI,7**

K.A. Grassick, J. Light and A.G. Nicol, 16 January 1966

A very fine climb, often on thinly iced slabs; generally, the more ice the easier it will become. Start about 10m up from the lowest rock in the Black Spout and climb a prominent V-groove for about 10m then go left into another groove and continue via a short chimney and cracks (35m). Go up into a corner and go right onto the slab. Climb up and left by a slabby fault to a stance (25m) – this needs some ice or it is very hard. Continue up vegetated corners to a steep wall then go right past this wall to a groove leading into Route 1 which is followed to the top. In very good conditions a more direct line can be taken to the top of the Pinnacle.

Route 1 200m V,6**

J. Smith and W.D. Brooker, 11 March 1956

An excellent climb on the right side of the Pinnacle. It first gains the Springboard, a large platform about 40m up, then moves onto the front face where route finding can be tricky. Start in the Black Spout beyond a vertical groove in a smooth wall. Climb the obvious slabby ramp past an overlap, and shortly above it traverse left and gain the Springboard by a short wall. Go up ledges above then traverse left into the left hand of three faults. Climb this out onto the front face then work back right, starting by a large flake, to gain the crest and follow this to the top.

The Link Direct 185m VII,7***

C. Cartwright, S.M. Richardson, 1 February 1998

An outstanding mixed route – sustained but never desperate. Start in a snow bay just right of Route 1, below a steep vegetated groove. Climb steep parallel cracks and continue up and left over steep slabs to reach a stance on the rib (30m). Step left into the groove and climb it to below a prominent triangular overhang. Move up and right round a huge block to a recess (25m). Pull over the overhang to gain a vegetated groove. Continue up this to a good stance on the left (25m). Continue up the groove for another 5m then step down and right, then move up to the groove running through the headwall (15m). Climb the groove to a good stance (20m). Pull over the overhang above (crux) (10m). Move up to join Route 1 which is followed to the summit of the Pinnacle (60m).

The Ice Ox 100m IV,5*

(no photo topo)

G. Livingstone and A. Matthewson, 24 December 1984

The big corner starting from the fork in the Black Spout is the line of the climb. It can be good early in the season.

Pinnacle Gully 2 90m II

(no photo topo)

A.W. Clark and W.A. Ewan, 28 December 1932

A good little route that starts high up the Left-hand Branch of the Black Spout and ends at the col behind the Pinnacle. Climb the gully direct. The blocked through route behind the chokestone is climbed on the outside and is often the crux; awkward in lean conditions. Above this continue on the right to the col. To gain the Pinnacle from the col, descend a little way on the other side then climb a crack going right, go round a corner and climb slabs to the top. An abseil return may be required.

Black Spout Left Branch 250m I***

(no photo topo)

The left-hand branch is steeper and more interesting than the normal route up The Black Spout. The scenery is magnificent.

Crumbling Cranny 60m II

(no photo topo)

Miss Inglis Clark, Mrs Hunter, H. Alexander, 21 December 1913

This is the wide chimney in the right wall of the Left Branch of the Black Spout. It can have a huge cornice which can require tunnelling.

The Stack 150m V,6*

(no photo topo)

J.M. Taylor, G.B. Leslie and T.L. Fallowfield, 20 November 1952

This sustained route lies on the buttress between the two branches of the Black Spout and can be very icy. Start in the Left-hand Branch and climb the icefall to a platform. Go to a chimney with jammed blocks which is climbed for a short way until a descending traverse left leads to a platform. Return right via two short chimneys to the main chimney which is climbed to a bollard (it is sometimes possible to avoid this detour). Step off the bollard onto a shelf on the right then go up a wall to a ledge. Move left then up a slab to broken ground. A terrace goes left below the final wall then a short step leads to the top.

The crags of Lochnagar appearing from the mist (photo: Paul Noble)

Winter Climbs in the Cairngorms

The White Spout 70m IV,4
M. Freeman and N.D. Keir, 2 February 1974
This is an icefall which can develop on the right wall of the Stack near the top of the Black Spout. Climb it rightwards then by the easiest line at the top.

The Black Spout 250m I**
J.H. Gibson and W. Douglas, 12 March 1893
The huge easy-angled corridor is straightforward. The cornice is usually avoidable on the right.

West Buttress Group   NO 246 859 Crag base altitude 900m East facing

This collection of buttresses and gullies lies at right angles to the rest of the cliff. On the left it is terminated by the Black Spout, and the right-hand side gradually merges into broken ground. It is generally more broken than the other groups but West Gully, with its lower icefall, is well defined and prominent. Conditions here may not be so reliable as on the other areas, particularly later in the season when these rocks are more affected by the sun.

Black Spout Buttress 250m III,5**
J. Tewnion, C. Hutcheon, D.A. Sutherland and K. Winram, 9 January 1949
A fine climb following the crest of the buttress immediately right of the Black Spout. Start about 10m right of the Black Spout and climb the chimney fault, which may contain ice. Above continue more easily to the step. Climb a ridge and a 4m chimney. Easier ground leads to a short wall (crux) which is started i
n the middle and finished by a corner on the right. Above this, another wall is turned by a right traverse into a gully. Return left to the crest as soon as possible.

Gargoyle Chimney 120m IV,4**
J.M. Taylor and W.D. Brooker, 20 January 1952
A good winter line up the obvious fault in the centre of the upper face. The Midway Terrace at the foot of the route is gained by one of the three faults right of Black Spout Buttress, the centre one being the easiest. The chimney itself is climbed direct and the lower section can contain much ice.

Prince of Darkness 70m VI,7**
S.M. Richardson and C. Cartwright, 20 December 1998
A fine steep and sustained mixed route which climbs the imposing tower rising from above the upper section of West Gully. Start by climbing West Gully for 180m to the

The upper section of Black Spout Buttress (photo: Billy Burnside)

foot of this tower. Climb up a turf ramp and move left to a ledge. Move back right to a niche, and then climb straight up to a second niche. Step right around the arête to reach a hanging groove and follow this to a good belay stance (25m). Climb the prominent right-facing corner above to another good stance (25m). Climb the steep cracks above to the top of the tower (20m).

West Gully 250m IV,4*
A. Fyffe and M.D.Y. Mowat (direct), 4 April 1966
The obvious gully on the right of the cliff. It starts with a fine icefall which is climbed direct and forms the crux. Above, the gully is impressive but straightforward. The central branch at the top gives the best finish but the left branch is easier.

Gelder Gully 250m II
M.C.S. Philip, J. Henderson and A. Grattidge, 25 January 1953
The shallow gully to the right of West Gully. Trend rightwards up a snow ramp to gain the gully, which is followed (via a possible ice pitch) to a large snow bay. Here the gully forks. The right branch quickly leads to easy ground, while the left continues with more interest to the top.

Looking down the crux of Shadow Buttress A (photo: Allen Fyffe)

Creag an Dubh Loch (NO 234 826)

Start	Spittal of Glen Muick car park NO 310 851
Time	2hr 30min
Crag base altitude	730m
Aspect	North to north-east
Route lengths	80–360m
Style	Requires cold conditions to come into nick, but then provides some of the best and longest icy mixed routes in the country.

Lying on the flank of Broad Cairn overlooking the Dubh Loch is the biggest cliff in the Cairngorms. It stretches for 1km as a relatively straight face and gives routes up to 360m in length. In the centre of the cliff is the enormous Central Gully; the only other easy faults, South-East and North-West Gullies, lie at the extreme left and right ends of the cliff respectively. Right of South-East Gully, at the top of the cliff, is Broad Terrace Wall. This vertical and overhanging wall lies above the inappropriately named Broad Terrace which runs out left from the great scoop of the Hanging Garden, separated from the Central Slabs by the left-facing fault of the Labyrinth. The Central Slabs themselves are huge and unmistakable.

Running diagonally right below the steeper Upper Tier is a terrace that can be used as an escape onto Central Gully Buttress. On the right the Central Slabs become more broken and end at Central Gully. Right of Central Gully, the Central Gully Wall looms over the gully, the massive overlapping tile-like formation giving one of the most impressive rock walls in the country. This wall then swings round to form a slightly less intimidating frontal face which is defined on its right by False Gully. This shallow fault starts as an open, grassy ramp and has another steep and massive right wall, the False Gully Wall. Right of this, the ground is again more hospitable before North-West Gully is reached and the cliff becomes much more broken.

Approach

The normal approach is from Ballater where the minor road up Glen Muick is followed for 15km to the same car park as for Lochnagar, at the Spittal of Glen Muick. The last 4km are across open moor and can be difficult with drifting snow. The car park can be very busy at peak holiday times. Walk along the unsurfaced road on the north-west shore of Loch Muick to the head of the loch and continue up the path on the north

Winter Climbs in the Cairngorms

Creag an Dubh Loch (left side)

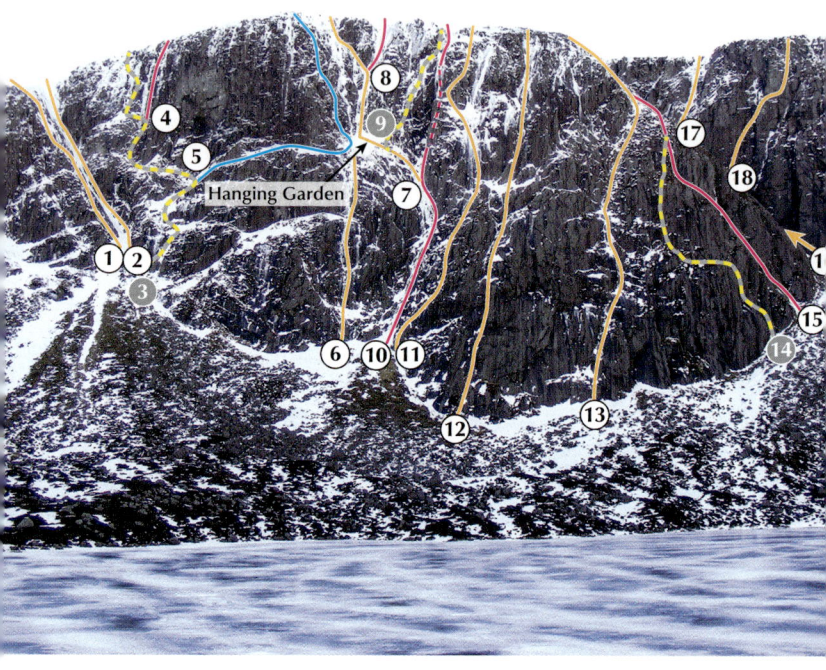

1. South-East Buttress II*
2. South-East Gully II**
3. The Snow Desert V,4
4. The Last Oasis VI,6**
5. Bower Buttress V,5**
6. The Aqueduct V,5**
7. Hanging Garden Route V,4***
8. Hanging Garden Route Right Fork V,4
9. Labyrinth Left-hand V,5*
10. Labyrinth Direct VII,6***
11. Labyrinth Edge IV,5*
12. The White Elephant VII,6**
13. Theseus Grooves III*
14. The Golden Thread IV,4
15. Centaur III
16. Central Gully I*
17. Sabre Cut IV,5*
18. Vertigo Wall VII,7***

Creag an Dubh Loch

side of the stream to the Dubh Loch. Cross to the south side of the glen, either at the head or the outlet of the loch depending on the part of the cliff to be visited. Cycling along the side of Loch Muick is a good option if there is no snow on the track.

Descent
Central Gully gives a convenient way down; the cornice is usually avoidable on the right when looking down. Either end of the cliff can also be descended, the north-west end being the better alternative with the outcrops being more easily outflanked.

Conditions
As the base of the cliff is fairly low at just over 700m, Creag an Dubh Loch is not as reliable a winter venue as its neighbour Lochnagar. However, when in good condition it offers superb icy mixed climbing with some of the most sought-after routes in this guidebook found here. Good conditions can be difficult to predict, with cold weather required for the ice to form, but if it is too cold then the springs can freeze at source. Unfortunately it can strip rapidly in a thaw, although the Hanging Garden area can hold ice for longer periods and later in the season. Sometimes the routes on Eagles Rock or Broad Cairn Bluffs can provide a good alternative should conditions on Creag an Dubh Loch not be as good as expected.

South-East Buttress 200m II*
F. Patterson and A. Alexander, March 1948
The buttress on the left of the cliff. The route follows the crest overlooking South-East Gully. After a slab corner pitch on the gully side of the buttress, the climbing is straightforward.

South-East Gully 200m II**
W.A. Russell, M. Smith and W. Stephen, 26 January 1947
The obvious gully which slants up to the left. The chokestone may give an interesting pitch early in the season but can bank out later.
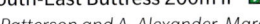
The following routes (with the exception of The Aqueduct which is on the lower tier) are usually approached by either zig-zagging up from the start of South-East Gully onto Broad Terrace, or by climbing the lower section of Labyrinth Direct and breaking left to gain the Hanging Garden. The route lengths given include these approaches.

The Last Oasis 300m VI,6**
A. Nisbet, N. Spinks, 30 March 1980
The left-hand of twin faults above South-East Gully; the right-hand fault is the right-facing corner of Sword of Damocles (VIII,8***). It can form an impressive icefall with a very steep finish which is unfortunately susceptible to the morning sun. The finish

may be turned on the left by the summer line (one nut and one peg for aid on the first ascent).

Bower Buttress 300m V,5**
J. Bower and G.R. Simpson, March 1970
A fine route which takes the edge between the vertical Broad Terrace Wall and the left margin of the Hanging Garden. In good conditions it can be all on ice; otherwise, it can give a fine mixed route. Start near the foot of South-East Gully and climb the zig-zag line of ramps up to the Broad Terrace. Go right below the vertical wall to where it turns into the Hanging Garden. Alternatively, this point can be gained by climbing Labyrinth and traversing left across the Hanging Garden. Climb grooves in the crest slanting left to the Gallery, a large ledge. Cracks trending slightly right lead to a shallow gully which leads to snow slopes and the cornice which is taken on the left.

The Aqueduct 120m V,5**
R.A. Smith and J. Moreland, 26 January 1975
In good conditions a fine icefall forms out of the left-hand side of the Hanging Garden. This gives a fine but serious direct route to the Hanging Garden.

Yeti 300m V,4**
(no photo topo)
R.A. Smith and J. Moreland, 26 January 1975
This takes the line of the slabby ramps between Bower Buttress and Hanging Garden Route. These can become sheathed in ice and give an exposed, sustained and serious climb. Gain the Hanging Garden by the first part of Labyrinth Direct. There may be two branches to the lower icefall, either of which can be climbed.

Hanging Garden Route 300m V,4***
A. Nisbet and A. Robertson, 6 January 1977
Another excellent ice route which has two forks. Climb the lower section of Labyrinth Direct for about 150m and go left to gain the Hanging Garden. Follow the gully above to below a steep, triangular buttress which separates the two forks. Go up the left fork until a wall forces a traverse left across an exposed, iced slab and follow snow to pass left of the cornice.

Right Fork V,4: Move down and right to gain a stepped icy fault that leads to a difficult cornice.

Labyrinth Direct 300m VII,6***
A.J. Bolton and P. Arnold, 11 March 1972
A superb but poorly protected ice route following the fault direct. One of the most sought-after ice routes in the Cairngorms. After an initial ice pitch, easier snow leads

The spectacular Labyrinth Direct (photo: Graeme Gatherer)

to the upper section. Climb the main fault into a steep groove and so to the cul-de-sac where there is a good belay on the right if the rock is visible (40m). 10m of very steep and perhaps thin ice leads to a steep groove which continues to reach easier ground (40m). Continue up easier ground to the top (40m).

Labyrinth Edge 300m IV,5*
W.D. Brooker and D. Duncan, 10 February 1959
This takes the left edge of the Central Slabs overlooking the fault line of the Labyrinth; difficulty increases with height. Start at the foot of the Labyrinth and go right onto the edge which is climbed to a bay. Follow grooves to a smooth area, the Sea of Slabs. Climb cracks on the left edge to a ledge on the left, then turn the Lower Tower above this on the right and go up to below the Fang, a rock tooth. Turn this on the left to below the Upper Tower. Traverse to a chimney on the tower's right and go up this then out right to easier ground and the top.

Mammoth 360m IV,4
(no photo topo)
J. Bower, J. Furnell, N. Blenkinsop and I. Rae, 31 January 1970
A huge route which goes diagonally right across the Central Slabs. Start at the foot of the Labyrinth and work up and right into the gully on the left side of the slabs, the Dinosaur Gully. Climb this gully taking the right fork and then continue up and right across shelves. Finish up the fault on the right side of the steep upper rocks or continue trending right to finish up Central Gully Buttress.

The White Elephant 320m VII,6**
R. Anderson and R. Milne, 12 January 1980
Can give a magnificent climb on ice which oozes from the Upper Tier and the big left-facing curving groove about 60m right of the top section of Labyrinth Edge and runs down the left side of the slabs. Unfortunately, the bottom section is slow to form. Climb ice up to and over the overlap and enter the gully system in the slabs, the Dinosaur Gully. Climb the right branch of this Y-shaped gully, or if conditions allow go direct, to reach the terrace running below the steeper upper rocks. Climb ice up a corner and into the big groove which is followed to the plateau.

Theseus Grooves 300m III* or
J.T. Campbell, B.S. Findlay, G.R. Simpson and G.S. Strange, 12 January 1969
The line of grooves on the right side of the main slabs. Start directly below the grooves at a shallow corner, possibly iced or even banked out. Climb this corner to enter the main groove system which is climbed to a snow field. From the top of the snow field, trend left up a depression until a line leads back right onto the crest of

Creag an Dubh Loch (right side) *(photo: Simon Richardson)*

1. Central Gully I*
2. Sabre Cut IV,5*
3. Vertigo Wall VII,7***
4. Mousetrap VII,8**
5. False Gully VI,7
6. North-West Buttress III

Central Gully Buttress which is followed to the top. In lean conditions IV,4 may be a more appropriate grade.

Centaur 300m III

A. Fyffe and D. Whitcombe, 14 March 1970

Takes a line of chimneys and ledges which lie to the left of and parallel to the crest of Central Gully Buttress, before joining that route above the steeper lower section. Start in a bay about 30m from the corner of the buttress. Climb either of two wide grooves and go up to the top of the fault. (The icefall above gives a IV,5 finish.) Go diagonally left, passing below a deep chimney, until a wide corner can be climbed and the buttress crest gained by going right.

Central Gully Buttress 300m II
(no photo topo)
T.W. Patey, March 1955
The ridge bordering the left side of Central Gully. Start either by an open chimney fault on the left of the crest or by a slab just inside Central Gully. Above the initial steep section the climbing is straightforward.

Central Gully 300m I*
Miss McHardy and Miss Stewart, February 1933
An easy but spectacular way up the cliff underneath the magnificent Central Gully Wall. The lower blocks often show through the snow and the cornice can be avoided on the left. A good descent route.

Sabre Cut 80m IV,5*
T.W. Patey, F.R. Malcolm and A. Thom, 13 February 1957
The large fault which cuts Central Gully Wall near its top usually fills with ice. Climb the main groove line which is steep. The cornice may be large and difficult.

Vertigo Wall 160m VII,7***
A. Nisbet and A. Robertson, 3/4 December 1977
A. Cunningham and A. Nisbet (FFA), November 1985
An extremely fine mixed route which takes the huge open corner below Sabre Cut. Early in the season it often holds ice in quantity, but later the headwall is often stripped by the morning sun. Start up Central Gully from the main line of the fault. Traverse right on a grass shelf and climb the corner to a platform (30m). Gain a large block then go right then left to reach slabs leading right to the main corner (35m). Climb the chimney (ice required) to a steeper section and go right for about 10m then back left into the corner (30m). Climb the slab to the headwall then traverse right along a creaking flake to a shallow corner (it is best not to belay directly below this flake). Climb the shallow corner then traverse right and go up to a belay (25m). Continue to the top (40m).

More Vertigo Finish 65m VII,8**
(no photo topo)
A. Melvin, R. Miller and H. Wackerhage, 12 March 2011
A fine alternative finish to Vertigo Wall which climbs through some unlikely looking terrain at a reasonable grade. Climb the first three pitches of the normal route. Climb thin ice up and left to get established on a small ledge. Traverse leftwards to the prominent icicles and continue steeply up to a belay (20m). Follow easy turfy ramps up and left to belay below a left-leaning off-width crack (15m). Climb the crack with

difficulty and continue to a sharp spike. Step up from the spike and boldly climb the slab on thin hooks and continue to the top (30m).

Mousetrap 180m VII,8**

M. Hamilton, K. Spence and A. Taylor, 19 January 1980

A big route which takes the grassy recess and cracks just where the Central Gully Wall changes angle. Start at the top of the mound where the face bends. Make a short right traverse, climb a corner to a ledge on the right (as for the summer route Predator; technical crux) and traverse right round a shelf under twin cracks. Continue right then climb into the grassy recess of The Mousetrap. From the top of the recess pull out on the left to gain a crack system which is followed to the top. This is sustained and thin but easier if iced up.

North-West Buttress 200m III

W. Church and G.S. Strange, 26 February 1995

The central line up the buttress starting at the break on the left side of the lower tier, up and right from the shelf leading onto False Gully. Go up and left in a shallow groove then go right to a terrace. Cross this and climb up right to follow snow then grooves and chimneys. Move left to finish.

North-West Gully 200m II/III**

(no photo topo)
T.W. Patey, W.D. Brooker, J.M. Taylor and J.W. Morgan, 29 December 1952

A good climb up the obvious gully on the right of the cliff. It may contain an ice pitch at the bottom and the top.

Ross Cowie on the crux pitch of Labyrinth Direct (photo: Graeme Gatherer)

Eagles Rock (NO 235 835)

Start	Spittal of Glen Muick car park NO 310 851
Time	2hr 30min
Crag base altitude	770m
Aspect	South
Route lengths	110–150m
Style	Some good mid-grade ice routes form in cold conditions early season. Strips quickly in the sunshine.

This is the band of broken cliffs which lie high up on the opposite side of the glen from Creag an Dubh Loch. It consists of several slabby buttresses which are south-facing and are something of a contrast from the shaded faces across the way. There is a conspicuous waterfall near the edge of the rocks and towards the right side is the large Diagonal Gully which slopes left to right.

Approach
As for Creag an Dubh Loch but stay on the north side of the Dubh Loch and ascend to the appropriate place.

Descent
Descend either well to the west of the waterfall, or by Diagonal Gully.

Conditions
These cliffs may hold ice in quantity in cold weather, even if there is little snow. However, later in the season much of the lower slabs may bank out and the cliffs are very susceptible to thaw and bright sunlight.

Waterfall Area   NO 231 835 Crag base altitude 770m South facing

The area around the waterfall.

The Waterfall 150m II*
N.D. Keir and J. Taylor, 2 January 1974
Climb ice on the left of the main fall. Escapes to the left are possible.

Eagles Rock

1. The Waterfall II*
2. Spectrum III**
3. Lethargy II/III*
4. Indolence III*
5. Nomad's Crack V,5*
6. Sliver III*
7. Gibber IV,3*

Winter Climbs in the Cairngorms

Spectrum 110m III*
D. Dinwoodie and J. Mothersele, 1 December 1971
Follows the obvious corners and grooves right of The Waterfall. Climb the ice leading into the V-groove near the top which gives a fine finish. Can give a sustained climb on water-ice.

Mid-West Buttress   NO 232 835 Crag base altitude 770m South facing

This is the highest and most continuous buttress to the right of the waterfall. The lower slabs may blank out completely.

Lethargy 120m II/III*
J. Bower and G.R. Simpson
The obvious corner on the left of the buttress usually forms a continuous line of ice. Climb the corner and go left above it. The obvious direct finish up the steep icefall above the corner is IV,5.

Indolence 140m III*
A. Nisbet and A. Robertson, 12 December 1976
The next icefall right of Lethargy which has its best and steepest ice high on the buttress.

Eagles Rock

Nomad's Crack 150m V,5*
A. Nisbet and A. Robertson, 26 December 1976
The next and best-defined groove right of Indolence can give a good route up a narrow ribbon of ice which forms in grooves. The lower slabs can bank out.

Mid-East Buttress   NO 233 835 Crag base altitude 770m South facing

This triangular mass is characterised by a big inverted L-shaped corner, the line of Gibber. It lies on the left of the obvious Diagonal Gully.

Sliver 150m III*
R.J. Archbold and G.S. Strange, 15 December 1974
This takes the continuous line of water-ice which runs up the right side of the broken ground between Mid-West and Mid-East Buttresses.

Gibber 130m IV,3*
A. Nisbet and N. Spinks, 2 February 1977
The big inverted L-shaped corner gives the line of this climb. The amount of ice is variable, and it may be poorly protected if the crack in the corner is not accessible.

An infinite variety of Scottish snow (photo: Paul Noble)

Broad Cairn Bluffs (NO 248 818)

Start	Spittal of Glen Muick car park NO 310 851
Time	2hr 15min
Crag base altitude	700m
Aspect	North
Route lengths	60m
Style	In cold conditions this crag provides a great cascade-style ice route and other easier lines.

This is the cliff on the left about a kilometre before the Dubh Loch. The main face is the left wall of an open gully. It may provide an alternative for a short day or when the going is extremely heavy.

Approach
As for Creag an Dubh Loch until a kilometre or so beyond the Stuic waterfall. This should allow a view of the crag to assess whether the route in in condition. Descend and cross the Allt an Dubh Loch then ascend the slope to the crag.

Descent
Descend the easy-angled gully beside the route.

Conditions
A great ice route but requires cold conditions to form.

Funeral Fall 60m IV,4**
(no photo topo)
M. Freeman and N.D. Keir, 3 March 1974
The prominent icefall gives a good climb.

The other routes here are **Coffin Chimney III**, the narrow chimney; **Rake's Rib III**, on its right; and **Yoo-Hoo Buttress III**, the front of the buttress facing the glen.

Glen Clova

Glen Clova lies to the south-east of the main Southern Cairngorm mass of Lochnagar and Creag an Dubh Loch, and is different in many ways from the rest of the guide. The rock is not granite, it is generally lower and more vegetated, and the area is only easily accessible from the south and east. However, it can be more sheltered from bad weather from the north and west, and there are several fine climbs, particularly in the lower grades. The two main winter climbing areas are The Winter Corrie of Driesh and Corrie Fee.

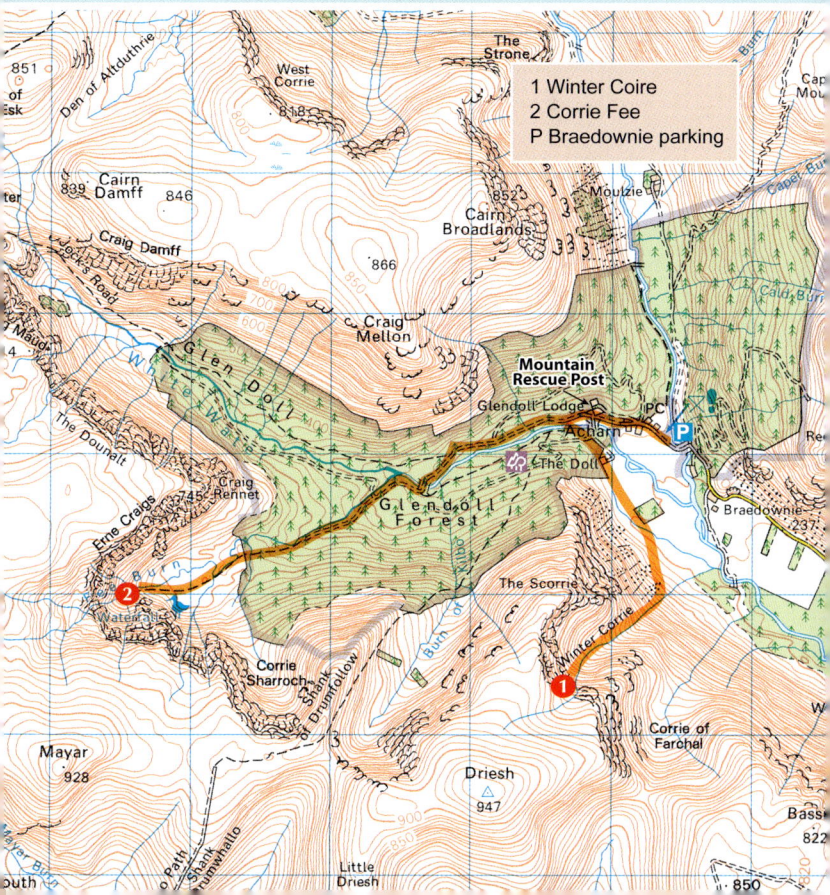

1 Winter Coire
2 Corrie Fee
P Braedownie parking

Winter Climbs in the Cairngorms

The Winter Corrie (NO 276 745)

Start	Braedownie car park NO 283 761
Time	1hr
Crag base altitude	650m
Aspect	North-east
Route lengths	70–200m
Style	A range of styles with some good routes in the lower grades.

The Winter Corrie is the obvious corrie overlooking the road-head and lies to the south of The Scorrie, a distinctive cone-shaped buttress. The rocks are very broken but do offer some interesting routes. The Waterfall is on the left of the main rocks. The Main Buttress is the highest section of cliff and is characterised by The Basin, a big snow patch in its centre.

Approach
From the car park at Braedownie follow the track into Glendoll forest and after 500m cross the bridge over White Water and head back out of the forest. Continue south-east by the fields to the burn draining the corrie then go directly into the corrie. Alternatively, go diagonally under the steeper rocks of The Scorrie to gain the corrie via some big boulders and awkward ground.

Descent
In good conditions, Easy Gully is the simplest descent. Alternatively, contour round the corrie edge and go down the northerly slopes of The Scorrie to the path in Glendoll.

Conditions
Several of the climbs are watercourses and come into condition quite quickly in cold weather.

The Waterfall 70m II/III*
(no photo topo)
The icefall high on the left side of the face gives the line of this climb. The easiest line is the inset corner on the left of the main stream, but if fully frozen it is better to start up the V-groove on the right and climb this to the main fall.

The Winter Corrie
(photo: Greg Strange)

- ① Central Gully II
- ①A Left-hand Branch II/III
- ② Easy Gully I
- ③ Backdoor Chimney II*
- ④ Backdoor Gully II*
- ④A Direct Finish IV,4
- ⑤ Diamond Slab IV,4
- ⑥ Diagonal Gully III**
- ⑦ Pinnacle Gully II
- ⑧ Wiggle III
- ⑨ The Shute I

Central Gully 120m II ◇ or ❄
In the centre of the corrie is an obvious deep gully. There is a left branch which is Grade II/III.

Easy Gully 120m I ◇
This is the straight, straightforward and obvious gully in the centre of the corrie.

Backdoor Chimney 200m III*
Where Backdoor Gully bends right, climb the deep chimney.

Backdoor Gully 200m II* ◇
The deep gully which cuts up behind the Main Buttress to reach The Basin. There, either move left as soon as possible to easier ground, or go to the top right of The Basin and finish up a gully on the right.
    Direct Finish 80m IV,4 From the top left corner of The Basin, climb ice to below a deep crack. Go right then back left to climb the wall right of this crack. Go up and slightly right to finish.

Diagonal Gully 200m III** ❄
In the middle of the Main Buttress a 30m icefall descends from a right-slanting chimney. Climb the ice and chimney into The Basin and go to its top right corner. Climb the icefall above till forced right to a block belay. Easier ground leads to the top.

Pinnacle Gully 120m III ◇
This is the deep gully leading to the upper part of Diagonal Gully. From the top of the snow here, finish up rightwards.

Wiggle 120m III
Right of Pinnacle Gully, climb some heathery grooves then go left and up to a steep wall. Climb the narrow chimney on the left to easier ground and finish up a broad ridge.

The Shute 120m I ◇
The wide snow gully on the right of the cliff.

Corrie Fee (NO 246 750)

Start	Braedownie car park NO 283 760
Time	1hr
Crag base altitude	550m
Aspect	North-east
Route lengths	60–200m
Style	Some good ice routes. Requires cold conditions to come into nick.

This is the biggest and best winter climbing area in Glen Clova. The corrie has two walls which meet at the Fee Burn. The South Wall is the more important and stretches south-east from the burn towards the Shank of Drumfollow. There are five gullies which split the crag and from left to right they are A, B, Look C, D and E. Look C is much less defined than the others and runs up the left side of Central Buttress, the steepest and largest mass of rock.

Approach
From the car park at Braedownie follow the track into Glendoll forest and cross White Water by the bridge at NO 267 758. Continue west along the track and continuation path to a stile at the edge of the forest and the start of the corrie.

Descent
A and D Gullies can be used for descent. Alternatively, follow the fence from the top of B Gully Chimney round to the Shank of Drumfollow and descend that to gain the Kilbo path and Glendoll forest.

Conditions
Requires some cold weather combined with some snow. Being slightly lower than the Winter Corrie, it usually takes a bit longer to come into good condition.

A Gully 200m I ◇
The gully in the left corner of the corrie is straightforward.

Corrie Fee
(photo: Greg Strange)

1. A Gully I
2. B Gully Chimney III,4**
3. B Gully Buttress III
4. B Gully II**
5. Look C Gully IV,4***
6. Wet Knees IV,4*
7. D Gully I
8. The Pyramid IV,5

B Gully Chimney, Pete Trudgill making the most of good ice conditions (photo: John Trudgill)

Pete Trudgill leading on the crux of Look C Gully (photo: John Trudgill)

A-B Integrate 200m II ◇ or ❄

(no photo topo)
Right of A Gully is a 100m easy-angled corner which can be icy early in the season. Finish up easier ground to the top.

B Gully Chimney 150m III,4** 🧊

D. Crabb and D. Lang, 29 December 1962
B Gully is well defined and the left branch, the obvious deep chimney containing several chokestones, is the best finish. After about 60m this route breaks out left. It can be icy although some pitches can bank out.

B Gully 200m II** 🧊

H. Raeburn, W. Galbraith and W.A. Reid, May 1915
This well-defined gully may have at least one ice pitch although it can be avoided on the right.

Look C Gully 200m IV,4*** ❄

C.L. Donaldson and J.R. Marshall, 15 February 1953
This takes the shallow fault in the left of Central Buttress and gives the best route in the area, although it does require a good freeze to come into condition. Climb up stepped ice to above a short chimney. Take the left-hand gully line into a basin then climb the rib on the right to below the main icefall. Climb the ice direct then continue up short pitches to where the gully forks. Above, easier ground leads to the top.

Wet Knees 200m IV,4* 🧊

N.D. Keir and A. Lawson, 30 January 1972
Takes a line of discontinuous chimneys immediately right of Look C Gully. Start up an ice-smear at the foot of Look C Gully. The last chimney is the best pitch.

D Gully 200m I ◇

This gully lies on the right side of Central Buttress and is straightforward.

The Pyramid 60m IV,5 🗻

A. Paul, G. Reilly, I. Reilly and W. Taylor, November 1985
The right and lower of the pyramids is climbed by a line close to the crest. Escapable between pitches.

E Gully 60m I ◇

(no photo topo)
This is the short, open gully high up at the right end of the face.

261

Creag Meagaidh

Approaching the North Pipe on Staghorn Gully, Coire Ardair (photo: Ali Rose)

Creag Meagaidh lies north of Loch Laggan in the Moy Forest, and is currently owned by NatureScot. It is noted for its native birch woods which NatureScot are trying to regenerate. Creag Meagaidh is situated roughly halfway between the west coast and the Cairngorms. The conditions found here tend to lie between what is found in those areas. There is generally more ice here than the Cairngorms, but it is less affected by thaw than the mountains nearer the sea. The main corrie, Coire Ardair, is about a kilometre east of the summit and is backed by an extensive plateau. The rock is mica schist which is generally fairly shattered and has a horizontal strata which dips back into the hillside. These factors, combined with the large amounts of vegetation present on the rock, means that snow and ice accumulate to considerable depths in places. This can produce very fine winter routes with some superb ice lines. It also unfortunately means there is often a significant avalanche hazard.

The main cliff of Coire Ardair is about 3km long and nearly 500m in height. The bulk of the cliff, as clearly seen from the lochan in the corrie bottom, is divided into three main buttresses divided by two large gullies. High up on the left is Bellevue Buttress which is separated from the impressive Pinnacle Buttress by the left-slanting Raeburn's Gully. Right of Pinnacle Buttress is the left-trending highway of Easy Gully,

above which rises the Post Face split by the four distinctive gullies or posts. At right angles to the Post Face and hidden from the lochan is the more broken Inner Corrie which stretches to the Window, NN 426 886, the prominent col on the north.

The rock varies from quite compact to shattered, and so a variety of nuts and pegs will be found useful. Ice screws are essential on the ice routes, with drive-in ice pegs such as warthogs and bulldog ice hooks useful in frozen turf. Longer ropes can be very useful on climbs here. There are some large snow fields which may require snow anchors, even on harder routes. The large cornices and open slopes on and above many of the climbs constitute a very real avalanche hazard both from windslab and during thaws.

The nature of the rock means these crags are cut by some prominent and distinctive ledge systems. These lend themselves to traverse lines and give what is probably the finest horizontal excursion in Scottish winter climbing, the Crab Crawl. This is described as its four constituent parts, but the pitches can be interchanged on other routes as well.

The approach to Coire Ardair, Creag Meagaidh

Coire Ardair (NN 440 883)

Start	Aberarder Farm car park NN 482 873
Time	2hr
Crag base altitude	850–950m
Aspect	North to east; also south
Route lengths	100–450m (up to 2400m for the girdle traverse)
Style	A major venue with many classic ice and icy mixed routes.

Access
This area lies on Ordance Survey Landranger 34 *Fort Augustus*. As the approach starts from the A86 (Newtonmore to Spean Bridge), the venues are readily accessible from both Aviemore and Fort William. Start from the car park NN 482 873 at the track to Aberarder farm which is well signed. Take the track to the farm and pass to the east of the buildings. Follow the very good path on the north-east of the Allt Coire Ardair, taking a high line parallel to the burn. This takes a big curve round into the corrie to eventually descend to the corrie floor then continue to the lochan. When there is heavy snow it may be best to keep high up on the right side of the glen until the approach into the corrie is obvious. Depending on snow conditions, the approach can be long and arduous.

Descent
The summit plateau is flat and featureless, and care must be taken when navigating to the descent routes. Raeburn's Gully and Easy Gully give quick descents for competent parties in suitable conditions. From climbs on Bellevue and Pinnacle Buttresses, the ridge of Sròn a'Choire leads back down to Aberarder farm. From climbs on the Post Face and the Inner Corrie, a descent by the Window to the corrie floor and the lochan is probably the easiest.

Conditions
These crags hold plenty of snow and ice and are usually in condition at some time during the winter. They get the snow from the west but avoid the worst thaws from that direction. In general, the gully lines are better than the buttress routes here and, as many of the routes are ice climbs, they tend to be better slightly later in the year when they have had a chance to build up. Some of the deeper and thicker ice routes can withstand a reasonable thaw.

Coire Ardair from the lochan on a settled winter's day

Winter Climbs in the Cairngorms

Crab Crawl 2400m IV,4***
T.W. Patey, 23 March 1969
One of the classic Scottish girdle traverses, this huge horizontal excursion is an aptly named and natural line. It is best from left to right and consists of The Scene, Appolyon Ledge, Post Horn Gallop and the Last Lap. For further detail refer to these routes which link in a logical manner.

Bellevue Buttress   NN 436 875 Crag base altitude 900m North-east facing

This is the buttress at the left or east end of Coire Ardair. On its right is the huge Pinnacle Buttress and between the two is the tapering Raeburn's Gully Buttress.

The Scene 400m II*
(no photo topo)
D. Grayand A. MacKeith, 15 January 1966
The first part of the girdle traverse. Follow the obvious horizontal ledge from left to right across the buttress into Raeburn's Gully. Spectacular and exposed in places.

Eastern Corner 300m III** ◇ or
C.G.M. Slessor and K. Bryan, 28 January 1961
At the right side of Bellevue Buttress where it abuts the smaller Raeburn's Gully Buttress is an obvious open corner. The corner is followed throughout with the lower

Some spectacular terrain on the approach to Eastern Corner (photo: Allen Fyffe)

section providing the more technical pitches (harder if it's continuous ice). The upper section is straightforward snow climbing.

Raeburn's Gully Buttress   NN 435 876 Crag base altitude 850m North-east facing

This is the long narrow buttress with a steep left wall lying between Eastern Corner and Raeburn's Gully. It contains some good mixed routes and can be a useful alternative early season, or when the big ice routes are not in condition. It is easy to descend Raeburn's Gully from these routes.

Barry White 130m IV,6*
A. Clarke, A. Perkins, I. Taylor and P. Thorburn, January 1999
A fine, reasonably well-protected mixed route. Start just to the right of Eastern Corner, where a curving fault runs rightwards. Climb this to a ledge below a crack which is followed to easier ground below a chimney. Climb this and continue more easily to the crest of the buttress.

Do What Thou Wilt 100m IV,4**
A. Powell and S. Grayson, 12 February 1994
Start in a snow bay by a small tower. Climb the snowy groove trending rightwards, then take an obvious unlikely looking ramp through a roof. Move right and climb a short wall to easier ground.

Raeburn's Gully 350m I***
H. Raeburn, C. Walker and H. Walker, 31 October 1903
The leftmost of the two large left-trending gullies is climbed direct below the spectacular wall of Pinnacle Buttress. There may be the occasional ice pitch or awkward cornice exit.

Pinnacle Buttress   NN 434 877 Crag base altitude 850m East facing

This is the steep and impressive buttress lying between Raeburn's and Easy Gully. There is a very steep wall rising above Raeburn's Gully which is cut by three parallel faults – the lines of Ritchie's Gully, Smith's Gully and The Fly. Pinnacle Buttress is also traversed by three horizontal lines, the central of which is Appolyon Ledge and the lower of which is Vanishing Ledge. The lower section of the front face has an

Winter Climbs in the Cairngorms

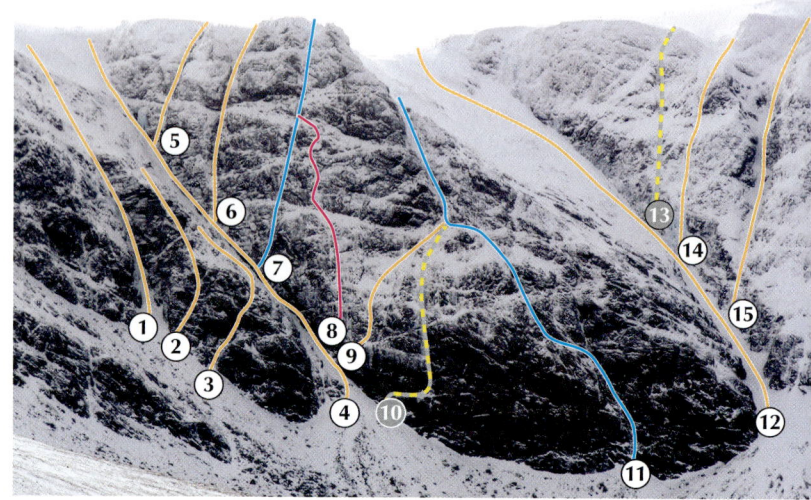

1. Eastern Corner III**
2. Barry White IV,6*
3. Do What Thou Wilt IV,4**
4. Raeburn's Gully I***
5. Ritchie's Gully IV,4**
6. Smith's Gully VI,5***
7. The Fly Direct VII,6***
8. The Midge VI,5*
9. The White Spider IV,4*
10. Pinnacle Buttress Direct VI,5**
11. 1959 Face Route V,4**
12. Easy Gully I
13. Missed The Post V,5*
14. The Last Post V,5***
15. South Post Direct V,4**

extremely steep initial wall with some lines of weakness on its right side. Higher up, this section tapers inwards and forms the left side of Easy Gully.

Appolyon Ledge 500m II** ◇

(no photo topo)

D. Gray and A. MacKeith, 16 January 1966

The second part of the girdle takes the middle of the three faults cutting across Pinnacle Buttress. Start in Raeburn's Gully about 90m from the top and cross the face by the middle of the three ledges. This is extremely exposed and spectacular, and leads to easy ground and into Easy Gully.

Ritchie's Gully 160m IV,4**
G.N. Hunter and N. Quinn, March 1969
The leftmost of the three parallel faults above Raeburn's Gully. Climb the initial icefall, turning an overhang on the right, and continue up to Appolyon Ledge. Climb the gully above with several ice pitches. The cornice may be difficult.

Smith's Gully 180m VI,5***
J.R. Marshall and G. Tiso, 8 February 1959
The steep gully cutting straight up Pinnacle Buttress from Raeburn's Gully gives a magnificent, sustained and serious ice route, one of the finest in the country. Unfortunately, it takes a while to come into good condition. Climb the gully to belay on the left above a snow bay (35m). An icy bulge leads to a belay in another snow bay (20m). Continue the still-steep gully to where Appolyon Ledge cuts across the face (45m). Climb the steep ice above (crux) to reach easier ground (45m). Easier snowy ground above leads to the top (35m).

The Fly Direct 240m VII,6***
M. Fowler and A. Saunders, 19 February 1983
The right-hand fault is a narrow gully, serious, sustained and superb when in condition, which unfortunately is not all that often. Start about 10m left of the gully and climb mixed ground up and right to reach the gully proper. Alternatively, start in a niche about 10m right of the gully, climb a groove then traverse left below a roof to the foot of the gully line. Climb the wide crack in the bulge into the gully and continue up the depression. Ascend a steep icefall then continue more easily to Appolyon Ledge. Go up the open chimney and exit right below the big roof then diagonally right to an icicle. Climb this and the icefall above to eventually gain an easy snow groove leading to the top.

The Midge 400m VI,5*
G. Harper and A. Nisbet, 19 February 1983
Another huge route up the wall right of The Fly. Ice is needed in the initial section and in The Fly icefall. Start near the foot of Raeburn's Gully where a fault, Raeburn's Ledge, slopes up to the right. Climb a steep icy corner for two pitches to the left end of a large snow patch. Go up a short groove, then left and climb iced slabs on the right of a big right-facing corner to Vanishing Ledge. Go left to belay below a second right-facing corner. Climb this corner, which leans right at the start with an exit left at the top. Continue up to belay below a roof. Turn this on the right, go left a short way

Good ice on Excasty (left; route not described) and The Fly Direct (right) (photo: Murdoch Jamieson)

and trend right to Appolyon Ledge. Traverse for about 30m left to join and finish up the top three pitches of The Fly Direct.

The White Spider 300m IV,4*
A.L. Wielochowski and J.P. Nash, 16 February 1976
A fine route. Start as for The Midge then traverse 30m rightwards along Raeburn's Ledge to a corner. Climb this to a snowfield (40m). Continue straight up (40m), and then climb a 20m ice pitch on the left to another snowfield. Traverse right for 60m and climb another 20m ice pitch onto a ledge. Finish up the final gully of 1959 Face Route.

A direct start, **White Knuckle Ride (VI,6)**, heads up diagonally rightwards to climb a thin ice pillar (50m), and then moves back left to the end of the initial traverse on the original route (10m).

1959 Face Route 450m V,4**
J.R. Marshall, J. Stenhouse and D. Haston, 9 February 1959
A fine mixed climb which takes a left-slanting line across the lower face to reach the central snowfields, above which the deep prominent gully right of the summit tower is followed. Start in a small bay right of the lowest rocks and about 80m right of Raeburn's Gully. Climb the left-trending depression for 60m then go left into a shallow gully which develops into ice chimneys. A pitch below the ice chimneys, traverse left for 60m to gain a slanting chimney with a prominent chokestone. Climb this for two pitches to the central snowfields. Above enter the obvious gully, turning its barrier icefall on the right, and follow this to the top.

The Post Face   NN 432 879 Crag base altitude 900m East facing

This is the face rising above the wide left-trending Easy Gully and extending right to Staghorn Gully where the cliff bends round into the Inner Corrie. It is characterised by the four large parallel faults of the Post Climbs. These are separated by large buttresses, the Pillars, which give climbs of IV,4 standard. To the right of North Post, the rightmost fault, is Great Buttress whose lower section is cut by two shelves which slant up to the right to two smaller parallel gullies known as the Pipes.

Easy Gully 450m I
W. Tough, W. Douglas and H. Raeburn, April 1896
The obvious wide left-sloping gully. It is narrow at first, widening out at about half-height into open snowfields. The easiest line moves left in the upper section. If used

in descent, keep well out from the Post Face initially, then cut back underneath it in the lower section.

The Last Post 240m V,5***
T.W. Patey and R.F. Brooke, 5 March 1962
An excellent ice route up the left hand of the major faults. Climb the impressive initial icefall starting about halfway up Easy Gully. Above, snowfields lead to the next icefall which is climbed in two pitches. Easy snow then leads to the final icefall, above which easy ground leads to the top. A variation that takes the left-hand side of the initial icefall, then the right-hand side of the second and avoids the final icefall on the left, reduces the grade to IV,4.

Post Horn Gallop 600m IV,4
(no photo topo)
T.W. Patey and R.F. Brooke, 28 February 1962
The third part of the girdle. Start by climbing the first pitch of The Last Post Variation to a ledge and follow this into the South Post below its second main pitch. Go up a short way and right onto a broad ledge, which leads into the Centre Post below its big ice pitch. Follow the ordinary route and continue diagonally to a spectacular ledge crossing the North Post. Continue into the snow bowl of Staghorn Gully.

South Post Direct 300m V,4**
T.W. Patey and R.F. Brooke, 5 March 1962
The second post from the left starts with an impressive icefall which is climbed to easier ground. This leads to the next ice pitch which is climbed diagonally from left to right (crux). Above, the gully and more ice leads to the top. The grade can be reduced to Grade III if the initial icefall is avoided on the right by climbing diagonally left from the base of Centre Post to join the main route, and if the crux pitch is avoided on the left.

Centre Post 400m III**
C.M. Allan and J.H.B. Bell, 21 March 1937
This is the third fault from the left. The first 250m are straightforward and lead to a huge icefall. Make a diagonal traverse up the right wall of the gully and climb an ice pitch to the snowfield above. This is climbed until a traverse back rejoins the main gully, which is followed to the top.

Centre Post Direct 60m V,5**
B. Robertson, F. Harper and E. Cairns, 22 February 1964
Centre Post Direct takes the huge icefall direct, the first half being the steepest but the top is only slightly easier. Can vary in size from about 45m to 60m in height depending on the build-up and can be very hard early in the season.

Winter Climbs in the Cairngorms

The steep crux of North Post (photo: Pete MacPherson)

North Post 400m V,5***
T.W. Patey, J.H. Deacon, G.R. McLeod and P. Danelet, 6 February 1960
The rightmost and narrowest of the posts gives a good route when in condition. Easy snow leads to a steep narrow chimney gully with a chokestone (crux). Above, the gully widens and a chimney in the left corner eventually leads to a ledge and then to a large platform on the right. Traverse back left for 25m across the face, overlooking the gully. A further 30m, first rightwards then leftwards, leads to open snow slopes and the top.

    Direct Finish 60m VI,5* ** Where the gully widens, climb a steep icefall instead of the chimney in the corner to reach the snow ledges of Post Horn Gallop. Above, thinner ice leads to the top.

Postman Pat 290m VII,7**
A. Perkins and M. Duff, 10 February 1991
A fine hard route combining steep ice and technical mixed climbing. Above the lower section of Staghorn Gully lies a sloping shelf above an overhanging wall. Two icicles sometimes form down this wall. Climb the left-hand icicle to the shelf and head along this to belay below a narrow turf ledge (45m). Traverse left along this ledge for about 5m until it is possible to climb steeply through the wall (crux) to reach a wide shallow

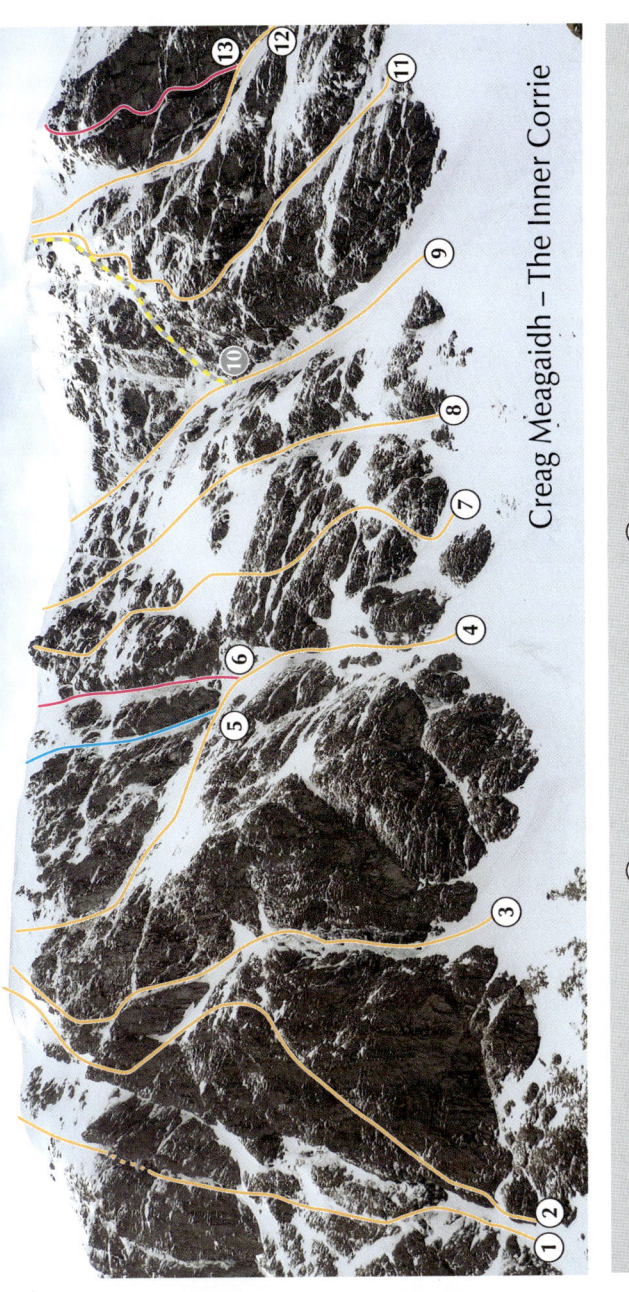

Creag Meagaidh – The Inner Corrie

1. South Pipe IV,4**
2. Trespasser Buttress IV,5**
3. The Pumpkin V,4***
4. The Sash II*
5. The Wand V,5***
6. Diadem IV,4*
7. Fairy Godmother III,4**
8. Glass Slipper II*
9. Cinderella II*
10. The Prow III
11. The Ugly Sister III
12. Crescent Gully II
13. Gully of the Sods VI,6**

gully (45m). Two pitches then lead to the Post Horn Gallop terrace (100m). Another two pitches up icy runnels and snow slopes lead to the top (100m). In good conditions it is sometimes possible to avoid the traverse left on pitch two by climbing the wall direct on ice.

Postal Strike 250m VII,6**

(no photo topo)

C. Harrison and S. Fortune, 30 January 2010

Another fine route starting up the obvious icefall up and right of the Postman Pat icicles, then taking a steep and exposed line up the buttress above. Climb the steep icefall to belay on, or just below, the sloping shelf (40m). Trend up and right to gain a turfy traverse line and follow this back left past a small groove to gain a large hanging groove. Continue up the left rib of this to belay where the angle eases (50m). Follow the left-facing corner to the big ledge of Post Horn Gallop and traverse left to join and finish up Postman Pat (160m).

Staghorn Gully 400m III*** ◇ or ⓧ

C.N.M. Allan, J.H.B. Bell, H.M. Kelly and H. Cooper, 29 April 1934

Where the Post Face bends round into the Inner Corrie, there are two parallel gullies in the upper part of the face. These are the South and North Pipes. Staghorn Gully finishes up the latter. It is a justifiably popular route. Start at the foot of North Post and climb a shallow gully and shelf diagonally rightwards to reach these chimneys. The right-hand chimney, the North Pipe, gives a series of short ice pitches leading to a snow bowl then the top. A more direct variation, which starts up and right of the main route and climbs a shallow gully to gain the North Pipe, can be climbed at the same grade.

South Pipe 250m IV,4** ⓧ

J.H. Deacon and T.W. Patey, 7 February 1960

Start up the Direct Start to Staghorn Gully then climb the South Pipe, the left hand of the parallel chimneys. This gives a fine, icy climb.

The Inner Corrie   NN 430 883 Crag base altitude 900m North-east facing

This lies between Staghorn Gully and the Window and is generally less steep and more broken than the other buttresses but may hold its conditions for longer. The main features of this cliff are firstly the large icy corner of The Pumpkin, then the twin icefalls of The Wand and Diadem higher up the cliff. Right again is the prominent gully of Cinderella, then the rocks become somewhat steeper and are bisected by the distinctive curve of Crescent Gully before diminishing in height towards the Window.

The Last Lap 900m IV,4*
(no photo topo)
A. MacKeith and M. Galbraith, 12 February 1966
The last part of the girdle. Climb the Shelf of Staghorn Gully to below the Pipes and traverse right on ledges into The Sash. Descend this to cross below the icefalls of The Wand and Diadem then go diagonally right onto the snowfield. Traverse this and descend into Cinderella then climb The Prow to a pitch below the top. Move into Crescent Gully and go down to above its ice pitch. Cross the right wall by a spectacular ledge on the vertical wall then continue across to the Window.

To link Post Horn Gallop to this route, go down The Sash from the snow bowl at the top of Staghorn Gully.

Trespasser Buttress 300m IV,5**
G.N. Hunter, H. MacInnes, D.F. Lang and N. Quinn, March 1969
The buttress between South Pipe Direct and The Pumpkin has a narrow chimney system which slants left to right. Start at the left corner of the buttress and climb up to gain the chimney system which is followed to a snow bay. Move right and climb another chimney to a large overhang. Move right to the Diving Board, an exposed ledge, then continue up easier ground to a large chimney. From the chimney, traverse left to the crest of the upper buttress and follow this. Finish by a small chimney then easier ground.

The Pumpkin 300m V,4***
R. McMillan, G.S. Peet and N. Quinn, 14 April 1968
A classic and very popular ice climb which takes the long right-facing corner right of Trespasser Buttress. The corner is climbed direct to easier ground, above which a left-trending chimney is followed to less demanding climbing and the top.

The Sash 300m II*
T.W. Patey, R.W.P. Barclay, M. Laverty and E. Attfield, March 1963
This starts in the narrow gully below the two parallel icefalls and then trends left across the face. Climb the lower gully direct to below the ice, then go up and left on a series of shelves and ledges to reach the plateau.

The Wand 260m V,5***
Q.T. Crichton, D.F. Lang, G.N. Hunter and N. Quinn, 2 February 1969
The left hand of the parallel icefalls gives a fine route. Climb The Sash to the ice then climb the ice close to the corner. Above the ice, a choice of lines leads to the top.

The final icefall of The Wand (photo: Ali Rose)

Diadem 260m IV,4*
J. Brown and T.W. Patey, 19 February 1964
The right hand and easier of the two icefalls is approached via The Sash. Climb the initial icefall then go up to a long iced corner which is followed to easier ground and then the top.

Fairy Godmother 260m III,4**
M.G. Geddes and N.G. Rayner, 27 December 1970
Between the gullies of The Sash and Cinderella is a buttress with a large central snowfield that gives a varied climb. Start halfway between the The Sash and the narrow initial chimney of Glass Slipper and climb a right-sloping ramp for a pitch. Work up and left by walls and ramps to a snow crest and central snowfield. Climb the obvious short gully which is the left of three faults above the snowfield. Go leftwards up a ramp to above Diadem and finish by the steep tower (crux).

Glass Slipper 240m III*
I. MacEacheran and J. Knight, March 1964
Start at the right of the buttress at a narrow chimney which leads in two pitches to the snowfield. Above this, climb the central of three breaks with one ice pitch to the plateau.

Cinderella 240m II*
W. Tout and T.W. Patey, February 1963
The prominent gully in the centre of the face is climbed direct. It can have a very large cornice which can be a real avalanche danger.

The Ugly Sister 210m III
M.G. Geddes and N.C. Rayner, 27 December 1970
Lies on the buttress between Cinderella and Crescent Gully. Climb a ramp sloping up left to a saddle, then go up the crest for about 6m. Traverse right to a better line going left to the crest and finish up this to a large cornice.

Crescent Gully 210m II ◇ or ⊛
J. Clarkson and R.J. Tanton, 17 February 1958
The curving gully on the buttress left of the Window. Climb a diminishing snow line going slightly left. An ice pitch then leads to the upper snowy amphitheatre.

Gully of the Sods 150m VI,6**
P. Davies and D. O'Sullivan, 29 January 2012
The imposing gully on the right wall of Crescent Gully. Follow the icy gully to a terrace (40m). Go up to the left of the overhanging recess until above the roofs, then make an exposed right traverse to regain ice and the upper gully. Belay on the left on blocks (40m). Easier ground leads to the top.

Winter Climbs in the Cairngorms

Inner Corrie, North Side   NN 432 888 Crag base altitude 900m South facing

This lies on the right side as you enter the corrie, below the summit of Stob Poite Coire Ardair (1053m). There are four buttresses with the largest on the right, separated from the second buttress by the big gully of The Soldier's Song (II/III). Good mixed climbing with an abundance of turf and cracks, with best conditions in early season or in cloudy weather after snow, as the sun quickly strips the routes. Large cornices can form above some of these routes.

Softairnuff 140m IV,4*
G. Ettle, J. Finlay and J. Lyall, 21 November 2016
Climbs the buttress right of the large gully, starting on a big ramp on the right, about 15m left of twin icefalls. Take the left hand of two grooves and the continuation chimney on the left to gain a large terrace. Go up the rib above and over a short wall to a belay ledge in a corner. Go to the right of the blocks above and up by brilliant cracks and edges to a ledge. Pass the final wall on the left.

Inherit the Wind 200m IV,5*
J. Lyall, S. Frazer and M. Twomey, 6 February 2018
Starts up easy mixed ground just right of the large gully to a ledge at 60m, then by corners just left of the crest, moving right at a roof to the edge and up this to a big shelf. Go easily up right to gain a fault left of the crest and follow this to a steep, narrowing chimney, passing a chokestone to a ledge, then easy ground to top.

Ardair Pillar 160m III,4**
J. Lyall and J. Preston, 5 December 2018
Weave a line up the lower scooped face left of the large gully to a big terrace. Sneak round to the right of a steep wall with a prominent crack. Regain the crest and follow the excellent pillar and climb the final snow slope.

Ardairnuff 160m V,6*
J. Lyall and P. MacPherson, 19 November 2016
Follow the left edge of the second buttress, taking in the prominent crack up the steep wall, then the excellent pillar.

Creag Meagaidh – Inner Corrie, North Side

1. Soldarnuif IV,4*
2. Inherit the Wind IV,5
3. The Soldier's Song – II/III
4. Ardair Pillar III,4**
5. Ardarnuif V,6*
6. Eyecatcher – III,4
7. Young Pretender – III,4

Pete MacPherson on the first ascent of Ardairnuff

Appendix A
Useful contacts

Weather

Mountain Weather Information Service: www.mwis.org.uk/forecasts, select 'Cairngorms NP Monadhliath' or 'Southeastern Highlands'

Met Office: www.metoffice.gov.uk/weather/specialist-forecasts/mountain, select 'North Grampian' or 'South Grampian and Southeast Highlands'

Weather data from Creagan Doire Dhonaich, above Drummochter Pass (south-west Cairngorms) at 700m: https://holfuy.com/en/weather/1531

Weather data from Stob Coire Dubh by Creag Meagaidh at 900m: https://holfuy.com/en/weather/1528

Cairngorm Mountain ski area links to weather and webcam images: www.cairngormmountain.co.uk/live-webcams

Avalanche forecasts and safety

Scottish Avalanche Information Service (SAIS): www.sais.gov.uk

Be Avalanche Aware (BAA) guidance: https://beaware.sais.gov.uk

Emergencies

Mountain rescue: tel 999 (ask for police, then ask for mountain rescue)

emergencySMS: www.emergencysms.net

Scottish mountaineering resources

Scottish Mountaineering Club (SMC): www.smc.org.uk

Mountaineering Scotland: www.mountaineering.scot

Scottish Outdoor Access Code: www.nature.scot

Accommodation

Mountaineering Scotland/BMC huts: www.mountaineering.scot/clubs/huts/national-huts

Raeburn hut, Laggan: www.smc.org.uk/huts/raeburn

Winter Climbs in the Cairngorms

Appendix B

Route summary table by area

Route name	Area	Route length (m)	Overall grade	Technical grade	Style	Rating	Page
NORTHERN CAIRNGORMS							
Northern Crags							
Short Ridge	Creagan Cha-no	45	IV	4	🟨		51
Mainmast	Creagan Cha-no	35	IV	5	❎	*	51
Cutty Sark	Creagan Cha-no	35	IV	4	❎	**	52
Auld Reekie	Creagan Cha-no	30	IV	4	❎		52
Direct Start	Creagan Cha-no	10	V	6	🟨		52
Chimney Rib	Creagan Cha-no	40	III	4	🟨	*	52
Recovery Gully	Creagan Cha-no	50	I		◇		52
Frozen Planet	Creagan Cha-no	40	IV	6	❎		52
Anvil Gully	Creagan Cha-no	45	IV	4	❎	*	52
Anvil Corner	Creagan Cha-no	50	VI	6	🟨	**	54
Wile-E-Coyote	Creagan Cha-no	50	IV	4	❎	*	54
Duke's Rib	Creagan Cha-no	55	II/III		🟨	*	54
Jenga Buttress	Creagan Cha-no	55	III	4	🟨	**	56
Daylight Robbery	Creagan Cha-no	55	V	6	🟨	**	56
Smooth as Silk	Creagan Cha-no	55	VII	7	❎	*	56
Arch Rival	Creagan Cha-no	50	V	5	🟨	*	56
Arch Enemy	Creagan Cha-no	50	V	5	❎	*	56
Mac's Crack	Creagan Cha-no	50	V	6	🟨	*	56
Swedish Meatballs	Creagan Cha-no	45	V	5	🟨	*	56
The Opening Break	Coire an t-Sneachda	100	IV	5	❎		59
Honeypot	Coire an t-Sneachda	90	IV	6	❎	**	59
Wachacha	Coire an t-Sneachda	90	VI	7	❎	*	61

Appendix B – Route summary table by area

Route name	Area	Route length (m)	Overall grade	Technical grade	Style	Rating	Page
No Blue Skies	Coire an t-Sneachda	100	VI	7	🗻	**	61
The Melting Pot	Coire an t-Sneachda	90	V	7	🧗	**	62
The Hybrid	Coire an t-Sneachda	100	IV	5	🗻	*	62
The Message	Coire an t-Sneachda	90	IV	6	🧗	***	62
Pot of Gold	Coire an t-Sneachda	90	V	6	🧗	***	62
Mariella	Coire an t-Sneachda	90	VI	7	🧗	*	63
Droidless	Coire an t-Sneachda	90	VI	6	🧗	**	63
The Messenger	Coire an t-Sneachda	90	V	6	🗻	*	63
Sharks Fin Soup	Coire an t-Sneachda	90	V	6	🧗		63
Yukon Jack	Coire an t-Sneachda	90	IV	5	🗻	*	63
The Haston Line	Coire an t-Sneachda	120	III	4	🗻		64
The Slant	Coire an t-Sneachda	120	II		◇ or 🗻		64
Hidden Chimney	Coire an t-Sneachda	110	III		🗻	**	64
Direct Start	Coire an t-Sneachda	40	IV	5	🧗	**	64
Jacob's Edge	Coire an t-Sneachda	90	II		🗻		64
Jacob's Ladder	Coire an t-Sneachda	100	I		◇	*	64
Aladdin's Couloir	Coire an t-Sneachda	180	I		◇ or ⊗		66
Original Route	Coire an t-Sneachda	100	IV	5	🗻	**	66
The Lamp	Coire an t-Sneachda	100	V	6	🗻	*	66
The Prodigal Principal	Coire an t-Sneachda	100	V	5	🧗		66
Doctor's Choice	Coire an t-Sneachda	110	IV	5	🧗	**	67
Doctor Janis	Coire an t-Sneachda	120	V	7	🧗	**	67
The Genie	Coire an t-Sneachda	110	V	7	🧗 or 🧗	***	67
The Magic Crack	Coire an t-Sneachda	100	VII	7	🧗	**	68
Salvation	Coire an t-Sneachda	100	VI	7	🧗	**	68

Winter Climbs in the Cairngorms

Route name	Area	Route length (m)	Overall grade	Technical grade	Style	Rating	Page
Patey's Route	Coire an t-Sneachda	120	IV	5		**	68
Terms of Endearment	Coire an t-Sneachda	100	III				68
Aladdin's Mirror Direct	Coire an t-Sneachda	45	IV	4		**	68
Aladdin's Mirror	Coire an t-Sneachda	180	I		or		69
Pygmy Ridge	Coire an t-Sneachda	90	IV	5		**	69
Central Left Hand	Coire an t-Sneachda	150	I		or	*	69
Central Gully	Coire an t-Sneachda	150	I				69
The Runnel	Coire an t-Sneachda	150	II			**	69
The Grooved Rib	Coire an t-Sneachda	150	III	4		*	70
Crotched Gully	Coire an t-Sneachda	150	II				71
Vortex	Coire an t-Sneachda	60	IV	5		*	71
Spiral Gully	Coire an t-Sneachda	150	II		or	**	71
Direct Finish	Coire an t-Sneachda	40	III			*	71
Wavelength	Coire an t-Sneachda	150	III	4		**	71
Fluted Buttress Direct	Coire an t-Sneachda	150	IV	5		***	71
Broken Gully	Coire an t-Sneachda	130	III			*	72
Fingers Ridge	Coire an t-Sneachda	130	IV	4		**	72
Red Gully	Coire an t-Sneachda	120	II/III			**	72
Western Rib	Coire an t-Sneachda	120	III	4			72
Goat Track Gully	Coire an t-Sneachda	120	II			*	72
Escapologist	Coire an t-Sneachda	55	IV	6			73
Straight to Jail	Coire an t-Sneachda	50	V	5		*	73
Houdini	Coire an t-Sneachda	160	VI	7		***	73
Stirling Bomber	Coire an t-Sneachda	55	V	7		**	75
Jailbreak	Coire an t-Sneachda	110	VII	7	or	*	75

Appendix B – Route summary table by area

Route name	Area	Route length (m)	Overall grade	Technical grade	Style	Rating	Page
Smokestack Lightnin'	Coire an t-Sneachda	140	VI	7	⛰	*	75
Fiacaill Couloir	Coire an t-Sneachda	150	II/III		◇ or ⊛	***	75
Trampled Underfoot	Coire an t-Sneachda	60	IV	4	⛰		76
Rampant	Coire an t-Sneachda	75	IV	5	⛰	**	76
Physical Graffiti	Coire an t-Sneachda	70	IV	6	⛰	**	76
Swan Song	Coire an t-Sneachda	70	V	6	⛰	*	77
Burning and Looting	Coire an t-Sneachda	70	V	6	⛰	*	77
Belhaven	Coire an t-Sneachda	75	V	6	⛰	**	77
Invernookie	Coire an t-Sneachda	120	III	4	⛰	**	77
Short Circuit	Coire an t-Sneachda	110	IV	5	⛰	*	77
Seam-stress	Coire an t-Sneachda	100	IV	6	⛰	**	78
The Seam	Coire an t-Sneachda	100	IV	5	⛰	***	78
The Hurting	Coire an t-Sneachda	35	XI	11	▮		78
Iron Butterfly	Coire an Lochain	150	III		⛰		81
Coronary By-pass	Coire an Lochain	110	V	7	▮	*	81
Auricle	Coire an Lochain	90	VI	7	▮	*	82
Ventriloquist	Coire an Lochain	90	VII	7	▮	**	82
Ventricle	Coire an Lochain	90	VII	8	▮	**	82
Daddy Longlegs	Coire an Lochain	70	VIII	9	▮	**	82
Inventive	Coire an Lochain	70	IV	5	⛰		85
The Vent	Coire an Lochain	100	II/III		⊛	*	85
Ventilator	Coire an Lochain	100	II/III		⛰	*	85
Chute Route	Coire an Lochain	90	V	5	▮	*	85
The Milky Way	Coire an Lochain	110	III		⛰	**	87
Appetite for Destruction	Coire an Lochain	110	V	6	▮	*	87
Andromeda	Coire an Lochain	120	IV	4	▮	**	87

Winter Climbs in the Cairngorms

Route name	Area	Route length (m)	Overall grade	Technical grade	Style	Rating	Page
Astroturfer	Coire an Lochain	120	III			*	87
Central Crack Route	Coire an Lochain	120	IV	5		*	87
The Crack	Coire an Lochain	20	VI	7		**	87
The Inquisition	Coire an Lochain	90	VI	8		**	88
Snow Bunting	Coire an Lochain	90	IV	5			88
Crow's Nest Crack	Coire an Lochain	60	III			*	88
The Couloir	Coire an Lochain	150	I			**	88
Ewen Buttress	Coire an Lochain	90	III			**	88
Ewen Buttress, Direct Start	Coire an Lochain	50	V	6		*	89
The Migrant	Coire an Lochain	100	VI	7		**	90
Migrant Direct	Coire an Lochain	90	VII	8			90
The Vicar	Coire an Lochain	70	VIII	8		***	90
Happy Tyroleans	Coire an Lochain	60	IX	9		**	90
The Overseer Direct	Coire an Lochain	60	V	6		*	90
The Hoarmaster	Coire an Lochain	60	VI	6		***	91
Hooker's Corner	Coire an Lochain	60	VI	6		**	91
Left Branch of Y Gully	Coire an Lochain	100	III				91
Stagefright	Coire an Lochain	50	VI	7		**	91
Grumbling Groove	Coire an Lochain	60	VI	6		*	93
The Head-hunter	Coire an Lochain	60	VI	6		*	93
Right Branch of Y Gully	Coire an Lochain	100	II			*	93
Oesophagus	Coire an Lochain	70	III	4		**	93
Deep Throat	Coire an Lochain	70	V	6		**	93

Appendix B – Route summary table by area

Route name	Area	Route length (m)	Overall grade	Technical grade	Style	Rating	Page
Gaffer's Groove Winter Variation	Coire an Lochain	80	V	5		*	94
Bulgy	Coire an Lochain	80	VII	7		*	94
Savage Slit	Coire an Lochain	90	V	6		***	94
Fall-out Corner	Coire an Lochain	90	VI	7		***	94
The Third Man	Coire an Lochain	100	IV	6		*	95
Sidewinder	Coire an Lochain	110	III	4		**	95
Western Route	Coire an Lochain	120	IV	6		***	95
Torquing Heads	Coire an Lochain	120	VII	7		*	95
North Gully	Lurcher's Crag	240	III			*	97
K9	Lurcher's Crag	180	IV	4		*	97
Window Gully	Lurcher's Crag	180	IV	4			99
Arctic Monkey	Lurcher's Crag	300	III	4		*	99
Central Gully	Lurcher's Crag	300	III			*	99
Diamond Gully	Lurcher's Crag	240	IV	4			100
Eskimo Gully	Lurcher's Crag	240	II			*	100
Doorway Ridge	Lurcher's Crag	200	IV	5		*	100
South Gully	Lurcher's Crag	150	I				100
Pinnacle Ridge	Lurcher's Crag	150	II				100
Drystane Ridge	Lurcher's Crag	100	III				100
Wolfstone Gully	Lurcher's Crag	80	VI	7			102
Quinn	Lurcher's Crag	80	III	4		*	102
Collie's Ridge	Lurcher's Crag	120	II			*	102
Deerhound Ridge	Lurcher's Crag	180	III				102

Winter Climbs in the Cairngorms

Route name	Area	Route length (m)	Overall grade	Technical grade	Style	Rating	Page
Polar Bear	Sron na Lairige	200	IV	5	mixed	*	104
Ghruvy Gully	Sron na Lairige	220	III		ice	**	104
White Hunter	Sron na Lairige	220	IV	5	mixed	*	104
Ghruling Gully	Sron na Lairige	220	III		snow/ice		105
Ghrupie	Sron na Lairige	200	V	5	mixed	**	105
Ghruve	Sron na Lairige	220	II		snow	*	105
Braer Rabbit	Sron na Lairige	130	IV	4	mixed	*	105
Idiot Proof	Sron na Lairige	130	IV	6	mixed	*	105
Gormless	Sron na Lairige	130	III		mixed	*	107
Pupster	Sron na Lairige	130	III		mixed	*	107
Sinclair's Last Stand	Sron na Lairige	150	III		snow/ice	*	107
Cerro Norrie Finish	Sron na Lairige	40	V	5	mixed		107
Lairig Ridge	Sron na Lairige	200	IV	5	snow/ice	**	107

Loch Avon basin

Route name	Area	Route length (m)	Overall grade	Technical grade	Style	Rating	Page
Rectangular Gully	Stac an Fharaidh	140	I/II		snow or ice		114
Apres Moi	Stac an Fharaidh	150	III		ice	*	114
Sermon	Stac an Fharaidh	120	V	6	snow/ice	**	114
Spirit Voices	Stac an Fharaidh	120	VI	8	snow/ice		115
Not Fade Away	Stac an Fharaidh	120	V	6	snow/ice	**	115
Rectangular Rib	Stac an Fharaidh	120	III		mixed		115
Narrow Gully	Stac an Fharaidh	160	I/II		snow or ice	*	115
The Overflow	Stag Rocks	45	III		ice		117
Cascade	Stag Rocks	45	V	5	ice	***	118
Cascade Right-hand	Stag Rocks	45	IV	4	ice		118
Truly, Madly, Chimbley	Stag Rocks	90	III		snow/ice	**	119
Afterthought Arête	Stag Rocks	150	III		snow/ice	*	119

Appendix B – Route summary table by area

Route name	Area	Route length (m)	Overall grade	Technical grade	Style	Rating	Page
CM Gully	Stag Rocks	140	II/III		🟩		121
Diagonal Gully	Stag Rocks	250	I		◇		121
Final Groove	Stag Rocks	70	II/III		🟦		121
Bambi	Stag Rocks	70	IV	5	🟫		121
Purge	Stag Rocks	80	IV	4	✕	*	121
Albino	Stag Rocks	80	IV	5	🟦	*	122
Apex Gully	Stag Rocks	150	III		ⓘ		122
Light Entertainment	Stag Rocks	140	III	4	✕	*	122
Groove and Rib	Stag Rocks	140	V	6	🟦 or 🟫	**	122
Honest Outlet	Stag Rocks	150	IV	5	🟦 or 🟫	*	122
Deception Inlet	Stag Rocks	150	IV	5	🟩		122
Monarch of the Glen	Stag Rocks	160	VI	7	🟫	*	123
Pine Tree Route	Stag Rocks	200	IV	4	✕		123
Amphitheatre Gully	Stag Rocks	220	V	6	🟦	***	123
Stagnant Gully	Stag Rocks	180	IV	4	🟩		123
Sneer	Hell's Lum Crag	120	II/III		ⓘ		125
The Escalator	Hell's Lum Crag	150	II/III		◇ or ⓘ	*	126
Auld Nick	Hell's Lum Crag	150	III		ⓘ		127
Kiwi Slabs	Hell's Lum Crag	150	IV	4	ⓘ	*	127
Kiwi Gully	Hell's Lum Crag	150	IV	4	ⓘ	**	127
The Wee Devil	Hell's Lum Crag	150	IV	5	🟦	*	127
Devil's Delight	Hell's Lum Crag	160	V	5	Ⓘ	***	127
Hellfire Corner	Hell's Lum Crag	160	VI	7	🟦	**	129
Salamander	Hell's Lum Crag	160	V	4	Ⓘ	**	129
Brimstone Groove	Hell's Lum Crag	160	IV	4	Ⓘ	**	129

Winter Climbs in the Cairngorms

Route name	Area	Route length (m)	Overall grade	Technical grade	Style	Rating	Page
Towering Inferno	Hell's Lum Crag	160	VI	5	ice	*	129
Nobody's Fault	Hell's Lum Crag	160	IV	6	ice	**	129
Deep Cut Chimney	Hell's Lum Crag	160	IV	4	ice or mixed	***	130
Hell's Lum	Hell's Lum Crag	150	II/III		snow or gully	***	130
The Chancer	Hell's Lum Crag	90	V	6	gully	**	130
The Gullet	Hell's Lum Crag	130	III		ice	*	130
Blunderbuss	Garbh Uisge Crag	150	III		mixed		131
Garbh Gully	Garbh Uisge Crag	150	III		gully	*	131
Quartz Gully	Garbh Uisge Crag	90	II		gully	*	133
Castle Wall	Shelter Stone Crag	210	IV	5	buttress		136
Breach Gully	Shelter Stone Crag	240	IV	5	buttress		136
Raeburn's Buttress	Shelter Stone Crag	240	IV	5	buttress	*	136
Sticil Face	Shelter Stone Crag	260	V	6	ice	***	136
Citadel	Shelter Stone Crag	270	VII	8	buttress	***	137
Citadel Winter Variation	Shelter Stone Crag	130	VI	8	buttress	**	138
Clach Dhian Chimney	Shelter Stone Crag	220	V	5	buttress	*	138
Postern Variations	Shelter Stone Crag	240	VI	6	buttress	**	138
Western Grooves	Shelter Stone Crag	220	IV	5	buttress	*	140
Unknown Gully	Shelter Stone Crag	150	III		ice	*	140
Games of Chance	Shelter Stone Crag	90	VI	7	ice	*	140
Pinnacle Gully	Shelter Stone Crag	250	I		snow		140
Eastern Approach Route	Carn Etchachan	100	IV	5	buttress	*	142
The Silent Approach	Carn Etchachan	110	IV	6	buttress	*	142

Appendix B – Route summary table by area

Route name	Area	Route length (m)	Overall grade	Technical grade	Style	Rating	Page
Western Approach Route	Carn Etchachan	110	III		⊠	*	144
Crevasse Route	Carn Etchachan	75	V	6	⊠	*	144
Equinox	Carn Etchachan	90	VI	6	⊠	**	144
Nathrach Dubh	Carn Etchachan	100	VI	6	◩	**	144
Snake Charmer	Carn Etchachan	90	V	6	⊠	**	147
The Guillotine	Carn Etchachan	100	V	6	⊠	***	147
Nom-de-Plume	Carn Etchachan	90	VI	6	◩	**	147
Pagan Slit	Carn Etchachan	90	V	6	◩	**	147
Route Major	Carn Etchachan	290	IV	5	⊠	***	147
Red Guard	Carn Etchachan	250	VI	6	⊠	**	148
Scorpion	Carn Etchachan	240	V	5	◩	***	148
The Sword	Carn Etchachan	250	V	5	⊠	**	149
Siberia	Carn Etchachan	210	IV	5	⊠		149
Sideslip	Carn Etchachan	150	III		◇ ◩	*	149
Castle Gully	Carn Etchachan	150	III		🌀		149
Castlegates Gully	Carn Etchachan	210	I		◇	**	149

Ben Macdui crags

Route name	Area	Route length (m)	Overall grade	Technical grade	Style	Rating	Page
Quartzvein Edge	Creagan a' Choire Etchachan	120	III		⊠	*	152
Bastion Wall	Creagan a' Choire Etchachan	150	IV	4	⊠		152
Original Route Direct	Creagan a' Choire Etchachan	150	V	6	⊠	*	153
The Corridor	Creagan a' Choire Etchachan	120	IV	5	🌀	**	153
Architrave	Creagan a' Choire Etchachan	120	IV	4	◩	*	153
Central Chimney	Creagan a' Choire Etchachan	120	III		◩	*	155

Winter Climbs in the Cairngorms

Route name	Area	Route length (m)	Overall grade	Technical grade	Style	Rating	Page
Square-cut Gully	Creagan a' Choire Etchachan	150	V	6	❄	**	155
Winter Route	Creagan a' Choire Etchachan	150	III		🗻		155
Carmine Groove	Creagan a' Choire Etchachan	150	IV	5	🗻	*	155
Flanking Ribs	Creagan a' Choire Etchachan	150	IV	4	🗻 or 🗻		155
Red Chimney	Creagan a' Choire Etchachan	150	V	5	❄	**	155
Djibangi	Creagan a' Choire Etchachan	140	V	4	🗻	***	156
Scabbard	Creagan a' Choire Etchachan	140	VI	7	🗻	**	158
Switchblade	Creagan a' Choire Etchachan	160	VI	7	⛰	**	158
Pinnacle Buttress	Coire Sputan Dearg	120	III		⛰	**	161
Red Gully	Coire Sputan Dearg	120	I		◇		161
Crystal Ridge	Coire Sputan Dearg	90	IV	4	🗻	*	161
Slab Chimney	Coire Sputan Dearg	120	II/III		❄	**	161
Ardath Chimney	Coire Sputan Dearg	120	III		❄	**	162
Anchor Gully	Coire Sputan Dearg	120	I		◇	*	162
Anchor Route	Coire Sputan Dearg	120	III		🗻	*	162
Snake Gully	Coire Sputan Dearg	130	II		◇	*	162
The Ladders	Coire Sputan Dearg	120	II		◇	*	162
Narrow Gully	Coire Sputan Dearg	130	I		◇		164
Cherub's Buttress	Coire Sputan Dearg	130	III		⛰		164
Flying Ridge	Coire Sputan Dearg	130	II		⛰		164
Left-hand Icefall	Coire Sputan Dearg	90	IV	4	🧊		164
Right-hand Icefall	Coire Sputan Dearg	90	II/IV		🧊	*	164
Flake Buttress	Coire Sputan Dearg	120	III		⛰	**	164

Appendix B – Route summary table by area

Route name	Area	Route length (m)	Overall grade	Technical grade	Style	Rating	Page
Terminal Buttress	Coire Sputan Dearg	70	IV	5			165
Cairn Toul/Braeriach amphitheatre							
Lochan Uaine Waterfall	Angel's Peak	100	II				170
Angel's Ridge	Angel's Peak	300	I			***	171
The Shroud	Corrie of the Chokestone Gully	160	III			*	173
Chokestone Gully	Corrie of the Chokestone Gully	150	III			**	173
Bugaboo Rib	Corrie of the Chokestone Gully	150	V	7		*	174
Sasquatch	Corrie of the Chokestone Gully	120	III			*	174
Crown Buttress	Garbh Choire Mor	120	III			*	177
Great Gully	Garbh Choire Mor	120	I				177
She-Devil's Corner	Garbh Choire Mor	120	IV	5		**	177
Vulcan	Garbh Choire Mor	100	V	4		***	178
Bunting's Gully	Garbh Choire Mor	100	III				178
Snow Bunting	Garbh Choire Mor	100	II			*	178
Solo Gully	Garbh Choire Mor	100	I			*	178
Sphinx Ridge	Garbh Choire Mor	100	III			**	178
Sphinx Gully	Garbh Choire Mor	100	II				179
Pinnacle Gully	Garbh Choire Mor	100	I			*	179
Pinnacles Buttress	Garbh Choire Mor	100	III				179
Phoenix Gully	Garbh Choire Mor	100	IV	4		**	181
White Nile	Garbh Choire Mor	100	V	5		**	181
Phoenix Buttress	Garbh Choire Mor	120	IV	4		**	181
Forked Lightning Route	Garbh Choire Mor	100	III			*	181

Winter Climbs in the Cairngorms

Route name	Area	Route length (m)	Overall grade	Technical grade	Style	Rating	Page
Billabong	Garbh Choire Dhaidh	150	III		®		184
The Culvert	Garbh Choire Dhaidh	130	V	4	®	*	184
The Great Rift	Garbh Choire Dhaidh	140	V	5		**	184
Pommie Granite	Garbh Choire Dhaidh	130	V	6		**	184
Boomerang	Garbh Choire Dhaidh	150	IV	4		*	184
Twilight Gully	Garbh Choire Dhaidh	150	II		◇ or ®	**	184
Helicon Rib	Garbh Choire Dhaidh	140	III				185
The Chimney Pot	Garbh Choire Dhaidh	140	II/III				185
Pioneers' Recess Route	Coire Bhrochain	200	III				188
Direct Route	Coire Bhrochain	200	IV	5		*	188
Vanishing Shelf	Coire Bhrochain	200	III				188
The Great Couloir	Coire Bhrochain	200	III		®	**	188
Ebony Chimney	Coire Bhrochain	80	VI	6		***	188
Domed Ridge	Coire Bhrochain	200	III			*	189
West Gully	Coire Bhrochain	150	I		◇		189
Bhrochain Slabs	Coire Bhrochain	200	III			*	189
Braeriach Direct	Coire Bhrochain	200	IV	3			190
Braeriach Pinnacle South Face	Coire Bhrochain	130	III				190
Braeriach Pinnacle Eastern Route	Coire Bhrochain	130	II				190
East Gully	Coire Bhrochain	130	I		◇	*	190

Appendix B – Route summary table by area

Route name	Area	Route length (m)	Overall grade	Technical grade	Style	Rating	Page
Near East Buttress	Coire Bhrochain	110	II		mixed		190
Tigris Chimney	Coire Bhrochain	100	II		mixed		190
Pyramus	Coire Bhrochain	110	I		snow		192
Thisbe	Coire Bhrochain	110	III		mixed	**	192
Beinn a'Bhuird							
Neptune's Groove	Coire na Ciche	100	IV	6	buttress		196
The Carpet	Coire na Ciche	110	VI	5	mixed or ice	*	198
Slugain Buttress	Coire na Ciche	130	III		buttress	*	198
Twisting Gully	Coire na Ciche	130	II		snow or gully	**	198
Hourglass Buttress	Coire na Ciche	120	V	6	mixed	*	198
Sickle	Coire na Ciche	110	IV	5	buttress	*	198
Jason's Chimney	Coire na Ciche	100	V	6	buttress	**	199
South Corner Gully	Coire na Ciche	120	I		snow		199
Alchemist's Route	Garbh Choire	230	III		snow or gully		201
Gold Coast Direct	Garbh Choire	180	V	5	ice	***	202
Crucible Route	Garbh Choire	210	VI	5	ice	**	202
Consolation Gully	Garbh Choire	200	II		snow		202
Comala's Ridge	Garbh Choire	200	II		snow or buttress	*	202
The Flume	Garbh Choire	200	II		gully	**	202
Left-hand Finish	Garbh Choire		IV	4	gully	*	202
The Flume Direct	Garbh Choire		IV	4	gully	**	202
South-East Gully	Garbh Choire	200	V	4	gully	*	205

Winter Climbs in the Cairngorms

Route name	Area	Route length (m)	Overall grade	Technical grade	Style	Rating	Page
East Wall Direct	Garbh Choire	220	IV	5		**	205
The Grail	Garbh Choire	250	V	5		*	205
Mitre Ridge	Garbh Choire	220	V	6		***	205
Cumming-Crofton Route	Garbh Choire	160	VI	6		***	205
North-West Gully	Garbh Choire	150	III			*	206

SOUTHERN CAIRNGORMS
Loch Muick crags

Route name	Area	Route length (m)	Overall grade	Technical grade	Style	Rating	Page
Perseverance Rib	Lochnagar	80	III				215
Gale Force Groove	Lochnagar	70	III			*	215
Lunar Eclipse	Lochnagar	85	III			*	215
The Gift	Lochnagar	80	II			*	215
Temptress	Lochnagar	80	III			*	215
Windfall	Lochnagar	80	III			*	217
Transept Groove	Lochnagar	90	IV	5		**	217
Transept Route	Lochnagar	100	V	6		*	217
Sepulchre	Lochnagar	100	V	6		**	217
Judas Priest	Lochnagar	100	V	6		*	217
Trinity	Lochnagar	100	VI	7		*	219
Cathedral Chimney	Lochnagar	80	IV	4	or	*	219
Magic Pillar	Lochnagar	80	IV	5		**	219
Forsaken Gully	Lochnagar	90	II				219
Central Buttress	Lochnagar	300	II			*	221
Mantichore	Lochnagar	60	VII	7		*	221
Central Buttress Direct	Lochnagar	90	IV	6		*	221

Appendix B – Route summary table by area

Route name	Area	Route length (m)	Overall grade	Technical grade	Style	Rating	Page
Centrist	Lochnagar	140	V	6	⛰	**	221
Shallow Gully	Lochnagar	300	IV	4	🧊		223
Shadowlands	Lochnagar	250	VI	7	⛰	**	223
Shadow Buttress A	Lochnagar	300	IV	5	⛰	***	223
Shadow Chimney	Lochnagar	220	IV	4	⛰		223
Moonshadow	Lochnagar	220	V	5	⛰	**	223
Giant's Head Chimney	Lochnagar	220	IV	4	🧊	*	224
Polyphemus Gully	Lochnagar	200	V	5	❄	***	224
Shadow Buttress B, Bell's Route	Lochnagar	200	V	6	🧊	**	224
Penumbra	Lochnagar	110	V	5	🧊	*	224
Douglas-Gibson Gully	Lochnagar	200	V	4	❄	**	224
Eagle Ridge	Lochnagar	250	VI	6	🧊	***	227
Tough-Brown Traverse	Lochnagar	300	IV	3	🧊	**	227
Parallel Gully A	Lochnagar	270	III		❄	**	227
Parallel Buttress	Lochnagar	280	VI	6	⛰	***	228
Parallel Gully B	Lochnagar	280	VI	5	❄	***	228
Trail of Tears	Lochnagar	130	VII	8	🧊 🧊	***	228
Mort	Lochnagar	130	IX	9	🧊 🧊	***	229
Tough Guy	Lochnagar	120	VII	7	⛰	*	229
Tough-Brown Ridge Direct	Lochnagar	250	V	6	⛰	**	229
Backdoor Route	Lochnagar	220	IV	4	⛰	*	229
Raeburn's Gully	Lochnagar	200	II		◇ or ❄	***	230
The Gutter	Lochnagar	80	III		❄		230

301

Winter Climbs in the Cairngorms

Route name	Area	Route length (m)	Overall grade	Technical grade	Style	Rating	Page
Scarface	Lochnagar	170	V	4		*	230
Pinnacle Gully 1	Lochnagar	200	III				231
Pinnacle Face	Lochnagar	200	VI	7		**	232
Route 1	Lochnagar	200	V	6		**	232
The Link Direct	Lochnagar	185	VII	7	or	***	232
The Ice Ox	Lochnagar	100	IV	5		*	233
Pinnacle Gully 2	Lochnagar	90	II				233
Black Spout Left Branch	Lochnagar	250	I			***	233
Crumbling Cranny	Lochnagar	60	II				233
The Stack	Lochnagar	150	V	6		*	233
The White Spout	Lochnagar	70	IV	4			236
The Black Spout	Lochnagar	250	I			**	236
Black Spout Buttress	Lochnagar	250	III	5		**	236
Gargoyle Chimney	Lochnagar	120	IV	4		**	236
Prince of Darkness	Lochnagar	70	VI	7		**	236
West Gully	Lochnagar	250	IV	4		*	238
Gelder Gully	Lochnagar	250	II				238
South-East Buttress	Creag an Dubh Loch	200	II			*	241
South-East Gully	Creag an Dubh Loch	200	II			**	241
The Last Oasis	Creag an Dubh Loch	300	VI	6		**	241
Bower Buttress	Creag an Dubh Loch	300	V	5		**	242
The Aqueduct	Creag an Dubh Loch	120	V	5		**	242
Yeti	Creag an Dubh Loch	300	V	4		**	242

Appendix B – Route summary table by area

Route name	Area	Route length (m)	Overall grade	Technical grade	Style	Rating	Page
Hanging Garden Route	Creag an Dubh Loch	300	V	4	❄	***	242
Labyrinth Direct	Creag an Dubh Loch	300	VII	6	❄	***	242
Labyrinth Edge	Creag an Dubh Loch	300	IV	5	⛶	*	244
Mammoth	Creag an Dubh Loch	360	IV	4	🗻		244
The White Elephant	Creag an Dubh Loch	320	VII	6	🗻	**	244
Theseus Grooves	Creag an Dubh Loch	300	III		🗻 or 🗻	*	244
Centaur	Creag an Dubh Loch	300	III		⛶		245
Central Gully Buttress	Creag an Dubh Loch	300	II		⛶		246
Central Gully	Creag an Dubh Loch	300	I		◇	*	246
Sabre Cut	Creag an Dubh Loch	80	IV	5	❄	*	246
Vertigo Wall	Creag an Dubh Loch	160	VII	7	🗻	***	246
More Vertigo Finish	Creag an Dubh Loch	65	VII	8	🗻	**	246
Mousetrap	Creag an Dubh Loch	180	VII	8	🗻 🗻	**	247
North-West Buttress	Creag an Dubh Loch	200	III		⛶		247
North-West Gully	Creag an Dubh Loch	200	II/III		🗻	**	247
The Waterfall	Eagles Rock	150	II		❅	*	248
Spectrum	Eagles Rock	110	III		❅	**	248
Lethargy	Eagles Rock	120	II/III		❅	*	248
Indolence	Eagles Rock	140	III		❅	*	248
Nomad's Crack	Eagles Rock	150	V	5	❅	*	248
Sliver	Eagles Rock	150	III		❅	*	248
Gibber	Eagles Rock	130	IV	3	❅	*	249
Funeral Fall	Broad Cairn Bluffs	60	IV	4	❅	**	252
Glen Clova							
The Waterfall	The Winter Corrie	70	II/III		❅	*	254

303

Winter Climbs in the Cairngorms

Route name	Area	Route length (m)	Overall grade	Technical grade	Style	Rating	Page
Central Gully	The Winter Corrie	120	II		◇ or ⦿		256
Easy Gully	The Winter Corrie	120	I		◇		256
Backdoor Chimney	The Winter Corrie	200	III		🪜	*	256
Backdoor Gully	The Winter Corrie	200	II		◇	*	256
Diagonal Gully	The Winter Corrie	200	III		⦿	**	256
Pinnacle Gully	The Winter Corrie	120	II		◇		256
Wiggle	The Winter Corrie	120	III		⛰		256
The Shute	The Winter Corrie	120	I		◇		256
A Gully	Corrie Fee	200	I		◇		257
A-B Integrate	Corrie Fee	200	II		◇ or ⦿		261
B Gully Chimney	Corrie Fee	150	III	4	🪜	**	261
B Gully	Corrie Fee	200	II		🪜	**	261
Look C Gully	Corrie Fee	200	IV	4	⦿	***	261
Wet Knees	Corrie Fee	200	IV	4	🪜	*	261
D Gully	Corrie Fee	200	I		◇		261
The Pyramid	Corrie Fee	60	IV	5	⛰		261
E Gully	Corrie Fee	60	I		◇		261

CREAG MEAGAIDH

Route name	Area	Route length (m)	Overall grade	Technical grade	Style	Rating	Page
Crab Crawl	Coire Ardair	2400	IV	4	🪜 🪜	***	268
The Scene	Coire Ardair	450	II		◇	*	268
Eastern Corner	Coire Ardair	300	III		◇ or ⦿	**	268
Barry White	Coire Ardair	130	IV	6	⛰	*	269
Do What Thou Wilt	Coire Ardair	100	IV	4	🪜	**	269
Raeburn's Gully	Coire Ardair	350	I		◇	***	269
Appolyon Ledge	Coire Ardair	500	II		◇	**	270
Ritchie's Gully	Coire Ardair	160	IV	4	⦿	**	271

Appendix B – Route summary table by area

Route name	Area	Route length (m)	Overall grade	Technical grade	Style	Rating	Page
Smith's Gully	Coire Ardair	180	VI	5	🧗	***	271
The Fly Direct	Coire Ardair	240	VII	6	🧊	***	271
The Midge	Coire Ardair	400	VI	5	🧊	*	271
The White Spider	Coire Ardair	300	IV	4	🧊	*	273
1959 Face Route	Coire Ardair	450	V	4	🧊	**	273
Easy Gully	Coire Ardair	450	I		◇		273
The Last Post	Coire Ardair	240	V	5	🧗	***	275
Post Horn Gallop	Coire Ardair	600	IV	4	🧊		275
South Post Direct	Coire Ardair	300	V	4	🧗	**	275
Centre Post	Coire Ardair	400	III		◇ 🧗	**	275
Centre Post Direct	Coire Ardair	60	V	5	🧗	**	275
North Post	Coire Ardair	400	V	5	🧊	***	276
Postman Pat	Coire Ardair	290	VII	7	🧊	**	276
Postal Strike	Coire Ardair	250	VII	6	🧊	**	278
Staghorn Gully	Coire Ardair	400	III		◇ or 🧗	***	278
South Pipe	Coire Ardair	250	IV	4	🧗	**	278
The Last Lap	Coire Ardair	900	IV	4	🧊	*	279
Trespasser Buttress	Coire Ardair	300	IV	5	🗲	**	279
The Pumpkin	Coire Ardair	300	V	4	🧗	***	279
The Sash	Coire Ardair	300	II		◇	*	279
The Wand	Coire Ardair	260	V	5	🧗	***	279
Diadem	Coire Ardair	260	IV	4	🧗	*	280
Fairy Godmother	Coire Ardair	260	III	4	🧊	**	281
Glass Slipper	Coire Ardair	240	III		🧊	*	281
Cinderella	Coire Ardair	240	II		◇	*	281
The Ugly Sister	Coire Ardair	210	III		🗲		281

Winter Climbs in the Cairngorms

Route name	Area	Route length (m)	Overall grade	Technical grade	Style	Rating	Page
Crescent Gully	Coire Ardair	210	II		◇ or ⓧ		281
Gully of the Sods	Coire Ardair	150	VI	6	🧊	**	281
Softairnuff	Coire Ardair	140	IV	4	⛰	*	282
Inherit the Wind	Coire Ardair	200	IV	5	⛰	*	282
Ardair Pillar	Coire Ardair	160	III	4	🧗	**	282
Ardairnuff	Coire Ardair	160	V	6	⛰	*	282

NOTES

NOTES

Listing of Cicerone guides

BRITISH ISLES CHALLENGES, COLLECTIONS AND ACTIVITIES
Cycling Land's End to John o' Groats
Great Walks on the England Coast Path
The Big Rounds
The Book of the Bivvy
The Book of the Bothy
The Mountains of England & Wales:
 Vol 1 Wales
 Vol 2 England
The National Trails
Walking the End to End Trail

SHORT WALKS SERIES
Short Walks Hadrian's Wall
Short Walks in Arnside and Silverdale
Short Walks in Dumfries and Galloway
Short Walks in Nidderdale
Short Walks in the Lake District: Windermere Ambleside and Grasmere
Short Walks in the Surrey Hills
Short Walks Lake District – Coniston and Langdale
Short Walks on the Malvern Hills
Short Walks Winchester

SCOTLAND
Ben Nevis and Glen Coe
Cycle Touring in Northern Scotland
Cycling in the Hebrides
Cycling the North Coast 500
Great Mountain Days in Scotland
Mountain Biking in Southern and Central Scotland
Mountain Biking in West and North West Scotland
Not the West Highland Way Scotland
Scotland's Best Small Mountains
Scotland's Mountain Ridges
Scottish Wild Country Backpacking
Skye's Cuillin Ridge Traverse
The Borders Abbeys Way
The Great Glen Way
The Great Glen Way Map Booklet
The Hebridean Way
The Hebrides
The Isle of Mull
The Isle of Skye
The Skye Trail
The Southern Upland Way
The West Highland Way
The West Highland Way Map Booklet
Walking Ben Lawers, Rannoch and Atholl
Walking in the Cairngorms
Walking in the Pentland Hills
Walking in the Scottish Borders
Walking in the Southern Uplands
Walking in Torridon, Fisherfield, Fannichs and An Teallach
Walking Loch Lomond and the Trossachs
Walking on Arran
Walking on Harris and Lewis
Walking on Jura, Islay and Colonsay
Walking on Rum and the Small Isles
Walking on the Orkney and Shetland Isles
Walking on Uist and Barra
Walking the Cape Wrath Trail
Walking the Corbetts
 Vol 1 South of the Great Glen
 Vol 2 North of the Great Glen
Walking the Galloway Hills
Walking the John o' Groats Trail
Walking the Munros
 Vol 1 – Southern, Central and Western Highlands
 Vol 2 – Northern Highlands and the Cairngorms
Winter Climbs in the Cairngorms
Winter Climbs: Ben Nevis and Glen Coe

NORTHERN ENGLAND ROUTES
Cycling the Reivers Route
Cycling the Way of the Roses
Hadrian's Cycleway
Hadrian's Wall Path
Hadrian's Wall Path Map Booklet
The Coast to Coast Cycle Route
The Coast to Coast Walk
The Coast to Coast Walk Map Booklet
The Pennine Way
The Pennine Way Map Booklet
Walking the Dales Way
Walking the Dales Way Map Booklet

NORTH-EAST ENGLAND, YORKSHIRE DALES AND PENNINES
Cycling in the Yorkshire Dales
Great Mountain Days in the Pennines
Mountain Biking in the Yorkshire Dales
The Cleveland Way and the Yorkshire Wolds Way
The Cleveland Way Map Booklet
The North York Moors
Trail and Fell Running in the Yorkshire Dales
Walking in County Durham
Walking in Northumberland
Walking in the North Pennines
Walking in the Yorkshire Dales: North and East
Walking in the Yorkshire Dales: South and West
Walking St Cuthbert's Way
Walking St Oswald's Way and Northumberland Coast Path

NORTH-WEST ENGLAND AND THE ISLE OF MAN
Cycling the Pennine Bridleway
Isle of Man Coastal Path
The Lancashire Cycleway
The Lune Valley and Howgills
Walking in Cumbria's Eden Valley
Walking in Lancashire
Walking in the Forest of Bowland and Pendle
Walking on the Isle of Man
Walking on the West Pennine Moors
Walking the Ribble Way
Walks in Silverdale and Arnside

LAKE DISTRICT
Bikepacking in the Lake District
Cycling in the Lake District
Great Mountain Days in the Lake District
Joss Naylor's Lakes, Meres and Waters of the Lake District
Lake District Winter Climbs
Lake District: High Level and Fell Walks
Lake District: Low Level and Lake Walks
Mountain Biking in the Lake District
Outdoor Adventures with Children – Lake District
Scrambles in the Lake District – North
Scrambles in the Lake District – South
Trail and Fell Running in the Lake District
Walking The Cumbria Way
Walking the Lake District Fells:
 Borrowdale
 Buttermere
 Coniston
 Keswick
 Langdale
 Mardale and the Far East
 Patterdale
 Wasdale
Walking the Tour of the Lake District

DERBYSHIRE, PEAK DISTRICT AND MIDLANDS

Cycling in the Peak District
Dark Peak Walks
Scrambles in the Dark Peak
Walking in Derbyshire
Walking in the Peak District – White Peak East
Walking in the Peak District – White Peak West

SOUTHERN ENGLAND

20 Classic Sportive Rides:
  In South East England
  In South West England
Cycling in the Cotswolds
Mountain Biking on the North Downs
Mountain Biking on the South Downs
Suffolk Coast and Heath Walks
The Cotswold Way
The Cotswold Way Map Booklet
The Kennet and Avon Canal
The Lea Valley Walk
The North Downs Way
The North Downs Way Map Booklet
The Peddars Way and Norfolk Coast Path
The Pilgrims' Way
The Ridgeway National Trail
The Ridgeway National Trail Map Booklet
The South Downs Way
The South Downs Way Map Booklet
The Thames Path
The Thames Path Map Booklet
The Two Moors Way
Two Moors Way Map Booklet
Walking Hampshire's Test Way
Walking in Cornwall
Walking in Essex
Walking in Kent
Walking in London
Walking in Norfolk
Walking in the Chilterns
Walking in the Cotswolds
Walking in the Isles of Scilly
Walking in the New Forest
Walking in the North Wessex Downs
Walking on Dartmoor
Walking on Guernsey
Walking on Jersey
Walking on the Isle of Wight
Walking the Dartmoor Way
Walking the Jurassic Coast
Walking the South West Coast Path
Walking the South West Coast Path Map Booklets:
  Vol 1: Minehead to St Ives
  Vol 2: St Ives to Plymouth
  Vol 3: Plymouth to Poole
Walks in the South Downs National Park

WALES AND WELSH BORDERS

Cycle Touring in Wales
Cycling Lon Las Cymru
Great Mountain Days in Snowdonia
Hillwalking in Shropshire
Mountain Walking in Snowdonia
Offa's Dyke Path
Offa's Dyke Path Map Booklet
Ridges of Snowdonia
Scrambles in Snowdonia
Snowdonia –
  30 Low-level and Easy Walks:
  – North
  – South
The Cambrian Way
The Pembrokeshire Coast Path
The Snowdonia Way
The Wye Valley Walk
Walking in Carmarthenshire
Walking in Pembrokeshire
Walking in the Brecon Beacons
Walking in the Forest of Dean
Walking in the Wye Valley
Walking on Gower
Walking the Severn Way
Walking the Shropshire Way
Walking the Wales Coast Path

INTERNATIONAL CHALLENGES, COLLECTIONS AND ACTIVITIES

Europe's High Points
Walking the Via Francigena Pilgrim Route – Part 1

AFRICA

Kilimanjaro
Walking in the Drakensberg
Walks and Scrambles in the Moroccan Anti-Atlas

ALPS CROSS-BORDER ROUTES

100 Hut Walks in the Alps
Alpine Ski Mountaineering Vol 1 – Western Alps
The Karnischer Hohenweg
The Tour of the Bernina
Trail Running – Chamonix and the Mont Blanc region
Trekking Chamonix to Zermatt
Trekking in the Alps
Trekking in the Silvretta and Ratikon Alps
Trekking Munich to Venice
Trekking the Tour of Mont Blanc
Walking in the Alps

PYRENEES AND FRANCE/SPAIN CROSS-BORDER ROUTES

Shorter Treks in the Pyrenees
The GR11 Trail
The Pyrenean Haute Route
The Pyrenees
Walks and Climbs in the Pyrenees

AUSTRIA

Innsbruck Mountain Adventures
Trekking Austria's Adlerweg
Trekking in Austria's Hohe Tauern
Trekking in Austria's Zillertal Alps
Trekking in the Stubai Alps
Walking in Austria
Walking in the Salzkammergut: the Austrian Lake District

EASTERN EUROPE

The Danube Cycleway Vol 2
The Elbe Cycle Route
The High Tatras
The Mountains of Romania
Walking in Hungary

FRANCE, BELGIUM AND LUXEMBOURG

Camino de Santiago – Via Podiensis
Chamonix Mountain Adventures
Cycle Touring in France
Cycling London to Paris
Cycling the Canal de la Garonne
Cycling the Canal du Midi
Cycling the Route des Grandes Alpes
Mont Blanc Walks
Mountain Adventures in the Maurienne
Short Treks on Corsica
The GR5 Trail
The GR5 Trail – Benelux and Lorraine
The GR5 Trail – Vosges and Jura
The Grand Traverse of the Massif Central
The Moselle Cycle Route
The River Loire Cycle Route
The River Rhone Cycle Route
Trekking in the Vanoise
Trekking the Cathar Way
Trekking the GR10
Trekking the GR20 Corsica
Trekking the Robert Louis Stevenson Trail
Via Ferratas of the French Alps
Walking in Provence – East
Walking in Provence – West
Walking in the Ardennes
Walking in the Auvergne
Walking in the Briançonnais
Walking in the Dordogne
Walking in the Haute Savoie: North
Walking in the Haute Savoie: South
Walking on Corsica
Walking the Brittany Coast Path

GERMANY
Hiking and Cycling in the Black Forest
The Danube Cycleway Vol 1
The Rhine Cycle Route
The Westweg
Walking in the Bavarian Alps

IRELAND
The Wild Atlantic Way and Western Ireland
Walking the Wicklow Way

ITALY
Alta Via 1 / Alta Via 2 – Trekking in the Dolomites
Day Walks in the Dolomites
Italy's Grande Traversata delle Alpi
Italy's Sibillini National Park
Ski Touring and Snowshoeing in the Dolomites
The Way of St Francis
Trekking in the Apennines
Trekking the Giants' Trail: Alta Via 1 through the Italian Pennine Alps
Via Ferratas of the Italian Dolomites: Vols 1&2
Walking and Trekking in the Gran Paradiso
Walking in Abruzzo
Walking in Italy's Cinque Terre
Walking in Italy's Stelvio National Park
Walking in Sicily
Walking in the Aosta Valley
Walking in the Dolomites
Walking in Tuscany
Walking in Umbria
Walking Lake Como and Maggiore
Walking Lake Garda and Iseo
Walking on the Amalfi Coast
Walking the Via Francigena Pilgrim Route Parts 2 and 3
Walks and Treks in the Maritime Alps

MEDITERRANEAN
The High Mountains of Crete
Trekking in Greece
Walking and Trekking in Zagori
Walking and Trekking on Corfu
Walking in Cyprus
Walking on Malta
Walking on the Greek Islands – the Cyclades

NEW ZEALAND AND AUSTRALIA
Hiking the Overland Track

NORTH AMERICA
Hiking and Cycling the California Missions Trail
The John Muir Trail
The Pacific Crest Trail

SOUTH AMERICA
Aconcagua and the Southern Andes
Hiking and Biking Peru's Inca Trails
Trekking in Torres del Paine

SCANDINAVIA, ICELAND AND GREENLAND
Hiking in Norway – South
Trekking in Greenland – The Arctic Circle Trail
Trekking the Kungsleden
Walking and Trekking in Iceland

SLOVENIA, CROATIA, SERBIA, MONTENEGRO AND ALBANIA
Hiking Slovenia's Juliana Trail
Mountain Biking in Slovenia
The Islands of Croatia
The Julian Alps of Slovenia
The Mountains of Montenegro
The Peaks of the Balkans Trail
The Slovene Mountain Trail
Walking in Slovenia: The Karavanke
Walks and Treks in Croatia

SPAIN AND PORTUGAL
Camino de Santiago: Camino Frances
Coastal Walks in Andalucia
Costa Blanca Mountain Adventures
Cycling the Camino de Santiago
Cycling the Ruta Via de la Plata
Mountain Walking in Mallorca
Mountain Walking in Southern Catalunya
Portugal's Rota Vicentina
Spain's Sendero Historico: The GR1
The Andalucian Coast to Coast Walk
The Camino del Norte and Camino Primitivo
The Camino Ingles and Ruta do Mar
The Camino Portugues
The Mountains of Nerja
The Mountains of Ronda and Grazalema
The Sierras of Extremadura
Trekking in Mallorca
Trekking in the Canary Islands
Trekking the GR7 in Andalucia
Walking and Trekking in the Sierra Nevada
Walking in Andalucia
Walking in Catalunya – Barcelona
Walking in Catalunya – Girona Pyrenees
Walking in Portugal
Walking in the Algarve
Walking in the Picos de Europa
Walking La Via de la Plata and Camino Sanabres
Walking on Gran Canaria
Walking on La Gomera and El Hierro
Walking on La Palma
Walking on Lanzarote and Fuerteventura
Walking on Madeira
Walking on Tenerife
Walking on the Azores
Walking on the Costa Blanca
Walking the Camino dos Faros

SWITZERLAND
Switzerland's Jura Crest Trail
The Swiss Alps
Tour of the Jungfrau Region
Trekking the Swiss Via Alpina
Walking in the Bernese Oberland – Jungfrau region
Walking in the Engadine – Switzerland
Walking in the Valais
Walking in Ticino
Walking in Zermatt and Saas-Fee

CHINA, JAPAN AND ASIA
Hiking and Trekking in the Japan Alps and Mount Fuji
Hiking in Hong Kong
Japan's Kumano Kodo Pilgrimage
Trekking in Tajikistan

HIMALAYA
Annapurna
Everest: A Trekker's Guide
Trekking in Bhutan
Trekking in Ladakh
Trekking in the Himalaya

MOUNTAIN LITERATURE
8000 metres
A Walk in the Clouds
Abode of the Gods
Fifty Years of Adventure
The Pennine Way – the Path, the People, the Journey
Unjustifiable Risk?

TECHNIQUES
Fastpacking
Geocaching in the UK
Map and Compass
Outdoor Photography
The Mountain Hut Book

MINI GUIDES
Alpine Flowers
Navigation
Pocket First Aid and Wilderness Medicine
Snow

For full information on all our guides, books and eBooks, visit our website:
www.cicerone.co.uk

CICERONE

Trust Cicerone to guide your next adventure, wherever it may be around the world…

Discover guides for hiking, mountain walking, backpacking, trekking, trail running, cycling and mountain biking, ski touring, climbing and scrambling in Britain, Europe and worldwide.

Connect with Cicerone online and find inspiration.

- buy books and ebooks
- articles, advice and trip reports
- podcasts and live events
- GPX files and updates
- regular newsletter

cicerone.co.uk